For my grandchildren,
Joey and Jennifer Rogers,
and all of the children of the
twenty-first century

To clarify any unfamiliar terminology
readers can refer to the glossary at the end of the book.

PART I

Stirrings

Prologue

Late nineteenth century, Tasmania—Three rapid rifle shots cracked the calm of the mountainside, and a gathering of yellow-eyed currawong birds flew into the nearest gum tree, their black wings shining in the spring mist. They were escape artists, thought Philo Hoffman, like all the native fauna since the British conquerors had invaded Tasmania. He pushed back his visored safari helmet and peered through his binoculars at the trail below. Probably a hunter, he shrugged, then let his binoculars fall on their strap while he recorded the number of currawongs in the gum tree. He preferred to call it a *moonah* tree, liking the flavor of the native name.

Considered a moonstruck dreamer by his proper Boston family, Philo had been tracing the path of primitive man throughout Asia for the past twenty years. He was looking for the key to human origins, what made man human, what could be called his soul. Here in Tasmania, soul was in short supply. It was a cruel country, Philo said to himself, as a cold gust of damp wind chilled the sweat on his neck. All mountains, impassable rapids, and fierce storms, not to speak of the convicts and ex-convicts that littered Hobart, the shabby little capital.

Philo's fine dark brows came together as he heard another shot. A solitary man, he had hoped to find ultimate solitude in these mountains at the tip of southern Tasmania. Now he could see first one hunter, then

1

two others running along the path fifty feet below the ridge on which he stood. Yapping dogs, mangy as their masters, ran ahead, their noses near the ground.

No doubt chasing a *lenah*, a bush kangaroo. The Brits were always chasing some animal, either to catch or to kill. They couldn't leave the landscape alone but were always worrying at it, building roads, monuments and their infernal prisons. At the hellhole he had visited in Hobart yesterday, any prisoner who complained was forced to wear a leather snout strapped to his head. Poor devils. Almost as bad off as the handful of natives still hiding in the hills.

Philo was about to turn the page of his notebook when he heard a long, haunting cry that dropped off suddenly, as if the one who uttered it had suddenly fallen from a cliff. Adjusting his binoculars, he saw the thin, naked body of a native, a Parlevar, as they called themselves, bent over and stumbling as he struggled up the side of the mountain, trying to elude the hunters. The man's skin was black, with a faint violet sheen, except near the left shoulder, where it was bright red with blood.

"Damn," Philo muttered under his breath, pulling out his pistol. "They're tracking him like a dingo." He fired into the air and called to the hunters when they looked up, "Let the poor fellow go, mates. He's done you no harm."

"Bug off, Yank!" one of the hunters shouted, "or we'll send you to Tassie hell along with him." They fired again, this time in Philo's direction, and a handful of fractured sandstone fell from the rocks overhead. Out of sight from below, he pressed his back against the cliff, deciding it was useless to argue about civilized rules with men who had none. With luck, though, he might save the wounded Parlevar.

Philo ducked around a rock and began climbing down the steep side of the cliff, trying to find the native. If the Parlevar had the strength, he would surely avoid the trail and go for the heights, scaling the cliff as Philo had seen natives do before. Suddenly the rocks gave way under Philo's boots, and he slid twenty feet down, scraping his cheek and palms as he flailed, groping for a handhold in the rough brush. He landed on a wide ledge, shadowed by an outcropping of rock and a *moonah* tree that had almost lost its moorings, roots straining to keep it from falling into the valley below. After brushing against his high, tanned cheekbone, Philo's hand came away bloody. His long, craggy face had so many scars that one more would not matter.

Philo heard a low moan from just below the ridge and saw a black hand groping for a hold. Then the other hand appeared. A low muttering in Parlevar followed, then a despairing cry as the hands began to slip. Bracing himself against a rock, Philo grabbed the aboriginal's hand and dragged him onto the ledge. The black man rolled over and stared up at the sun, his eyes glazed and unblinking. "*Lumeah*," he whispered. "I rest here."

"You'd best have some of this," Philo said in the native dialect as he pulled out his brandy flask. "Looks like you've lost a lot of blood." He checked the man's wound and shook his head. The bullet was not in the shoulder, as he had thought from a distance, but nearer the heart. How this man had climbed a hundred feet straight up with such a wound, Philo could not guess.

The yapping of the dogs following the trail of blood told him the hunters were close. Philo leaned over, his head shadowing the Parlevar's face. "We've got to move on," he said. "Where? You know these hills."

"Turn, turn," the black man whispered. "Behind the vines, a cave. I must end there."

Brushing aside the growth of trumpet vines, heavy with their red and yellow cone-shaped flowers, Philo saw a dark, irregular hole in the rock. Bent almost double, he pulled the aboriginal inside, then went out again, opening his flask. The dogs were not far away; he could hear them growling and sniffing as they worked. Philo poured brandy over the blood that had spread under the Parlevar's body, then lit it with a match.

Just as the first dog's head appeared above the narrow ledge, the fire roared up, consuming the blood and leaving no human scent. The dog yipped and backed off. Philo could hear it racing down the hillside, taking the other dogs along. Wrenching off a dried branch that hung from the *moonah* tree, he stuck one end into the fire, then took the torch into the cave, letting the thick vine curtain fall behind him.

The Parlevar had crawled deeper into the cave, around a corner and into a large cavern. Lifting the torch, Philo could see red and black wall paintings, in which humans and animals were intertwined.

"Put your torch on the place of fire," the Parlevar whispered, pointing at a circle of stones with blackened wood inside. "It will burn a long time after I am gone."

The black man's face was full, like his lips, and his nose was broad, with a curve at the top. As he lay on the bare rock, the flickering light cast shadows under his eyes, highlighting his deep wrinkles. Philo rested his hand on the dying man's head, trying to soothe his pain. The thick, black hair was coarse to the touch and prickled against his palm like live wires.

"How are you called?" the man asked, his eyes opening suddenly, their brown depths lit by the torch. "Of what family and race are you? What is your Dreaming?"

"My dreaming?" Philo was unsure how to answer.

"Your God, as you call it." The Parlevar groaned and rolled over on his side. "The spirit of those who came before." He waved his hand vaguely.

"I'll start with my name, Philo Hoffman." He felt as if he had never said his name before and heard it roll off his tongue slowly, like a mantra. It was strange to be asked about his family, for Philo had always identified himself by his professorship at Harvard. Few people had ever asked about his race or his God. "I am as much Jewish as anything," he said, feeling ashamed that he knew so little of his ancestral faith beyond his bar mitzvah training. "I do not know God, but imagine God as better than I am. Different from what I am. And you, my friend, what is your name? Who is your God?" The Parlevar's breath was becoming erratic and shallow, and Philo feared he would soon die. Knowing this man's God suddenly seemed very important.

"White men call me Jocko, because none can pronounce my name. I will tell my real name to you." He mumbled a many-syllabled name that flowed incomprehensibly past Philo's ears. "And my God, as you call the Dreaming, is that One who gave birth to all. The Old Woman."

Jocko sighed and held up his hand, watching his fingers turn transparent in the firelight. "Philo Hoffman, I am last of my people, last to carry the old secrets. May I give you my story? Yes?"

Philo felt his heart beat out of phase, as if it might stop. Like the dying man, he gasped for air, and wondered if he, too, would die in this cave where the walls crawled with life. He knew of the goddess Jocko called "the Old Woman." She was called Great Mother by the people of Old Europe, six thousand years ago. Jocko called her old because his people thought old meant full of power. "Yes," Philo whispered. "Tell."

"Long ago, when the continents were one, my people lived here on this spot. We were the earliest race of men, and it was to us the Old Woman came each night, like a mother singing her children to sleep. Her name was Pra, and it was she who gave birth to the world."

"Is Pra the word for love in the ancient language?" Philo took a notebook from his pocket and began to write.

The black man nodded and went on. "Mother Pra is the one we see when eyes are open and when eyes are closed. She takes care of us even to this day. She came in flesh long ago, half a world away from here. As a man with the heart of a woman."

"You mean Jesus, the Jew of Nazareth?" Philo's pen stopped, poised above the notebook.

"Yes." The Parlevar tried to nod, but his head fell to the side. He coughed, and blood ran from the corner of his mouth. "But that Incarnation was not the first. From the spirit world her divine children come when needed to save earth from destruction. She is already here on earth, but in a hidden place. Later Pra will come again as a small, black man with great powers. After that she will return in such a form that we will not know if she is man or woman, so motherly will be her heart."

The black man's breath rasped in his throat, and his eyes closed. His knees curled to his chest as he rolled onto his side.

"Jocko, tell me," Philo said, forgetting to keep his voice down. "Where is the place? Where has the avatar come back to earth?" Echoing against the painted walls, his voice sounded deep and far away.

The old shaman opened his eyes and held Philo's. "Go to a land where old laws are kept, where men give their lives to sacred oneness of mind and body, where women are still incarnations of the Old Woman. Look for a tall man, with a white beard and ash on his forehead. I see him behind my closed eyes, wearing a white robe, in a small village by the sea, surrounded by many people, his spiritual children. He is called Baba—Father. His names are on my ring. Go to Baba. He will tell you what to do." The shaman's voice trailed off like a child's drifting into sleep, and he was gone.

Philo touched Jocko's eyes in a ritual gesture, but they were already closed. On the black man's finger was a gold ring, with an inscription inside that he could barely make out: Shirdi—Sathya—Prema. The last two he recognized as the Sanskrit words for Truth and Love. The first was a village near Bombay. If the winds were fair, he could sail there in a week. Philo put the ring in his pocket, sprinkled the old man's face with dust as a burial gesture, and said the words of the ring for a blessing, if such a man as this required a blessing for his passage.

1

Gina Hoffman was not in the best of moods. In fact, she was thinking that any minute she would hit the bottle. She had avoided alcohol for twenty years, but was holding it in reserve for her fiftieth birthday and thereafter. Her birthday would be tomorrow, and "thereafter" loomed as a long, downhill slide. She had held her youth well, but now had to cover the gray in her thick, shoulder-length hair with a chemical solution called medium ash-brown. On dark days, of which there had lately been many, it looked more like dirty blond. The crow's feet and dimples that once had crinkled prettily when she smiled didn't go away when she stopped smiling. Gina wasn't smiling much today, because she hadn't sold a house in the past month.

For the first five years after leaving her ex-husband's real estate firm to start her own, she had sold at least one house every week, and during the previous year had made enough to buy her first mansion. She had done it by knocking on the door of every house in Santa Barbara that was worth more than three-hundred thousand. By handing out ten thousand note pads with her name and phone number on every page. By mothering every buyer and seller she found, until one night she dreamed she had a hundred teats and somebody hanging from every one of them. Now, the office phones hardly ever rang.

Your big mistake was sinking all your savings six months ago into that new Spanish-style oceanfront villa, Gina complained to herself. Bad timing. Once the dreaded year 2000 had passed, she had been certain that real estate prices would go through the roof. Gina tapped her polished red nails with a pencil imprinted with the words "MOVE FAST! Call Gina Hoffman, 964-3996." If she had waited even two months to buy, the price would have dropped by twenty-five thousand. *Maybe fifty*, nagged a little voice that had lately begun to argue with her, confusing her previously well-organized brain. No, the biggest mistake had been hiring Jerry North because he was in love with her and because her ex-husband had dumped him as an agent. Jerry had a weakness for poor young couples who wanted more house than they could afford and whose loans were never approved.

Gina had hoped Jerry would handle her low-end offerings, leaving her free to go after the quality listings. "Skim the cream" had always been her motto, but now even the cream wasn't selling. And her broker's insurance payment was due, along with multiple listing fees, and the twelve-thousand-dollar mortgage payment on her oceanside extravaganza. "For a live buyer I might even turn religious," Gina muttered, breaking the pencil point as she stabbed it into her fashionably mauve blotter. "I might even pray, if I thought it would do any good."

She actually had prayed once or twice, awkwardly, like a rusty key turning in the lock of an old house, but nothing had come of her prayers except the small, argumentative voice at the back of her mind, a voice she could just as well do without. The bottle was probably a better idea, Gina thought, staring out the large plate-glass window that was supposed to give her a good view of the next customer.

The mail carrier, her rear barely covered by a gray mini-skirt, stopped outside to talk with another young woman who wore a stained, sagging sweatsuit. A red-faced baby with a runny nose rested uneasily on the woman's hip, his arms flailing as she talked. That child has a fresh cold, Gina thought wearily, feeling an attack of motherliness coming on. This silly girl shouldn't have taken him out on such a cold morning, and Gina would tell her so, now that the girl was coming in.

She quickly sized up the young mother, who was having trouble closing the door. Another unlikely customer, Gina thought, smiling her professional smile and offering her hand. Probably wants a fifty-thousand-dollar condo with no down payment.

"I'm Annie Blake," the girl said, sniffling. She obviously had a cold, too. "Have you got any condos about fifty thousand, with nothing down?" She sat on the edge of her chair. "Oh yeah, here's your package. The mail girl's a friend of mine."

Gina glanced at the sturdy square box, noticing that it came from her cousin, Phyllis Hoffman, on the East Coast. "You can't get anything without a down payment unless you're a veteran. I would guess you aren't." She took pity on the squirming, stuffed-up baby and handed him her key chain.

"I gotta get a place," Annie said, tears brimming in her pale blue eyes. "My landlady's daughter is coming home, so I'm outta my apartment. Renting's no good. They can throw you out anytime they want. That's no way to live." The baby dropped Gina's keys and howled, kicking his mother in the stomach as he threw his head back.

Gina found some clean towels and a pile of tissues, then took the baby in her arms. He stopped crying and let her wipe his nose. "Let's put him on the floor. He'll be more comfortable and we can talk," Gina said, covering the baby with another towel. He went to sleep instantly as she had been sure he would. "Now, Annie, tell me. Do you have a job? Any income at all?"

"Three hundred a week, counting welfare and baby-sitting," Annie said. "I work about sixty hours a week, but don't tell the social worker." She smiled confidentially, leaning on Gina's polished mahogany desk.

Gina sighed, knowing Jerry would have this woman fill out a loan application and fight for her at the bank, then lose, as he always did. "Look, Annie. I can try to get you a temporary room at a home for single mothers. It's run by a church. No drinking or smoking or men allowed. You can live with that?"

"I don't know." Annie's face clouded. "My boyfriend just got laid off his landscaping job. We thought we'd try to buy a place together and get married."

The usual dream. Gina's heart ached as she saw behind Annie's round, sallow face an army of young parents with no place to raise their children. And here was Gina, with her sprawling five-bedroom house, and only her son, Kief, home now and then from his university job, to share it with.

No, she said to herself. No guilt. I earned that house, even if I'm too busy to clean it. I work sixty hours a week. *So does Annie*, said the voice inside her. Ignoring the voice, Gina dialed the number for the church shelter. When she heard that the last room had just been filled, Annie sat up straight, her rough red hands folded in her lap. *Notice her hands.* The voice kept nagging. *She does housework as well as baby-sitting.*

Gina could remember, even as a little girl, talking to herself or to an imaginary friend that she alone could hear. At first she even thought the voice might be her conscience, but she wasn't concerned since she seemed to have won her share of disagreements. Now, however, she realized that it had a personality all its own, quietly persuasive, while Gina's style was about as subtle as a slam dunk.

"Okay," Gina said. "I could use a yardman and housekeeper. Bring your young man around to my place tomorrow afternoon about five-thirty and we'll talk. If we all like each other, you can rent my guest cottage for a hundred a month. It has only one bedroom, plus the kitchenette and living room, but it should do for now. I'll need references, of course," she added, as if to show the interfering voice that she was still in charge.

"Sure, I got 'em." Annie picked up the baby, looking down with a frown. "Oh Lord, Jason's snotted up your nice towel. I'll wash it and bring it back when I come tomorrow afternoon, okay?"

"Fine. Here's a card with the address. You'll have to call in at the gate. Now take that baby back to a warm room before he gets the croup," Gina said, waving as Annie left. Once alone, she listened for the voice again, but it was quiet. Maybe it had gone to torment poor, big-hearted Jerry. Or maybe she had caught it from him like a virus. Suddenly she heard the voice again, *Call your company Heart Homes.*

"Oh, gimme a break," Gina said out loud. The voice persisted, *Heart. The real estate company that gives ten percent of every commission to help homeless mothers and children.*

But Hoffman Homes has a track record. I can't give up the name. *Well then*, said the voice, sounding more and more familiar. *Change your ad. Put a heart around the name and say right up front what you're going to do for women like Annie.*

Gina made a rapid sketch, then got up and began pacing back and forth in front of the window. Why not? she thought. Things can't get any worse. If I do some charity, maybe this voice will shut up and leave me alone. I might even get an extra deal or two by putting ads in church and synagogue bulletins. An ad campaign began to unroll in her mind, and Gina sat down to sketch out a logo. Hearing a car door slam, she glanced out the window. Maybe the good deed had won her a customer already.

Jerry was coming up the walk, smiling at her. He held up a contract in one hand and made a victory sign with the other. A good omen for the new promotion plan, Gina thought, if it didn't involve another hopeless loan application.

"Jerry, have a look at our new logo," she said as he came in.

He loosened the tie around his thick neck, as he always did when no customers were around. Jerry was a big man, with shoulders and chest that were too broad to look comfortable in anything but a sweat suit. His graying blond hair stood on end like a cock's knot, because he often scratched his head in consternation at a world and a profession he couldn't understand. He had a bad case of scalp psoriasis, brought on by nervous tension and a conviction that he would have been better at preaching or social work than at selling. His wide, surprised blue eyes and big, dazzling smile should have pulled in more business than they did. Trouble was, the smile was likely to be followed by a self-effacing remark that alienated prospective home sellers before Jerry could make his listing pitch.

"I like it," he said, studying the new logo. "Ten percent of our commissions go to homeless mothers and children. Great, Gina. I'd feel good with that. But first I've got to get a commission."

"So show me the contract," Gina said. "We could both use a commission around here." Her eyes ran down the figures. Oh fine. Another young couple offering a five-thousand-dollar down payment. And an offer twenty-five thousand below the listing price. "Forget it." She sighed and laid the contract down.

"Oh, what the hell," she muttered, more to herself than him. "Submit the offer. At least our seller will know you've shown his hovel. First time we've even had a looky-loo on it." Right now she'd even settle for one of those nosy women with nothing better to do than wander through other people's houses. At least he'd get to practice making his pitch. *Come on,* said her small, interior voice, sounding friendlier since she had drawn the logo. *You're going to get a break. You're working with me, now, remember. You're my hands in this world. Would I let you down?* Gina shook her head, thinking she'd better go home and sleep. Twenty hours of cold-calling must be making her crazy, like a prisoner of war under relentless lights and blows.

"Hey, take a look at that Rolls out there!" Jerry tightened his tie. "Is this guy a diplomat or what?"

Gina looked up and saw a tall, thin man in an elegantly tailored, cream-colored suit coming up her walk. Large, dark aviator sunglasses covered his eyes. A narrow mustache and well-trimmed goatee almost hid his thin, tight mouth. As the man entered, his attendant held the door open. A third man, in semi-military livery, stood at attention beside the gleaming black Rolls. We got one, thought Gina. Arab oil money. Holy Aunt Hannah, we finally got one. Her knees trembled, but she smiled and bowed, knowing better than to shake hands. These Middle Eastern types, she had heard, didn't like to be touched by strange women, who might be ritually unclean.

"Jerry, sit at the desk," she whispered through her locked smile. "You handle this one."

"Huh?" Jerry turned red. "Oh yeah. Please sit down, Mr. . . .?"

Good, thought Gina. He remembered that Arabs do business only with men. But Gina sat close behind him, ready to coach.

"Nazim." The man snapped his fingers, and the attendant handed him a long, thin cigarette from a platinum case with a rosette of diamonds on the front. "I come just now from Lebanon and require house at once."

"You want to rent or buy, Mr. Nazim?" Jerry picked up a rental form and handed it across the desk. Ignoring him, the Arab began talking to his assistant in Arabic.

Gina nudged Jerry hard and whispered behind her hand, "Buy, buy. Don't even think about rent."

"Just now it's better financially to buy, Mr. Nazim." Jerry kept talking, not missing a beat. "High quality rentals are hard to find."

"I pay cash," Nazim said, flicking his ashes into the attendant's cupped hand. "I want to buy big place. Must have five bedrooms at least, front on ocean. Much privacy and gate of security. Security very important. Very." He gave his attendant the cigarette and snapped his fingers again. Juggling the burning cigarette and the platinum case, the attendant pulled out a pen and an embossed leather checkbook. Nazim wrote out a check and handed it to Jerry. "Two hundred thousand dollars, payable to Hoffman Homes, memo—down payment," Gina read over Jerry's shoulder.

"You will find me house today," the Arab said. "I do not have to see. By tomorrow night, I must be in."

Gina thought fast. None of her listings fit Nazim's requirements. Nothing vacant, certainly. If she went to another broker, half the commission would be lost. Only one thing to do. Her oceanside extravaganza would have to go. Gina immediately felt lighter, as if a burden had dropped from her back.

"Mr. Nazim," she said, bowing and trying to look stupidly meek, the way Arabs in the movies expected women to look, "may we present you with furniture already in place? And a caretaker couple with a six-month contract?"

"Yes, yes, but be sure all personals are gone from house when I arrive." Nazim unfolded his long legs and stood up. "I come back tomorrow morning to sign papers. Have them ready."

Gina scribbled a quick note and pushed it across the desk to Jerry.

"Uh, Mr. Nazim," Jerry mumbled. "The price of the house is two million dollars. That includes a hundred thousand for the furniture. Will cash be a problem?"

"Cash when I come back to sign papers." Ignoring Gina, the Arab bowed slightly to Jerry, then left.

They waited until the car door closed, then, holding hands, began to whirl around the room. "Wow, cash!" whooped Jerry. "We live again."

"No more house payments," Gina laughed, kicking her heels together.

"No more house." She stopped in the middle of the dance, frowning. "Call Santa Barbara Movers," she said. "And write up a rental contract for me on that little Olive Street dump. I've got some fast packing to do."

Already Gina had decided to take only her familiar, beat-up furniture from the rec room, leaving the unpaid-for, neo-Spanish clutter with the house. Fortunately, most of her belongings were still in boxes stored in the garage. After the closing tomorrow, she would pay off the eighty thousand she still owed for furnishings and finish packing. She would be free. Suddenly she heard the voice again. *You owe much to the mothers and children. Remember.* Ten percent of my profits is what they get. I promise. For the first time since moving into the house six months before, Gina felt like she belonged to herself.

"I'll take you out to lunch." She hugged Jerry. "You buy the champagne. I'm celebrating my birthday a day early." Tucking the package from cousin Phyllis under one elbow, she hung a "Sorry" sign in the front window and locked up the office. Gina wasn't sorry at all. Her profit on the house, even after taxes—and the tithe for homeless moms, she added, to forestall the little voice—would be four hundred thousand dollars. Hoffman Homes was back in business. Her ex would not be happy to hear about it.

∽ာၑ

A born-again Christian, Jerry North was unused to champagne, and his head felt like it had insufficient room for his brains. If Gina hadn't insisted, he would gladly have settled for club soda. But when her dark blue eyes sparkled at him, and she played with his hands across the table top, Jerry caved in, as always. His minister, Homer Healey, had said he shouldn't marry a Jewish woman, but as St. Paul said, it is better to marry than to burn.

"Don't get me wrong," Homer said, "I'm a great supporter of Israel. The greatest. But Jews and Christians should marry their own."

"Why is that?" Jerry watched Homer Healey's wide, full-lipped face turn faintly pink. The minister was having a conflict between his biblical belief that Zion belonged to the children of Israel and his certainty that God would damn them as unbelievers. Since Jesus himself had been a Jew, the conflict seemed irreconcilable. Homer's sudden flush was the sign of a moral short circuit that only the grace of a subtle intelligence could have put right. But that grace was one the Lord had not seen fit to grant the Reverend Healey. He prided himself on his simplemindedness, since the only things that counted in the sight of God were faith, hope and love.

"Well, you know." Homer picked up his Bible and put it down, sparing Jerry a quotation. "The children. They get confused."

"Gina can't have any more children," Jerry explained, wanting to avert Homer's moral crisis. "She's past menopause." As the minister looked down, the pink in his cheeks deepened into scarlet. When he preached on television, he had to be thickly painted with ivory blush so viewers wouldn't think he was snockered.

"You came for some other reason than this marriage?" Homer asked, running his fingers over the black, bark-textured Bible, tracing its golden letters.

"I brought my tithe," Jerry said, laying a check on the desk. "A thousand dollars. We'll be closing a major deal tomorrow. Praise the Lord!"

"To him be the glory," Homer gasped, holding up the check, his palms closed around it in a gesture of prayer.

As a member of the church board, Jerry knew that Reverend Healey's dream was to build a glass temple to rival the Crystal Cathedral in Los Angeles. From this theater of light he would preach to the unsaved multitudes. Homer Healey knew he could do better for the Lord than any of those phony, pushy pitchmen who ranted, sweated and stomped as they preached the word on TV. Soft words were what won hearts to Jesus, loving words that let sinners know they were in the tender arms of God. He had an easy, offhand manner before the camera, "a cool presence," one TV producer told him, adding, "It's too bad your little cinderblock church looks like a third-world classroom." With make-up to cover his blotchy face and a glass temple facing the ocean, Homer could break into the Sunday morning big leagues. Many souls would be saved, souls Jesus thirsted for. Reverently he laid Jerry's check in the Bible, like a bookmark. "God bless you, Jerry," his rich basso quivered. "You've brought the kingdom of heaven one step closer to earth."

Homer Healey's whole life was a guided missile headed for the Parousia, that ecstatic moment when Christ would return on a cloud and rule for a thousand years. Homer knew that the time was growing near. Wars and rumors of wars abounded. Earthquakes split the fabric of the groaning earth, as it awaited delivery from sin. His heart grieved and burned at the thought of so many sinners who would be lost on that glorious day—glorious, that is, for the Lambs of God. Tears came to Homer's eyes when he preached about the poor lost ones who would never see the Lord, who would not be caught up with him in the Rapture. They were the reason why he had to build his great temple and bring God's message to the nation. Homer travailed in a terrible labor for the birth of souls into the kingdom of heaven, as Jerry had reported the minister's words to Gina Hoffman. She had laughed nervously, uncertain if dear, credulous Jerry was making a joke.

The secretary knocked, then opened the door before Homer could answer. "There's some kind of Arab sheikh to see you," she whispered, her hand at her throat. "He came in a Rolls-Royce. With a bodyguard, can you believe!"

"Nazim," Jerry said, jumping up to look out the window at the car. "That's our buyer. He's got some kind of pipeline from the Middle East. Oil flows in one end, and dollars come out the other."

The minister stood up so fast his chair fell over, and his face went florid with a wild surmise. "Hallelujah! God has sent him to us. Show him in. No, Jerry, don't leave. You're a board member, and you know this man. Stay right here."

Jerry bowed to Nazim and waited to sit down again until the Arab had settled into an easy chair. Only when the minister had assured Nazim that Jerry was a power in the church and must remain, did Nazim consent to his presence.

Ignoring the "Thank you for not smoking" sign on Homer's desk, Nazim snapped his fingers for a cigarette, and his bodyguard stepped forward with the platinum case. After the Arab had taken a reflective puff, he looked down his long, arched nose at Reverend Healey.

"You talk well on television," he began. "Why do you not yet have your own show?"

Except for the Parousia, Homer's media career was his favorite subject, and he was glad this aloof, graceful man had brought it up. "Kind of you to ask, Mr. Nazim. It's in the works, just waiting on the building of our glass temple. You know about the temple?"

"I know." Nazim flicked ashes into the cupped hand of the body-guard, who took them to the wastebasket. "You have heard speakers of your faith supporting Zionism on television? A scandal, yes?"

Jerry looked uneasily at Homer, who was developing faintly purple patches under the thin skin of his cheeks. If the minister agreed with Nazim, his solidarity with evangelical Christians in support of Israel was compromised. If he defended his belief in Zionism, the glass temple would remain a dream. Homer's flush faded as he hedged. "It's true the Evangelical Media Association has officially endorsed Zionism," he said, gripping his Bible. "But not all of us agree. Wholeheartedly agree, that is." The light gray eyes, that caught the lights on camera and shone like a saint's, were fixed on Nazim, trying to read his face.

"I will not beat bushes," Nazim said, recrossing his legs and brushing one long, elegant hand over his immaculate lap. "We in the Middle East wish you to quickly stop with support. We want no more Bible talk of Palestine as land of Jews. Arab land, only Arab people there, Inshallah." As Nazim's hand stroked his mustache, Jerry saw his fingers tremble. Once land had been conquered for Islam, Jerry knew, the Arabs could not give it up. Letting that sacred land revert to the Jews had been a sac-rilege, an abomination before Allah. Nazim's narrow mouth was grim.

"You think I could bring pressure on the association to cut back its support for Israel? Mr. Nazim, I am nobody. Just a voice crying in the wilderness." Homer clutched his Bible and swallowed hard. He did not mention that his voice had cried more than once for Israel's protection.

"When you have this glass temple," Nazim said, snapping his fingers for the checkbook, "you will have big influence. Will you not?"

"More important, yes," Homer said, his palms so wet that the black, bark-textured cover of the Bible gleamed. "But certainly not able to . . ."

Nazim handed him a check. "You begin construction. I arrange your loan. As you speak for us against the Jews, loan is paid for you. Greater influence, greater talk for us, then greater pay for loan. You see what to do? Or you give my money back?" He held out his hand.

Reverend Healey stared at the check, then showed it to Jerry. "Two million dollars," Jerry breathed out loud. And more when that ran out. Endlessly more. The minister's aorta pulsed and red blotches spread across his cheeks. A done deal, Jerry told himself. I'm no great salesman, but I know when a buyer is on the hook. Homer Healey had just broken with gospel Zionism.

"You are too generous, Mr. Nazim," Homer said, reverently taking the Arab's hand. Jerry thought he might kiss the hand, but Homer only wrung it between his own, as if to milk it for yet another check. "I will do as you ask. Discreetly, of course. Too quick a turnabout would be questioned, for my support of Israel is well-known, you understand."

Nazim stood up. "We will watch," he said gesturing for his man to open the door. "You have these temple plans ready? Yes? Then begin at once. Little time to waste." He ignored their bows and left, leaving a faint smell of musk hanging in the air.

"The glass temple is God's will," Homer said in a low voice, not looking at Jerry. "I must ask your promise not to reveal this conversation."

"No one in the church will hear of it from me." Jerry would not break a promise, but he would not be sinning when he told Gina Hoffman what he had learned about the new owner of her house.

❧

Late the next afternoon, Gina took a break from packing her "personals," as the Arab had called them, and opened the box from her cousin Phyllis. Inside was a letter from Phyllis, taped to a second package which was wrapped in faded brown paper. The letter said little, for the cousins had never been close. Gina scanned it quickly, in a hurry to get back to wrapping her French crystal wineglasses. The second package was a box of letters from Phyllis' grandfather, Gina's great-uncle

Philo, which for some reason he had insisted should go to Gina after his death. She vaguely remembered meeting a gaunt old man, with shining eyes and a gentle voice when she was five and he as old as God, as it seemed to her then. "So this is the girl," he had said, taking her on his lap. "I will remember her."

At the time, her family had thought Philo meant to remember her in his will, for he had a considerable fortune. But his money had been given to charity, and all that remained were these letters, which he had instructed should be given to his grandniece Gina on her fiftieth birthday.

As she opened the inner box, the stiff brown paper crumbled in Gina's hands. On top of the yellowed letters, tied with faded ribbon and decorated with East Indian designs, was a packet folded in tissue paper. Inside was another letter, written to her by her great-uncle, and a gold ring inscribed with some words in a language she did not recognize. The ring fit her wedding finger, which had been bare for the five years since her divorce. Wondering what the words said, Gina put on the ring. Perhaps the letter would tell. She read it quickly, looking for an explanation, but Philo wrote only that the ring had been given to him in Tasmania by a dying aboriginal. Someone named Shirdi Sai Baba had instructed Philo to pass it on to his younger brother's oldest grandchild.

"How could he have said that?" Gina sniffed through her long, arched nose. "I wasn't even born back then. Uncle Philo must have been a crackpot, like the whole family thought."

The letters were postmarked Shirdi, India, which she learned from her atlas was near Bombay. Out of curiosity, she opened the first one and began to read. Philo wrote about finding a holy man spoken of by the Tasmanian. He was called Baba, meaning Father, by the devotees who surrounded his small temple, waiting for him to come out every morning and bless them. He was tall, with a white beard like Philo's grandfather, who had been known for his piety and his jokes. This Baba, however, seemed to be ascetic and stern, telling his followers that they must give up their worldly desires.

Gina sniffed again and put the letter down. Maybe an Indian ashram was the place for Uncle Philo, but the world of earning and spending was the only one she knew. For a moment she felt a pang at the loss of her neo-Spanish estate. The little house on Olive Street was quite a comedown. Her friends would feel sorry for her, and Gina hated pity. She picked up the letter again. Baba had told Philo to live simply, in a state of prayer, helping the poor. He was a great healer, and Philo saw many sick people cured under his hands. Few could accept Baba's strict discipline, however, and his close group of followers remained small.

"I'd have left like a shot," Gina murmured, turning the page. "Forget sleeping on a dirt floor. And getting whacked with the old guy's stick when I asked for a hamburger." But her great-uncle had loved Shirdi Baba, as the holy man was called.

Philo was sending her the ring, because Baba had said she was to give it to her first grandson, and it would lead him home. "Grandson?" Gina shrugged. She had no grandson. Her only child, Kief, was already thirty-two and had shown little interest in women. He was a gentle, scholarly professor who spent his university sabbaticals reading inscriptions in the Egyptian desert, and she more than half suspected that he was gay. The unlikely grandchild, according to Philo, would be a reincarnation of himself. This child would be blessed, for he would live in a time when Sai Baba returned to bless the world. "Oh, sure," said Gina, tossing the letter into the box. "Kid me not, Uncle Philo. You are dead and gone and that's how it is." But she kept the ring on her finger.

The phone rang while she was looking for a box big enough to hold her silver-rimmed crystal salad bowl. Her son, Kief, was calling from his university in Santa Cruz. "Guess what, Mom," he said in his soft baritone voice. "There was this Swedish archeologist I had an affair with in Egypt last year. I just got a telegram from her. Turns out we have a son, and they're flying in tonight. His name is John Philo."

"Philo?" Gina's crystal bowl crashed to the tile floor. "How come Philo?"

"Because it's Greek for love, and the baby was born in Greece. His mother's name is Kori. She won't marry me, because I'm eight years younger than she is, and besides, she thinks that marriage ruins relationships. We'll be driving down this Friday, if that's okay with you." He spoke in a rush, as he usually did, probably fearing that she would interrupt if given a chance.

Kief should have told her about this woman before, Gina reflected as she hung up. She wasn't the kind of mother who would have scolded him. In fact she would have been glad. It had been so long since Kief had been involved with a woman. And now this grandson with Philo's name. She turned the ring on her finger and made a mental note to read the rest of her great-uncle's letters. This Shirdi Baba seemed to have known a thing or two.

The phone rang again, and it was Annie, asking to be let in at the gate. A few minutes later the little family pulled up in a dilapidated blue truck. A tall, gangling young man got out first. He had a light brown ponytail that was surprisingly thick, considering that he had no hair at all on top of his head.

Carrying baby Jason on one hip, Annie held out a neatly folded towel. "Here it is," she beamed. "I washed it at the beach and dried it in the sun. Is it clean enough? This is David. He's a lot stronger than he looks."

"I think once he's had some steak and potatoes, he'll be fine," Gina said, holding out her hand.

"I'm a vegan, Ms. Hoffman," the young man said. "I don't even eat eggs." When he smiled, she saw that at least he had a good set of teeth.

"Too bad. I was going to suggest you could keep chickens here. There's a coop behind the guest cottage." She led them out the back way and down a flagstone path lined with flaming red bougainvillea bushes that met overhead on the arched trellises framing the walkway. "The cottage is pretty close to the main house," she said, "so you might not have much privacy." She stopped in front of a low, white stucco building with gray cracks where the last earthquake had left its mark. "It smells a bit moldy," she warned, "but you can air it out by opening the windows and the French doors."

They followed her inside and looked up at the beamed ceilings, then over at the stone fireplace. A blue bird sat on the casement windowsill looking in at them. Hibiscus flowers were waving overhead, touched by the wind. Sitting at the round wooden kitchen table, Annie lowered her head and began to cry.

"What's the matter?" Gina hurried to open the windows. "It could smell better, I know."

"Not that, not that." Annie wiped her eyes with her sleeve. "It's so nice. I never thought we'd have a place that was nice."

David patted her shoulder and took the baby so she could cry. "We'll take good care of the place, Ms. Hoffman. I've done a lot of gardening and fix-up work in my time." He looked at a picture on the table and then at Gina. "He has your eyes," David said. "Your son?"

"Yes, Kief Feuerstein. That's his father's name. I went back to Hoffman," Gina said, studying the picture for a moment before putting it in her shoulder bag. "That was when he first grew his beard, at an archeological dig. He's bringing his new baby home this weekend."

She laid a contract on the table. "You should know that you'll be working for someone else. Just today I sold this place to an Arab guy named Nazim. He's agreed to take you on for six months as caretakers. He'll want to deal only with David. No alcohol on the premises. And don't let him know you're not married. He's probably one of those fundamentalists."

Like Jerry's Reverend Healey, Gina thought, walking back alone to the main house. She could not understand narrow-minded fanatics and felt uneasy when Jerry tried to explain that there was only one truth, which everyone had to believe or burn in hell. His explanations always fell flat, perhaps because Jerry himself was too kindhearted to believe them. Perhaps, too, he was embarrassed that his church condemned Gina's own people to damnation.

She remembered visiting her orthodox aunt and uncle in the Galilean hills, where Uncle Philo's branch of the family had lived for a hundred years. They always kept the Shabbat, and while living with them in Zefat, Gina had kept it, too. Through the curtain, she used to watch the men nodding over their Torah scrolls at the minyan on Saturday mornings. In the afternoon, Aunt Hannah would often send her to bring home strangers who didn't have a place to eat the Shabbat dinner.

The Arabs of Zefat had burned down the Hoffman house in 1948, when the partition of Palestine turned Arabs and Jews against each other. After fleeing down the mountain to Tiberias, her family hid for a week until the Zionists took back Zefat. Then it was the Arabs' turn to flee, and they had never returned.

This Nazim, Gina thought uneasily, tossing the last of her personals into her dark green Volvo station wagon, had the bitter look of a man who had been done out of an inheritance. He would probably not have bought the house if he had known she was a Jew. She must warn Jerry not to tell him. Closing the carved front doors of her Spanish mansion for a last time, Gina paused to gaze at a sunset that was turning the western sky a pale lavender. The marble fountain burbled gently, reflecting the rays and scattering them into splinters of light as the water fell back into the pool. *This too shall pass,* the small voice said, keeping her company in her loss. *There is much joy to come. Much joy.* Gina looked down at the ring, touched it, and smiled. Olive Street would not be so bad. She was free.

∽∾◡∾∾

Jerry was waiting for her in the living room of the new place. He had cooked steak and corn on the outdoor grill and had a salad waiting on the table. "To you." He held up his glass with a look in his eyes that said he wanted to stay the night. "To the new house and us."

After the meal, Gina looked across the candlelight at Jerry. "This

Nazim really bothers me. What's he here for, anyway?"

"I happen to know," Jerry said, getting up to toss another log on the fire. "He came to Homer Healey's office today with an offer. More than he offered us."

"Don't tell me. He's going to buy your church and turn it into a mosque. You remember when all those people committed suicide near San Diego? The ones that wanted to ride the Hale-Bopp comet? Ever since, I've been waiting for some new religious cult to start up here." She sat on the faded sofa facing the fireplace and watched the dying sparks land on the stone hearth.

"Not so far off," Jerry said, sitting down beside her with his arm along the back of the sofa, lightly touching her neck. "Nazim's bribed Reverend Healey to stop supporting Israel and go undercover for the Arabs."

"Dammit!" Gina set down her glass and clasped her long, nervous fingers around her knees. "He wants to turn the evangelicals against Israel, so nobody in America will care when the Arabs take back Palestine." Ignoring Jerry's comforting arm, she began pacing back and forth in front of the fireplace. "Next time there's a pogrom in the world, Jews will have no place to run."

For years Gina hadn't thought about going to shul and watching from behind the curtain as the men in their white shawls bowed rhythmically in prayer. A sudden backwash of memory carried her to Uncle Chaim's tiny living room in Zefat, with its balcony overhanging the narrow cobbled street, the balcony where hand-washed *tsizsit* hung, drying in the sun. She remembered the pace picking up as sunset approached on Friday. Everyone hurried to finish all the work before the sun dropped behind the mountains. After laying out the challah bread, Aunt Hannah would cover it with an embroidered cloth. The grandchildren's job was to tear up toilet paper, putting it in plastic bags by the toilets, for not even the tearing of paper was permitted on the holy day. Finally nothing was left to do but eat, pray and breathe. Then Aunt Hannah would light the sabbath candles and put her hands over her eyes so she would be in the darkness of prayer while saying the ancient words, *"Baruch atah adonai, elohainu melech ha-olam* . . . Blessed are you Lord, King of the Universe . . ."* Gina had forgotten the rest, but had a sudden urge to look up the prayer she had heard so often as a child.

Very happy, very happy. Do not forget the prayers. The voice spoke softly in her head, and instead of impatience, Gina felt a soft peace fall over her like a shawl. Without arguing, she smiled and turned to stare at the flames. Perhaps she would celebrate Shabbat when Kief arrived with his Swedish girlfriend and their new baby. Kief would not mind, for he was "into religion," as he put it. Not that what he called religion would be recognizable to Uncle Chaim and Aunt Hannah. Idol worship, they would call Kief's little meditation altar with its incense and statue of the Buddha. Having always prided herself on being tolerant, Gina now realized that her tolerance was really indifference. I've been ungrateful, she thought. I could at least have been Jew enough to keep Shabbat.

"Jerry, how do we stop this Nazim?" She leaned over the fireplace, her hands curled tightly around the edge of the faux marble mantelpiece.

Watching the way Gina's pale blue silk dress moved over her full hips, Jerry felt his heart would burst, as he did when monthly communion time came at the church. He forgot himself in love, in contemplation of this woman who seemed so much a part of him that his eyes blurred when he thought of her, feeling no difference between them.

"Jesus," he breathed, "give me Gina to care for, and I will, I will." For years she had taken care of him. Now he longed to protect her from un-nameable demons, from the frantic pace that seemed built into her as if she were a racing metronome, from the dark rages that came over her when deals fell through or when clients pushed her patience beyond its limits.

Her Jewishness fascinated him. She was somehow ancient and fragile, as if she herself had suffered all the wrongs done to her people. She was of the same body as his Christ, made up of the same flesh and bone that had introduced God into the world. Jerry could not understand why Homer Healey objected to marriage between Jews and Christians. The very existence of Gina and her people was living proof that God had interrupted the world in its headlong flight to ruin.

"We should try to keep an eye on Nazim," Jerry said.

"Through Annie," Gina agreed, tapping her fingers on the mantelpiece. "We've got him bugged and we can blow the story to the newspapers at the right moment." Gina snapped her fingers and smiled. "Besides, Kief's coming home this weekend. There's a woman and a baby to celebrate. Mazel tov time." She turned to Jerry and held him close, feeling the warmth of his body through her silk dress.

❧

Nazim sat in the moonlight beside the sparkling fountain, savoring the stars as he imagined his desert ancestors had. The first step in his western venture had landed solidly, he thought, wanting to call Abdul for a cigarette, then deciding simply to taste the night air. He wished that his wives would arrive, sturdy Fatima, with her newborn baby girl, and the dewy-eyed Yasmin, only sixteen. They were inseparable, like mother and daughter, and had refused his offer of separate mansions.

Nazim laced his graceful fingers behind his head and looked up at the stars, wishing that, like the Prophet, he could hear the voice of Allah. Instead, he had only his feelings to guide him. He thought of unkempt, hollow-cheeked women squatting in refugee camps. He thought of angry young warriors, who in another age would have carved out an empire for Allah, but were now reduced to cutting down the occasional Arab merchant who sold to Israelis.

His people were not enjoying fountains and mansions by the sea but were waiting in their tents for him to deliver them, for him to drive out the unbelievers from the Holy Land. *Holy to whom?* asked a nagging voice in his head. Jerusalem had never been as sacred to the Arabs as it was to the Jews and Christians. The Koran did not refer to it as a holy city. Mohammed's ascension from the site of the Temple Mount was only a dream, a legend. Nazim knew that, for he was well-educated in Muslim literature and history. Nevertheless, land once conquered for Allah must remain his and his alone. Inshallah. The will of Allah must be done, he vowed, his slender shoulders shivering in the sudden cool breeze from the sea. The barbarous Western practices of free love and materialism must not win over the simple, holy message of the Prophet to love Allah and serve him utterly.

The waves crashed on the shore, shaking the ground under Nazim's feet. He smiled, thinking how easy it would be to land commando boats by night on this unguarded coast, how easy to bring ashore infiltrators and assassins, devoted to winning America for the cause of Allah. The Jews of New York would pay for the suffering of the Palestinian people. The time was not far off. Years before, their plan to blow up the World Trade Center had been moderately successful, but his people had been careless about whom they brought into the organization. Had it not been for an infiltrator who betrayed the cause, the subways and tunnel systems of Manhattan would have been destroyed. He must be more careful in the future.

Already the economy of the Great Satan was beginning to crumble and it was only a matter of time before angry, dispossessed mobs in the cities turned on each other like dogs. Then, if prophecy were accurate, once-powerful America would fall into separate, more vulnerable states, with a few rich and many poor, like most of the wretched third-world governments. No longer did fear of the communist empire hold America together. The decadent Americans would soon go the way the godless communists had gone, and this wide, rich land would be taken by those with the will to take it.

Gazing up at the stars again, Nazim imagined that he was back in Lebanon, in the embroidered tents of his Bedouin ancestors, who had watched and prayed under those same stars. He was sure that the Arabs' wealth had been given by Allah so they could conquer the world for him. Arabs controlled the oil and were amassing weaponry for the final jihad that would cause the Crescent flag to fly over every nation. The world would become a paradise where order and simple piety ruled. All men would kneel to Allah, and all women would kneel to their men. Remembering that it was time to read his nightly ten pages from the Koran, Nazim rubbed his cold hands together and went into the living room, which now held no personals but his own.

2

Gina took a break from scrubbing the kitchen cupboards of her new home, wondering whether to line the shelves with contact paper, preparing for a long stay, or to tack down shelf paper. After all, she might be here only a little while. She felt an itch to go somewhere, to do something that was not part of making money for Hoffman Homes. Maybe she would travel to Israel again. Never having made the pilgrimage to the land where his Lord had taught and died, Jerry had been urging her to visit Jerusalem with him at Easter time. Gina found it hard to imagine that the God of the universe would take human form. In her mind, God had as little to do with mankind as possible, except to blast it from time to time with plague, earthquake or genocide in punishment for sins that most people did not even know they had committed. Jerry explained that if you were trying to talk to ants in an ant colony, you would have to become an ant and speak ant language. That was what God had done by incarnating as Jesus. Gina thought he was oversimplifying, but that was dear Jerry.

She picked up Uncle Philo's letters again, wondering what sort of God he had believed in that took him so far from home. In one envelope she found a photo of Shirdi Baba, a bony man with deep-set blue eyes and a shaggy white beard. He wore a babushka over his forehead, tied in back. His eyes seemed alive, and, for a moment, she saw them dance, as if he would have shared a joke had they spoken the same language.

She tucked the picture into the corner of the window over her sink, looking again at the eyes, which no longer danced but seemed to stare through her. Then she sat down with one of the yellowing letters from Shirdi.

"The master says," Philo wrote in his neat, delicate hand, "that we must give as much as we can to those who ask us for help. He himself gives away whatever he receives. When rich people come, he sometimes asks for a hundred pounds. They may squirm, but few refuse. Then, right in front of them, he distributes it to poor women with children and others in need. Then he laughs, as if delighted with a joke. Today I asked him how I should lead my life. Should I go to the mountains and meditate? 'No,' said the master. 'Stay and face your responsibilities. Serve others, but do not forget to renew yourself in prayer. Do not forget to contemplate the God who lives in you. Devote yourself to love. Do not think so much. Love me and trust me, for I am not merely who I seem to be.'"

Gina uneasily put the letter aside, for the words reminded her of those she had been hearing in her head and Jerry's quotations from Jesus. The idea of a God who lives inside you seemed to her much more sensible than Jerry's theory about ants. Still, having known Uncle Chaim, she could perhaps believe in holy men like Shirdi Baba. Who, she wondered, are these beings, these men who drop into human history for a brief moment and confuse the honest issues of making a living and caring for one's family—and maybe having a little pleasure in life? Survival came first. Maybe these masters, these Godmen, as Philo called them, could make food out of nothing and heal people with the wave of a hand, but the rest of us have to pay for groceries and health insurance.

Trust me, her inner voice said faintly, as if heard through heavy static. *The price the world asks is too high, and the soul must not pay it. Trust me.* Gina shrugged the voice away, thinking that the last time someone had asked for her trust it was her ex-husband, who had walked away with the business they had started and both homes they had built. The world has not improved much since the days of Jesus and this Shirdi Baba, she thought, checking her refrigerator to see if she had enough shmaltz herring. Kief was coming for the weekend, and she was going to prepare a Shabbat table that would make his Zen meditation altar look pitiful.

∽∾∾

Just as Kief's multicolored Volkswagen was pulling into the driveway, the telephone rang. Cradling the phone between her cheek and shoulder, Gina pushed a loaf of challah bread into the oven and dropped matzoh balls into the boiling soup.

"This guy Nazim has two wives." Annie's voice was breathless and low, as if she were afraid of being overheard. "They just got here. Along with some men carrying those rifles that look like machine guns. Y'know what I mean?"

"Assault rifles, I guess they are, Annie," Gina said. "And those men must be his bodyguards. Look, Annie, my son and his family are just coming up the front walk. Anything else?"

"Yeah. David saw a pile of checks on Nazim's desk. Made out to American senators. He knows the names. Big checks, Gina."

"Oh God," Gina said. "What's his game, anyway? Look, don't phone me. Just come over or mail me a note. It won't be long before he bugs your phone, if he hasn't already. Talk to you tomorrow, Annie. Stay cool, okay?"

As if Annie's message had dirtied her palms, Gina wiped her hands on her apron. She uncomfortably remembered Realtors from San Diego telling her about secretive Arab deals for oceanfront houses with security. Her ex had mentioned one sale on the south shore of Long Island. So they were buying up U.S. land, along with the Chinese, and anybody else whose country hadn't been bankrupted by arms spending. Why they were buying senators was anybody's guess. Maybe for the next vote on aid to Israel. She heard the car door slam and footsteps on the walk.

Kief didn't bother to ring but pushed the door open so hard that the handle left a dent in the drywall. Gina pulled off her apron and ran to meet him. It had been a year since she had last seen her son, and now he was bringing home a woman and their child. She would not think about Nazim until tomorrow.

Over Kief's shoulder Gina saw a blond woman, as tall as he and just as slim. These two, she thought, must be living on roots and berries, like the skeletal vegan, David. She hoped the baby was getting milk rather than carrot juice smoothies, but vowed not to ask.

"This is Kori, Mom. And John Philo." He put his arm around the woman, whose wisps of ash-blond hair stirred around her incongruously childlike, triangular face. Seeing Kori's dazzling smile, framed by dimples in her pink cheeks, Gina was won over. She hoped the baby would have Kori's looks, for Kief, with his broad face, had never been particularly handsome, and two orthodontists had given up on his teeth. Luckily he had wide shoulders, thick curly hair like the baby in Kori's arms, and a good set of brains, though God, he used them in weird ways. Probably so did this woman archeologist. Gina guessed that in Egypt they had sat around the campfire at night gluing five-thousand-year-old clay pots back together. Well, he would not have cared for any other sort of woman. Being careful not to scare the baby with too sudden a movement, Gina gathered mother and child in a single embrace.

John Philo looked up at her with his astonishingly pale blue eyes, and for a moment she stared back. She had seen eyes that color before, but they were old and tired, under broad white brows. Feeling strangely timid, she put her left hand on his head and said his full name softly. The baby laughed and reached up, grabbing her finger so he could examine the ring. His brow furrowed.

"You would think he recognized it," laughed Kori. "He doesn't usually pay attention to jewelry. Just to things that move." Her voice was musical and low, and her eyes, light blue like the baby's, were clear as the California sky.

Kief could have done a lot worse, Gina decided. She wondered about her son and this woman. Did they love each other, or had they just made this baby by accident? After meeting Kori, Gina felt reassured. If Kief didn't love this woman, he was even odder than she had feared. For a moment a pang of jealousy shot through her, and she felt old, unlovable. Once Kief had loved her as this grandson of hers loved his mother. Now, she wondered what he felt for her, other than a vague, awkward friendship. It had been a long time since she felt that he really cared about her. During their few visits in recent years, they had talked only of his interests. Perhaps he was simply bored with her and the real estate business. Kori obviously had more to offer, and it was no wonder that Kief's eyes kept straying to her, even when he spoke to his mother.

"I like the new house," Kief said. "It's homey. Not like the mansion you wrote about. What happened to the mansion, anyway?"

"Sold it to an Arab," Gina said shortly. "Like a lot of folks have been doing lately."

Kief surprised her by showing interest. "It's happening up in Santa Cruz, too," he said. "There's talk of an Arab fundamentalist movement spreading throughout the U.S. They're not just buying land in the inner cities, but setting up brainwashing bases for the unemployed and homeless. Conversion centers, they call them." He sat on the hassock near Kori's feet and watched as she settled the baby on her lap and began to nurse him.

"What use could such men be to Arabs?" Gina handed Kief a glass of iced tea and set another glass on the table beside Kori, who had become quiet and remote as the baby sucked noisily. "I've never heard of fundamentalists doing social service."

"I think the idea is to start with terrorist bombings. Next they'll try to organize the poor into a revolutionary army," Kief said, stirring the ice with one finger. Gina used to be annoyed when he did that, but now she watched without wanting him to change.

Kief went on speaking softly, as if to himself. "Maybe they're trying to enlist the fifty million people in this country who have nothing to lose. A jihad, they call it. A holy war against the decadent West. The Great Satan, remember? They haven't changed their strategy. Just their tactics."

Gina remembered what Annie had said about the big checks on Nazim's desk and wondered what favors Nazim was buying. She thought of Annie and gentle David living out of their truck. Not likely they would join some wild-eyed foreign army bent on destroying the handful of corporations that owned most of America. "You think the poor in this country could get that kind of act together?"

"With help, they could." Kief took the baby from Kori so she could button her blouse. John Philo drooled a bit of milk from one corner of his round pink mouth, and his eyes drifted shut. "There's talk up in the Bay Area of a People's Army. Apartment buildings are being bought and renovated for the faithful. You join up and swear to stay off drugs and booze, and they give you a nice apartment. Maybe even a gun."

"I've heard they do training missions up in the Sierras," Kori said, her low voice faintly singsong, rising with a Scandinavian lilt in unexpected places. "We have seen big trucks full of men going up into the mountains."

"And nobody stops them? The FBI? The CIA? What are they doing about it?" Gina's hand shook as she picked up Kief's empty glass. "God knows they take enough of our money to deal with a few revolutionary nuts."

"The government's looking the other way and so is the media." Kief laid the baby on his fluffy white blanket, then rubbed John Philo's back until he burped and went back to sleep. "A lot of money that used to go to the CIA is going into other hands. Nobody thinks we need spies, now that the U.S.S.R. has dropped out. I didn't used to think so either."

"We hope to make a safe little place for ourselves," Kori said, putting her long, slender hand on Kief's shoulder. "The day after I flew in, we bought a piece of land, fifty acres in the mountains above Santa Cruz.

There's a little cottage and a studio. Kief thinks you might like to come and stay with us if troubles come to the cities. It should be safe up there."

Gina felt a leap of joy that Kief had thought of her, wanted her. Perhaps having this child had made him realize how much she had loved him, still loved him. She looked at her son with his wide mouth, irregular nose and unruly black curls, for a moment remembering how beautiful he had seemed to her when he was little. It was as if no time, no space had come between them. *You see how it is,* said the voice in her head. *Only the now—no time, no space. What use are plans? Games played with water and wind is all they are. What you have is here, now, and that is all you have.*

I see what you mean, she answered silently, wanting to disagree, but having no arguments in this moment, feeling that she was part of Kief, Kori and their child. But I must plan, I must. What if all they say is true, and bad times are coming? There's a child to think of now. "We have police to handle any trouble in the cities," Gina said.

Kief shook his head. "They're from the same class as the rebels. You think they will fire on their own people? Nobody thinks the government cares about them anymore. Some of our friends in Berkeley are talking revolution."

"Oh, Berkeley," Gina shrugged. "Some guy gets up on stage with a guitar and a big mouth, everyone gets stoned, and a few windows get smashed. No sweat. We've been through that before. You were there yourself once upon a time. Getting arrested, as I recall."

"They aren't stoned now." Without looking, Kief reached up to hold Kori's hand. "They're drilling with gas masks and assault rifles and putting their kids in schools where they learn math and science and how to make explosives. It's happening in other cities, too. Even Washington D.C."

"We are thinking," said Kori, "that it might be wise to set up our own little community. Raise vegetables, have a generator." She looked at Gina inquiringly. "Generator is what you call it? Yes? What do you think?"

Gina had never expected her dreamy, pacifist son to turn into a survivalist. "I think that's premature," she said, getting up to put lunch on the table. "The economy's weak, it's true, but it's gone up and down before. In a year or two, most people will be back to buying jet skis and vacation homes."

"Well, if you ever need it," Kief said, putting the plates on the embroidered linen tablecloth, "you have a place to stay. Free veggies, too. We're vegetarians now, preparing for India."

Not registering the word India at first, Gina smiled at him, wondering that she had ever thought him plain. Since reaching thirty, he had become quite beautiful, in a rough, masculine sort of way. Or perhaps she thought so because he had invited her to live with them. "I'll come visit," she said, a glad ring to her voice that made the baby stir and flutter his eyelids, "but not because I need a place to run to. It's been a long time since I've had a taste of family. I'd like to get to know my grandson." Her eyes clouded as she looked down, wondering what to do with her suddenly trembling hands. "And what's this about India?" Rubbing her cold palms together, she had a quick vision of skinny brown people lying in heaps along the streets of Calcutta.

"Kief, perhaps I should explain. Yes? It will sound like craziness." Kori passed her hands over her short, pale hair and sighed. "You have not, I think, heard of a great healer and holy man in India? He has built schools, hospitals and universities. Millions of his people have gone into Indian villages to teach and build clinics and water supplies."

"And he does miracles," Kief interrupted, waving his hands the way he did as a child when he wanted his mother's attention. "Sick people, dying people, are healed. He materializes objects out of thin air."

Kori gently placed her hand over his mouth. "Too much, too fast," she said. "It is enough to know that this being called Sai Baba is changing India and the world, doing much good for the people. We want to see him, Mother."

It was the first time Kori had called her Mother, and Gina felt awkward, as if she had been given a present by a stranger. Kori's gift made it harder to argue against the words Gina had just heard, but she could not let them pass. "You're both educated people," she began, feeling a lecture coming on, like the kind Kief had turned off when he took up Buddhism, shaved his head and lived for weeks on a mountaintop, eating odd food. "You have a real life. A child. I hope you don't go chasing after foreign gods and chanting Hare Krishna songs, like those characters in the yellow robes, the ones that beg and dance in the street."

Kori put her hand over Kief's mouth again, as he started to answer. "No strange gods," she said. "Sai Baba is not starting a new religion. He says there are enough religions already, that we should keep whatever one we grew up in, if we want to. People should love God and serve mankind. It sounds to me like what Jesus taught, and I believe it."

Gina felt her arguments dry up and blow away, except for one, her ace. "I know who Sai Baba is," she said, in the tone of somebody throwing down a winning card. "He died years ago in Shirdi, near Bombay. My Uncle Philo sent me letters about him. Your Sai Baba is a fake." Gina felt the same exhilaration as when she could deflate one of Kief's silly childhood notions by pointing to a page in the encyclopedia.

"That was the first Sai Baba," Kief said, pushing away Kori's hand, his voice so loud that the baby woke up and began to cry. "This one is Sathya Sai Baba. When he was fourteen, he announced to his parents that he was the same being as Shirdi Baba, then left home to teach and do miracles."

"Just a minute, just a minute," Gina said, clinking her gold bangles together warningly. "My Uncle Philo said . . ."

"I would like to read these letters from your uncle." Kori scooped up the squalling baby and pushed him into Kief's arms. "It is curious to me that you know of the first Sai Baba. But now, Mother, we have not spoken about Kief and me. How all this came about. I would like you to know it. Kief, my love," she said, with a smile like the one Gina imagined Helen of Troy had launched a war with. "Will you take the baby out for a walk? I would like to tell your mother some things."

Gina was relieved when Kief went outside with the baby. She patted the cushion beside her on the couch. "Sit here, Kori, next to me. I want to hear how you and Kief got from there to here." She felt more comfortable, back on the familiar turf of human relationships, loving, quarreling, making a life. For a moment Gina sat in silence, looking at Kori's smooth, childlike face and incongruously aged, intelligent eyes. "I think you have come a long way to be with us," she said, her voice faltering as Jerry's did so often. "You don't seem to me like an ordinary person."

Kori had come a long way indeed, as it turned out, and was not at all ordinary. She had been trained as an Egyptologist by her father, whose coldness had turned her against marriage and men, while her passive mother had turned her against marriage and women. Kori admitted she had been a hard case, given to solitude and scholarship, intent on making the reputation her father intended for her. She and Kief had connected over a bottle of sour Egyptian wine, near a dying campfire long after the other archeologists had gone to bed. It had been a ritual occasion, her first brush with religious emotion. Kief had offered to teach her what he knew of tantric sex, which was supposed to end, not in consummation, but in union with divinity. For them, it had turned into sex of the common kind, but pleasant enough that they kept it up for the two months left of Kief's stay in Egypt.

He had wanted Kori to come back with him to America, but she was studying the old goddess lore with a female shaman who knew many stories from the ancient days when the mother goddess had ruled the earth. These stories had been published in Kori's new book, which was now making her a sensation in feminist academic circles.

Kief had just returned to California after a long stay at a dig in New Mexico, when he learned from Kori that they had a son. She had agreed to come and live with him, if they could find a home far away from the city. On their first drive into the mountains, they had found the property they wanted and immediately bought it. Gina groaned inwardly at the price Kori quoted and wished they had let her negotiate the deal.

But, for whatever reason, Kief had never let her in on decisions until it was too late to change them.

While Kori was telling Gina about the new place, Kief came in with the baby. His face brightened as he described the vegetable garden and the way the pine trees rose through the early morning mist. "It is a good place," Kori said offhandedly, as was her way. "We hope to harvest the vegetables before going to India."

Gina's fists clenched, and she was ready to fight again. It was clear that this Indian escapade was Kori's idea. "Can't you go alone? I'd be glad to take care of the baby. And Kief." The baby was Kori's gift to them both, Gina thought, stroking John Philo's soft, smooth back. She felt a sudden surge of anger at this foreign worshipper of mother goddesses, who wanted to take Gina's men off to a place where people suffered needlessly and died on filthy sidewalks. She hated herself for sounding hostile, showing the unattractive side that she was usually able to keep under wraps.

"The ashram is clean," Kori said, taking no offense. "Many children are brought there and do very well. Kief and I are used to simple living, and the baby takes only breast milk. I think now would be quite the best time to go." She gathered up the baby, whose arms waved like Kief's during an argument, kissed Gina on the cheek, and went upstairs.

Long after Kori and Kief had gone to bed, Gina lay awake watching the moonlight through the treetops from her second-floor bedroom window. What a crazy idea, this notion of theirs to go off to India and live in an ashram. The baby would get sick from the filthy water, and the doctors would likely want to apply leeches. She tossed off her quilt and punched her pillow, trying to give it a little life. The good plump pillows had hastily been put on the bed in the guest room, although Kief and Kori, given their strange, Oriental notions, probably didn't even use pillows.

Gina kicked off her flowered sheet and went to the window, letting the wind blow through her hair and flutter her full, embroidered nightgown. Maybe she could convince them to leave the baby with her while they played at being *tzaddiks*. The Hebrew word came back to her, sounding surprisingly like the Sanskrit word, *sadhus*, that Kori had used. Uncle Chaim had come from a long line of tzaddiks and was the happiest man Gina had ever known. The deep laugh lines around his eyes and mouth were drawn by the finger of God, Uncle Chaim said. Out of respect he said *Ha-Shem*, instead of God.

Once, Gina had gone to shul and watched through the curtain as he danced around the Torah, arms outstretched as if to embrace the whole world. Maybe this tzaddik madness was in the genes, she thought uneasily. Maybe Kief had inherited it from Uncle Philo and Uncle Chaim, like nearsightedness or scoliosis. To her, their beliefs were a jumble of dreams, a curtain like the one that divided her from the men dancing in ecstasy around the Torah.

As the full moon sailed into view, she smiled at the round, shadowed face which seemed to smile back, as it had when she was a child. Feeling that she could sleep now, Gina sighed for a moment and leaned her forehead against the window frame. In a shower of sparks behind her closed lids, she saw a small dark man in an orange robe, with a shock of black hair and a face that shone like the moon. *Who do you think has been calling you?* he asked, his full lips in a half smile. *It is I. Your Uncle Philo knew me and you wear my ring. Why do you fear? I want you to come to me. I want you to come as a married woman. Are you waiting for a telegram?*

Gina jumped back from the window as if it carried some exotic disease. She thought of India, imagining the water and food Kief's little family would be eating for the next six months of their lives. Why had they chosen to visit such a dirty, charmless place? Had they put some sort of spell on her, with their talk of ancient gods and new religions? She felt the need for a prolonged submersion in the Jacuzzi and began to miss her mansion with its spotlit pool and bubbling hot tub.

The phone on the nightstand rang and she fell onto the bed, trying to answer before the baby woke up. Dim in her maternal memory was the sense that it was better to die in battle with the phone than to let it ring and wake the baby.

"Gina?" The voice was Jerry's. "I know it's the middle of the night, but I've just had a dream. I've got to talk to you. Somebody told me that I should go to India. In my dream, there was a man wearing an orange robe. He said not to be afraid, but that I should come and see him. Gina?"

She sank her face in the pillow sobbing. "I don't want this person in my life, Jerry. He's got Kief and my grandson. I'm wearing his ring, and I keep hearing his voice. Maybe I should talk to your minister. Maybe I'm possessed."

"Gina, I'm coming over right now." Jerry's voice was full and deep, not tentative as it usually was. "We've got to decide if we're going to get married. It's not something to play with anymore. I've been told we are to marry."

"Oh God," Gina said, the tears burning under her eyelids. "I have, too. So come over and stay for breakfast. I'll introduce you to the family."

⁂

Kief sat at the kitchen table, showing Jerry a map of India taken from a satellite photo. "Strange," he said. "In this picture, everybody sees the face of Sai Baba. Not the one from Shirdi who died eighty years ago. This one is living now in the south central part of India."

"I don't believe it," Gina said, serving up bagels and lox. Her head ached, and the Sai Baba they were talking about was different from Uncle Philo's. "Sai Baba's been dead for a long time. Look, here's his ring. Whoever this other one is, I don't know him."

Little John Philo crowed and threw up his hands, as if he'd just won the triathlon. "You be quiet," Gina said, thrusting her face close to his. "You may think you're Uncle Philo, but you're just a baby with something dirty in your pants."

Kori got up. "You are right about that. I will change him. Kief, can you explain all this to your mother?"

"I don't think so." Kief carefully smeared cream cheese and chives on his bagel, sprinkling pepper over it, reliving one of the few Jewish rituals he had grown up with. "All I know is that our South Indian friend in Santa Cruz says we should go to see Sai Baba, that he's the same as the other one. Don't ask me how. Reincarnation, I suppose. He does miracles, they say. Raises the dead, heals the sick and sacred ash falls from his fingers. Vibhuti, it's called. Our friend gave us some. Here."

Jerry opened the little packet decorated with curling Sanskrit symbols. "In my dream, he put this on my forehead. Sai Baba, I mean. Smeared on a whole handful. There was a big streak of gray across my face. I fell down and put my forehead against his feet."

"Oh, come on," Gina said roughly, snatching away the packet. "I thought you were a Christian."

Jerry laid his large hand over hers and looked at her so hard that she backed off. "I was never so much a Christian as when I was at his feet. In the dream he gave me a ring, and Jesus' face was on it."

"Yes," Kief said, carefully scooping up the gray ash and returning it to the packet. "He materializes objects like that. Sometimes with the face of Jesus. Sometimes with his own face or a Hindu symbol. His idea is that staying with your own religion is best, but you shouldn't knock anybody else's. He says there's only one religion, the religion of love."

"Well, that sounds safe enough," Gina snapped. "Who's going to argue with love?" She turned to Jerry, slamming her hand on the kitchen table. "I suppose now you plan to go on this harebrained trip to India? Everybody I love is going to wind up with dysentery or elephantiasis, falling at the feet of some guru who's pretending to be Uncle Philo's Baba." For a moment the ring seemed to burn on her finger, and she twisted it up to her knuckle. *I am who I am,* the voice said. *So are you. Wake up. Come.*

"Will you go with us, Mom?" Kief laid his hand on hers. "We'd like your help with the baby and to keep us all from freaking out. That can happen, our friend said."

Gina remembered the face in the moonlight and the words that came like a cry from her own heart. "I'll think about it," she said. "But only because of the baby."

"Let's get married first," Jerry said. He turned to Kief. "You should, too. Sai Baba wants couples to be married, not just living together."

"Tell Kori." Kief crossed the knife and fork carefully on his empty plate. "She's the one who doesn't believe in marriage."

Jerry tried talking to Kori, who shook her head. "I'm going to India, but not with anyone else's name. It is a belief I have. Bear with me." She laid the baby on the bed and lightly tickled his bare tummy until he kicked his feet and laughed. "Gina, why don't you play with him while I take a shower? The two of you should be together more often. I will try not to be jealous."

Kori slung a bath towel over her shoulder and headed out the door, then turned back for a moment. "I wish my mother had lived to hold this baby," she said, her voice so even and cool that Gina felt goose-bumps rise on her arms. "She killed herself because I had put her out of my life and gone to live with my father. Now that I have a child of my own, I understand."

Before Gina could answer, Kori was down the hall, and shower water was splashing furiously in the bathroom. That young woman is carrying a heavy burden, she thought, wanting to tell Kori that when people kill themselves, they are trying to take you with them. In death they can possess you as in no other way. Holding little John Philo close to her heart, Gina went outside on the front porch. It was no wonder Kori kept herself aloof from marriage, from any connection that might drag her down the same black hole her mother had disappeared into.

Gina felt dampness on her arms and looked up as the sun was beginning to burn through the foggy marine air. Light-blue jacaranda petals, the color of Kori's eyes, were falling from the treetops. One fell into the baby's hand, and he held it close to his eyes, smiling. She noticed that this baby looked at things first and then put them in his mouth, which was the opposite of what most babies did. Checking out the food supply seemed not so important to him as seeing all there was to see. A born dreamer, like my Uncle Philo, she thought. For a moment she could have sworn that the baby winked at her, but it was probably just his response to the petal touching his eyelid.

It took Gina a moment to realize that someone was calling her name. Annie had just stepped out of her truck with baby Jason under one arm, his arms and legs dangling. From this distance he looked like a small pink pig. Annie herself was wearing some sort of gray, shroud-like caftan that billowed around her in the gentle breeze. Nazim hadn't wasted any time getting her covered up and invisible.

"You're probably wondering why I'm wearing this thing," Annie said breathlessly, as she sat down beside Gina in the small front yard. "Hey, is that your grandson? Give him a kiss, Jason." She held her baby close to John Philo, who lunged backward against Gina's shoulder and began to cry.

"Funny, babies usually like each other," Annie said, trying to hold down Jason's flailing arms.

"Why are you wearing that thing?" Gina asked, frowning. "Nazim afraid you'll seduce him?"

"No, I haven't even talked to Mr. Nazim." Annie put Jason down and gave him a cookie, which disappeared messily into his mouth. "The two wives came this morning and had a talk with me. They're really nice. Friendly with each other, which I can't hardly believe. I'd kill any woman who tried to share my David. Anyway, Fatima, that's the older one, gave me this cover-up. Says I gotta wear it all the time except in my room or alone with my husband."

"Bummer," said Gina, thinking of the hot summer days Annie was going to spend under that robe, trying to cook and clean with her sleeves falling into the soup or the slop pail. "You think the job is worth it?"

"Actually, yeah," Annie said. "Fatima explained that men gawk at women and think bad thoughts and maybe even rape us because we wear sexy clothes, y'know?" Jason kicked her and she gave him another cookie. "Somebody tried to rape me once, right in the homeless shelter. When they pulled him off, he said it was because I was wearing a halter top and shorts. Which I was, actually. So maybe Fatima is right. Anyhow, I'm wearing the thing and it doesn't feel so bad."

"What does David think of it?" Gina carefully held John Philo beyond the range of Jason's wet, waving cookie.

"At first he thought it was weird looking, but then he said that at least nobody would try to take me away from him. Wasn't that sweet? As if I was great to look at, or something. David really likes Mr. Nazim. They've been talking about how to help homeless people, and he asked David where he could meet some. David's taking him down to the meat rack today."

Gina knew where she meant, down on the lower east side, where jobless men stood around waiting until someone hired them for a day's work. She had just read in the paper that some Arabs were renovating an apartment house in Florida for the homeless. Like the Arabs in Washington and Santa Cruz and God knows where else, Nazim was recruiting himself an army. "Did he promise them guns?" She avoided looking at Annie, not wanting the girl to realize that her trust in the two of them as spies was fast evaporating.

"Oh no, nothing like that. He says he's going to build a school for them and their children, so's they can get ahead. A real good school, starting with babies. Day care, y'know. Maybe an apartment house, too, like one his friends are building in Florida. David and I are real excited about getting Jason into a free school. Mr. Nazim says it's going to be the best. Even better than those fancy private schools."

So the revolution has come to Santa Barbara, Gina said to herself, wondering if Annie was right about the guns. Maybe David hasn't told her. Women are supposed to tend to the food and the kids, Nazim would say. Leave them out of men's work. Gina wondered if she'd ever hear more about the checks payable to important senators. The best way would be to jolly Annie and David along, not letting on that she knew what Nazim was up to. "Well, Nazim really does sound terrific, Annie," she said, hating the falseness in her voice. "I guess you lucked out."

"You betcha," Annie smiled, picking up Jason and tossing the now-formless cookie into the eugenia hedge. "It's biodegradable," she explained, catching Gina's frown. "I know about that stuff. Mr. Nazim says we're all responsible to God for keeping the world neat and clean, especially us women."

"Not exactly a new idea," Gina muttered. Then she smiled brightly, hiding her discomfort. "You come by again next week and tell me how it's going for you, okay? I really want to know."

As Annie drove off, Gina wondered if her son would be willing to play at being homeless for a day. If Nazim hired him, Kief might be able to learn more than she could now expect to get from Annie.

∞◡◠◡∾

The next day, Kief put on his old pair of ripped dungarees, a dirty T-shirt and a crumpled safari hat that sat low on his forehead, then took a bus to the meat rack. It had been fifteen years since he had lived in Santa Barbara, and Kief figured that his recently grown beard would prevent anyone from recognizing him. He had also developed strong arms, having dug his share of archeological trenches in Egypt during the two years of his university grant.

Kief had been waiting no longer than ten minutes when a short, stocky man with a red bandanna tied around his head came up and looked him over.

"You got hands that's done some work," the stocky man said. "Not like some of these guys who just play the guitar and open beer cans." The man looked contemptuously over the rest of the wall-sitters. "I'm Bill Stuckey," he said, holding out his palm.

"O'Keefe," Kief said, slapping the man's hand. "Think there's gonna be any work today?"

"Maybe. You new here?"

"Just down from Santa Cruz. Nothing much happenin' there."

"Here we got some action." Bill nudged him. "A guy's gonna build a school over on Ortega Street. We're tearing down an old Quonset hut that the homeless used to live in. Wanna go over and sign up?"

"Sure. What's the pay?" Kief easily caught up with Bill, whose short legs slowed his pace.

"Ten bucks an hour, along with lunch. No drinking, though. The boss says if he catches anybody sneaking a beer, the guy's outta there."

Kief nodded and walked the rest of the way in silence, mentally reviewing Gina's list of questions. His mother was shrewd, and with the right information she might be able to reach someone high enough up to stop Nazim in his tracks. Still, it might be hard to stop somebody from doing good works using his own money. Who could argue with a school for the homeless? He looked over the site, wondering if Nazim's ideas were so bad after all.

The fierce Santa Ana winds blowing in from the desert and the blazing noonday sun reminded Kief of Egypt. He pulled off his drenched T-shirt and hung it on a fencepost, letting the breeze dry him off. After three hours of hauling away lumber and metal, Kief was ready to quit. He thought of Kori's slim body lying under cool cotton sheets as she took her afternoon nap and wished he was beside her.

When Bill Stuckey offered him a sandwich, Kief paused before digging in, noticing that it was ham and cheese. Though his family had retained almost nothing of its Jewish heritage, Kief had always felt a vague disgust at ham. Now that he was mostly vegetarian, the pink, slightly slimy flesh that lay on top of the cheese was even less appealing. Absorbed in trying to chew and talk at the same time, Bill did not notice when Kief slid the ham from his sandwich and pushed it under the log they were sitting on.

"That is good," said a silky, foreign voice behind him. "Not to eat the meat of pig."

Kief turned around and looked up at the slender, elegantly dressed man who stood observing them. The man's face was deeply lined, and his lips were thin and straight, as if they'd had little practice smiling.

Shoving his sandwich back into the paper sack, Bill Stuckey turned red and quickly tried to swallow. "Didn't see you there, Mr. Nazim. We're just taking ourselves a little break."

Nazim nodded. "You will bring this one tonight," he said. "I can see a man of character." His back erect, the Arab walked slowly over to talk with the engineer and architect who were bending over their drawings.

"Hey, you're in good with him," Stuckey said. "Nazim don't usually let the new guys come to night drills."

Kief took a deep breath to keep his heart from beating too fast. "What kind of drills? Sounds like boot camp."

"You'll see." Stuckey suddenly seemed wary. "We gotta finish getting that junk into the dumpster. The backhoe's coming to dig the foundation this afternoon."

That evening, after sharing a pizza with the other workers, Kief called Gina from a pay phone to say he'd be at Nazim's for some kind of military drill and would learn more about the operation. Predictably, she had wanted him to come straight home and not mess with Nazim's undercover army, but Kief cut her off. No one would recognize him, and it was a way of getting into the organization fast. A few days was all it would take to blow Nazim's cover to the state police.

Until he arrived with the truckful of men, Kief had not seen the estate his mother had briefly owned. He wondered how she had been able to give it up. Her dream had been to live in a Spanish-style villa by the ocean, and for years she had talked of little else. He had tuned her out, wondering how he had been born to this woman who longed for possessions more intensely than other women longed for love. Kief was content with the little cottage in the mountains and wanted nothing more than to have Kori and John Philo stay for good. He especially enjoyed carrying the baby in a little sling in front of his belly and going out to pick berries or bringing back an occasional cherimoya for Kori, who had never eaten one before she came to America. But since she refused to get married, he wondered how long he would keep this sudden family.

The fierce heat increased, as the scorching wind from the mountains turned into one of the dreaded sundowners that sometimes whipped fires through the canyons, forcing people to leave with nothing but their pets and jewelry. He remembered his careful mother renting a storage space down near the ocean where she kept special papers, jewelry and photos, rather than risk their loss in the vulnerable home where Kief had grown up. They had almost lost the whole place during the great Sycamore Canyon blaze. He recalled helping to load her real estate records into their station wagon while the flames danced overhead and sparks landed on the roof, which Gina fortunately had equipped with sprinklers. Even as a child, he was not concerned with familiar surroundings or lost objects. What preoccupied him was the sense that nothing is permanent. "None of this is real," he had said to his mother. "When we die, it will be gone anyway. Or belong to someone else."

Gina had yelled at him and smacked his rear with the flat of her hand. "It's real enough to pay for your private school, you pumpkinhead. Get in the front seat and buckle up. I'm going back for my ledgers." Eyebrows singed and hair smelling of smoke, she drove wildly down the narrow canyon road, as flames darted across the road behind them.

Now Kief stood next to the splashing fountain and watched the moon through scudding clouds. He remembered Gina's last letter, the one which said she had finally found her dream house. Like all dreams, he thought, it was only smoke. In the little Olive Street house with Jerry, she seemed happier than he had ever seen her. Perhaps even she could learn to live without grasping at the straw of security. As if people could live forever, not allowing their impersonal atoms to scatter into the cosmos, becoming new, undreamed of beings. Suddenly thinking of India and the holy teacher he would soon visit there, Kief's heart jumped with joy, as it had when he first learned he had a son.

"Come on, O'Keefe," Stuckey called. "We're going down to the beach. Come through the house and out the big double doors to the patio. You gotta carry your shoes."

His sneakers in one hand, Kief hung behind while the other men picked up rifles from a pile near the double doors. One door was open, revealing what looked like a study, and he darted in. It would take him only a moment to glance through the papers on the desk. Sure enough, one was from a major network owner offering to sell his controlling interest to Nazim. Another was from a states' rights organization agreeing to support Nazim's program for local rule and complete elimination of the federal government.

Kief stuffed both letters into the back pocket of his sweaty jeans and was turning to leave the room when he saw a plain, blonde girl in a gray caftan. She frowned at him and shook her finger. Lifting his hands, as if in surrender and innocence, Kief smiled and backed out of the room, hoping that she wouldn't yell for the assault riflemen. The girl stared at Kief as if she dimly recognized him. Hoping she was friendly enough not to turn him in, Kief ran for the porch. He felt foolish picking up a rifle, since the only weapon he had ever fired was a BB gun he had briefly owned in the fourth grade.

"You, over here," yelled the young man who seemed to be in charge. "What's your name?"

"O'Keefe." Saying the alien name made Kief feel awkward. He wasn't used to lying, and his voice betrayed him. Someone turned a spotlight on him, and he blinked, feeling the light strafe his eyes.

"You're Gina Hoffman's son," someone said. "You're not one of us," another cried out. The group of men surged toward Kief as he tried to protect his eyes from the brilliant light. He didn't even think about using his rifle, except as a club to fend off the arms and legs coming at him from all directions. Falling on his knees, he swung the rifle ineffectually at the men, who kicked in his front teeth and pushed him face-down in the sand. Kief was more concerned with coughing out the teeth so he could breathe than with protecting his back from the pounding rifle butts. After the first blow to his lower spine, he could feel nothing.

Kief's breath caught in his throat as he drifted out of his body. He looked down on the scene with distant interest as one man pushed the others away. "He's gone," the man cried. "I'll take him out to the Wilcox property and dump him."

Kief woke up under a ragged, swaying eucalyptus tree and stared through its branches at the moon. Somebody was wrapping him in a blanket, and he tried to focus his eyes on the thin young man, who had no hair on top of his head. An extraterrestrial, perhaps, Kief thought dreamily. Have I been abducted? When he tried to speak to the extra-terrestrial, his lips moved but there was no sound.

"Look, you'll be okay," the young man said. "Just keep quiet about what happened or I'm dead."

"Why did you . . .?" Kief's voice faded again.

"Because I know your mother and she's a nice lady." The young man turned away. "I'm going to call 911. The paramedics'll pick you up in a couple of minutes. Don't tell. Promise?"

"Promise." Kief felt his lips framing the word, but fell back into sleep before he could speak.

Nazim had heard shouting from the drill grounds on the beach, but did not know what had happened until informed later by the drill-team captain. Now he sat cross-legged on the embroidered cushions in his paneled study and stared at a flowered wallhanging. It would be useless to blame the men, he reflected, since their intention was to be loyal and to protect him. Still, the law of hospitality had been offended by this at-tack on a stranger and Nazim was uneasy. The possibility of being tried for accessory to murder did not concern him, for he knew his billions would protect him in the American courts. He bowed down with his face to the floor and prayed for guidance. Behind his closed eyelids, he saw the face of his old teacher Al-Hallaj, named after a saint who was crucified in the tenth century for crying out in spiritual ecstasy that he was God. Actually, the saint had cried out that he was Reality, All-being. Like his master, Nazim understood that the human soul is like a moth burned to ashes by the flame of God. Nazim wished his soul had the wings of a moth, but instead it felt like lead.

"Now I have known, O Lord, what lies within my heart," he chanted aloud. "Though from my deepest gaze your holy face is hidden, I feel you touch my inmost ground." Tears rose to his eyes and he was still, the breath so slight within him that he hardly needed to breathe at all during the long moment of this communion.

Nazim sighed, wondering if the face of his teacher would ever stop reproaching him for leaving the scholar's world to become a warrior. The Koran had been his life, until this task of winning the West for Allah had been laid on him by the militant imam who had replaced Al-Hallaj as his guide. It was said among the Sufis that something of the master's spirit always remains in the student, so that the student will not stray too far from the high path he had been taught. Al-Hallaj would have urged him to retire into prayer and fasting for at least a month after a man had been killed on his property. But the imam would have offered grateful prayers that one more infidel was dead. Between the holy man and the warrior in himself, Nazim had long experienced a personal jihad, which Muslims regarded as more serious than holy war with weapons. The spiritual jihad was between a man's instinct and his faith. Nazim knew his love for Allah was often darkened by his desire to see Allah's rule on earth. He was scholar enough to know the difference, but too much the warrior to give up his cause.

Laying aside the keffiyeh, which made him sweat, Nazim sat bareheaded at his desk to study his correspondence. The letter from the network president must be answered at once, since the jihad needed media support, now that the work was spreading across America. He rifled through the papers on his desk, then pulled open the drawers, one after the other. The letters he had left on the desk were gone.

The members of the household were called together immediately, and Nazim paced up and down in front of them. "Letters are missing from my desk," he said, staring into the frightened faces of his family and staff. "One of you took them. Who was in the study tonight?"

Annie sat in the back behind Yasmin, and nervously fiddled with the tassels on the young wife's robe.

When Nazim's eyes settled on her face, she turned red. "You know of this?" He walked across the room and stood over her, his voice soft but with an edge. Yasmin started to cry, but he hushed her with a glance. "What?"

"I was walking by the door." Annie's voice cracked and she tried again. "Just passing by and I saw this man with a beard standing next to the desk. Gina Hoffman's son, maybe it was. I let him know he'd better leave, and he did. Right fast."

"Gina Hoffman's son. He has them." Nazim snapped his fingers, and the two bodyguards jumped to their feet. "Find the body," he told them. "Take my letters from the pocket. No walking. Run."

The household waited silently for an hour until the men returned with David, who had gone along to show where he had laid the body. They had found the place, with flattened, blood-stained grass, but no body.

"No one must see my letters," Nazim muttered, pacing again. "Must have the letters back."

Annie stood up, trembling. "I'll try to get them for you," she said. "It's my fault they're gone and I'll sure try."

"You know the man's family," Nazim nodded, half turning toward David. "I think it is good idea, David. You will let her go." Just yesterday, he had married David and Annie in a small private ceremony. Fatima and Yasmin had insisted on bringing flowers and on dressing the girl in an embroidered red robe. They missed the extended family left behind in Lebanon. Annie and her baby were now part of their harem, their house of women.

"Tomorrow you go," Nazim said, opening the Koran and settling himself on a cushion. "Now we read the holy book and make ready for prayers." He opened to the eighth sura, one of his favorites, and cleared his throat. "In the Name of Allah, the merciful, the compassionate," he read. *"Bismi-llahi al-rahman al-rehim."* As the words flowed from his mouth, he forgot the lost letters, the killing and the reproachful face of Al-Hallaj. The prophets had promised that whenever the Koran was recited with purity, Allah's peace, his sakina, would descend. And so it did on Nazim, whose finger followed the graceful letters of the text, whose heart danced with the holy writing on the page.

⌁

The call from Cottage Hospital came just after Gina and Kori had gone to bed. John Philo had been fussing all evening, so they took him along to the hospital. They found Kief in the emergency room lying on his side while the doctors were doing something painful to his back that caused him to moan into his pillow. When she saw his bleeding, swollen mouth, Gina cried out. Kori said nothing, but her face turned white. A nurse took the baby from her and carried him to the pediatric ward.

Gina pulled one of the doctors aside, her red fingernails digging into his shoulder. "I can't talk to you now," the doctor said. "We're getting him ready for a myelogram."

"Don't give me that," Gina said fiercely. "Myelograms are a waste of time. Only idiots do myelograms anymore. Can't he walk? Does he need an operation?"

"He has no sensation in his lower body," the doctor replied unwillingly. "Look, I don't even know who you are. I'm not supposed to tell you anything."

Gina's eyes blazed as she shook him. "That's my son in there, and you'd better the hell tell me what's wrong with him, so I can call my orthopedist at Sansum Clinic. No myelogram until Dr. Hyde gets here. You guys just keep him comfortable and don't practice your smartass internship on him. You hear me?"

A few minutes later she was talking to Dr. Hyde, a back specialist who had the best reputation in California. In less than thirty minutes he was examining Kief, while muttering his findings into the tape recorder around his neck. Gina could understand none of it. Kori sat beside Kief, her face pale and blank, her fingers gently touching his forehead, his hair, his swollen, smashed lips.

Dr. Hyde motioned for Gina to come with him into the hall. Standing under the harsh, blue lights, she remembered lying under such a light at the same hospital when Kief was born. "It's bad, Gina." Dr. Hyde touched her shoulder. "The x-rays show that his fourth and fifth lumbar vertebrae have been crushed, along with the spinal cord. He'll be able to use his upper body, but nothing below the waist."

"An operation?" Gina gasped, her eyes wide and furious. "Some kind of therapy?"

"Nothing will help. You're tough enough to take the truth and I'm giving it to you." Dr. Hyde moved toward the door to return to his patient. "He'll be able to use a wheelchair. Be glad they didn't get him a little higher or he'd be quadriplegic."

Gina sat in one of the burgundy leather chairs, bending over until her face touched her knees. She had done this to Kief, let him take this chance, asked him to. This precious body of bone and muscle, this love-making, joyful son of hers was a crippled, helpless mess, all because of her. *You don't take care of Kief. I take care of Kief,* came the intruding voice. *Bring him to me and don't cry.* Don't you even talk to me, she raged silently. You let my son be wrecked, turned into a cripple. Why should I listen to you? I'll never come to India to see you. Never. It's all just a lie. You play with us like a kid with an ant farm. Like hell you love us. *I'm telling you.* The voice was even and remote, like stars on a cold night. *Bring him.*

Gina?" Jerry came running up the hall, his face red and sweating. "How is he? I heard from Dr. Hyde's nurse. Why didn't you call me?"

She stared at him numbly. "You'd have given me some religious baloney about how suffering makes us holy. Or how we each have to carry our cross."

Jerry put his arms around Gina, stroking her back until her stiff body softened and curved against his. "Nothing hurts as much as loving." She could feel his tears against her cheek and his voice in her ear. "I feel so bad, so bad."

Her body shaking, Gina began to cry, gasps wrenching her throat until she thought she would vomit. "Tell me I'm not awake, Jerry. Tell me it's not real."

"We have to pray," Jerry said, his voice low as if he feared to offend her. "It's all we can do." He knelt down on the tile floor, bowed his head into his hands, and for a long time did not move. Gina waited awkwardly, hands at her sides, feeling as though he was leaving her. Suddenly the words from the Mourner's Kaddish came to mind, words she had heard every Friday in Zefat and every year at the temple when she went to honor her father's death day. *"Yis gadal, v'yiskadash shmai raba. . . .* Let us recall the lives of those who were close to us, and who have now gone to their eternal rest." The words were too joyful for mourning, she thought even as she said them, but she said them anyway.

Jerry looked up suddenly. "We should take Kief to India," he said. "That's what we should do."

"In a wheelchair?" Gina laughed harshly, the words from the Kaddish dying in her mouth. "I'm going to put him in the rehab clinic for the next year. For as long as it takes. I'll be with him every minute until he walks." The voice returned, *You don't take care of Kief. I take care of Kief.*

"Dammit," Gina cried, slamming her hand against the polished pink wall. "He's mine. He's my son." She pulled Jerry into Kief's room and knelt beside the bed.

"He woke up." Kori's voice was thin and faraway. "He wants to get married. I said yes, of course. Can you find us someone to say the words?"

"I'll call Homer," Jerry said. "He'll set something up. Can we get married at the same time, Gina?"

"Why not?" she said wearily. "Two for the price of one."

Kori touched her shoulder. "Kief and I are still going to India. I hope you will go with us, Mother. But whether or not you do, we must go. I've been told to come." She stood up, supporting herself on Gina's shoulder. "Stay with him, please. Kief reminded me that I must feed the baby."

Gina laid her head on the starched sheet covering Kief's half-dead body. The tears came slowly, as if from a rusty tap. If Sai Baba was taking care of Kief, she had a lot of reasons to question this Indian teacher. Who was he and why was he talking to her as if he had only the best intentions? It had always been her sense that God was not kind. Too many of her relatives had died in the holocaust for her to think of God as anything but a cat playing with a mouse whose luck had run out.

Kief's eyes, sunken into dark blue bruises, suddenly opened and lit up. His words were hard to make out, but Gina heard him say, "Have hope. We are being cared for." When his cracked, broken lips tried to make a smile, she saw what had happened to his teeth. As his eyes closed again, she saw a cloud of gray ash falling onto his lids. Vibhuti, gray ash, came from the hands of Sai Baba, Kief had said, but Sai Baba was not here. Sobbing, Gina threw herself across her son's still body, gripping his legs, willing that they come to life.

3

For Homer Healey the week had not been easy. Two walls of his new glass temple had cracked in the aftershocks of a 5.2 earthquake, and he worried that, after all, God might have decided against the Temple of the Parousia. Homer had been trying to tell his tight-lipped benefactor, the unreadable Nazim, that the American fundamentalist public was well aware of the Arab bloc's intention to drive the Israelis into the Mediterranean Sea. Nazim merely smiled his grim smile and said that the American public knew only what the media told it and that the media, like Homer Healey himself, could be bought. The minister was silent, and his face turned a mottled red. He had suspected that Nazim despised him as an infidel, and now he was sure of it. Still, he told himself, for those who loved the Lord, all things worked together for good. Nazim's money would be turned to winning souls before the Last Days engulfed the world in chaos.

On the first of his new nationwide programs, filmed in the just-completed southern end of the temple, Homer had tentatively suggested that the children of Ishmael were also the children of God's promise and deserved their own homeland. Furious letters poured in from everywhere, especially Texas, arguing that the Arabs already had all the land in the Middle East except for Israel, a country no bigger than Massachusetts. One billionaire oilman called from Dallas and thundered at him for ten minutes. How, he demanded, did Homer Healey expect Jesus to gather the multitudes of the saved into the new Jerusalem if the Arabs were allowed to turn the holy city into rubble, as they had in 1948?

Homer would have to tread more carefully, he decided, doodling on the script of his talk which was due to be taped the next morning. Yet he would need Nazim's approval of the script if he expected to receive this month's half-million-dollar check. The minister laid his cold palms over his hot, flushed cheeks. His hands always felt cold whenever Nazim was due to arrive, which was any minute. In his heart, he still believed that preachers should stay out of politics and that he should not render unto Caesar the things that were God's.

But the Last Battle between the forces of good and evil was taking shape. Homer Healey had long believed that when Armageddon arrived, he would be on the side of the righteous, opposing the godless secular idealists and the New Agers, who believed God existed in everyone and that the Oriental religions were just as good as Christianity. He added into his script a blast against the notion that everyone would wind up on God's side. Scripture warned that some would be drawn away, deceived by a miracle-worker, a servant of the devil who would seem to be Christ come again. Then, to placate Nazim, he wrote that today's Israelis were not the same as the Israelites to whom God had promised the Holy Land. Most Israelis were socialists from decadent Europe who had largely abandoned the God of Abraham, Isaac and Jacob, thereby forfeiting his protection.

"Very nice," said Nazim, a half hour later, tapping his long, slender finger on the passage about God having abandoned the Israelis. "An argument new, but I like. The Holy Land is belonging to us who live pure. We know God's laws must be mocked not." He snapped his fingers for a cigarette and leaned forward to take the light from his servant's hand.

"Amen," breathed Homer. A feeling came to him that he had much more in common with Nazim than with the strange, money-driven woman who his deacon, Jerry North, wanted to marry. He began to wonder if perhaps the Rapture were meant not for the Jews, but for the Muslims who were, after all, of the same Semitic stock. The minister scribbled down this idea for his talk, then, cheeks bright red and nose throbbing with passionate intensity, he read it aloud to Nazim.

"Again, good." Nazim flicked his long ash in the direction of the wastebasket. "You must tell your people this world will fall to bits if they do not turn back to old ways. Say Rapture will soon come. People must put their minds on this. No more rich politicians, no more talk that big government is God. Tell that people need only little government, for all will be pure in heart. No need for big tax, for armies. Just good people with little governments near to their homes. Yes? You see what to say?"

After Nazim had left, Homer Healey sat rewriting his speech. It would be as the Arab had said. Before the Rapture could come, all good men must join forces. Many fundamentalists were clamoring for a third political party devoted to cleaning up the filth in the media and to getting women back home with the children, where they belonged, where they would be safe from the rising tide of rape, violence and corruption of their innocence. He himself might even lead this fundamentalist party. The new party could begin right in Santa Barbara and expand throughout the whole nation. Who would not be glad to end the flow of dollars to Washington? What did the government have to do, anyway, now that the communist empire was gone? Pay artists to produce pornographic, anti-Christian trash and prevent public schoolchildren from praying? As his pen moved over the script in stabbing, scratching indignation, he prepared a television sermon that would set hearts on fire. And those whose hearts were not moved by the Spirit would at least be happy to see an end to the federal income tax.

When his script was finished, Homer stayed late, reviewing his plans for the completion of the glass temple. In his inner ear he heard a choir heralding the return of the Savior, whose voice was like thunder, stronger than earthquakes, yet softer than the voice of God speaking to Moses out of the burning bush.

The television program was staged under bright, blue lights in the chapel under construction. "The Rapture is at hand," Homer had preached in his soft, melodic voice, "and all it takes to join is a flick of the emotional switch. Prepare for the Judgment Day, the Second Coming. Bring your government close to home where you can make sure it serves the Lord. When Armageddon comes and the world stands under judgment, those who love God will be caught up in his everlasting arms." Reverend Healey had read these words from the TelePrompTer with the passion of a lover. Promising repentance and donations, people phoned in from all over the country, until his newly hired answering service was swamped.

∽ಲ಼ಬ

By the time the wedding party arrived, Homer was frantic. His thick, salt and pepper hair was standing on end and his face was crimson. If the weddings had been arranged by anyone but Brother Jerry, he would have canceled. "Once you are a public figure," Nazim had told him seductively, "you will have others do the little works."

"Did you watch the program?" The minister shook Jerry's hand, wringing it distractedly. "I had my secretary call you at your . . . um . . . fiancée's."

"Yes, we saw it," Gina answered, stepping in front of Jerry. "You're trying to hand Israel over to the Arabs, you son of a—"

Jerry put his hand over her mouth. "We have to tell the ambulance people where to bring Gina's son," he said. "Kief insisted on coming here, but he's on a stretcher, with an I.V. The guys will have to roll the stretcher in. Where's the ramp?"

"The sacristy," Homer said. "I'll get it." He had a strong desire to escape from Gina, whose shaggy hair was flying around her face like an avenging angel's and whose words pierced his heart.

"Jerry will never give you another cent for this church," Gina shrieked after him. "He has tithed his last tithe, you hear me?"

"Don't be angry with her." Jerry hurried along to help with the big wooden wedge that served as a ramp for the handicapped. "Like I told you, after her son was crippled in that attack, she's not been herself."

The minister looked around at Gina. Eyes blazing fiercely and fists balled on her hips, she looked as if she was being very much herself. He kept busy helping Kief's paramedics roll the stretcher up the ramp and down the aisle toward the pulpit, where Kori and Gina stood waiting.

Kori wore a long, gray-green dress made of a light, gauzy material. A wide straw hat framed her small, perfect face. As the stretcher approached, she handed the sleeping baby to Gina and walked beside Kief, holding his hand. Homer had not known there was a baby and wondered vaguely if he should hold off the wedding until he had investigated the suspect spiritual status of Gina's son and this tall woman, with her pale, alien beauty and bastard infant.

Kori turned her blue eyes on him and said, "May I have a flower or two from your altar? My mother would not have wished me to be married without flowers in my hand."

Homer brought two pink roses from the church bouquets, which had started to droop since the Sunday service two days before. Wrapping his clean handkerchief around the stems, so the bride would not prick her fingers on a thorn, he asked, "Who is giving you away?"

"Myself. I give myself away." Kori's voice was low and steady.

"Perhaps Brother Jerry, our deacon?" Homer tried again, wanting to get this strange, otherworldly female under some control, mindful of Nazim's warning that women in the West were ruining their families and churches with their heathenish feminism.

"Let us do the words now. Kief must return to the hospital quickly." Kori closed her eyes, keeping one hand in Kief's. "I give myself. That is enough. What else have we to give but ourselves?"

Homer scurried about, looking for his Bible and copies of the wedding certificates. Such women as this, with no confiding smiles, no small talk and no apologetic flutters, confused and upset him. Not knowing what to do, he looked helplessly at Jerry.

"It's all right," said Jerry. "You can change the words of the service." He glanced at Gina. "For us, too. Gina will give herself away."

Gina watched with mutinous eyes, as if any marriage Homer celebrated would mean zip to her. She probably did not even regard this marriage as holy, the minister thought, wondering if he should refrain from reading the words about Jesus turning water into wine during the marriage at Cana. Unless a Jew was married by a rabbi, perhaps she was not really married? For Jerry, he would do it, but there was misgiving in his heart as he nervously blessed them. Neither of these women was his idea of a wife.

That night Homer sat late in his office reading the messages that had poured in over the fax machine and listening to his voice mail. Christian evangelicals throughout the country were declaring their support for his new Fundamentalist Party of God. Most agreed that income tax payments should go mainly to local government, with the IRS receiving only enough to fund the national guard, the post office and interstate highways. Forget about foreign aid. The U.N., supervised by the Joint Chiefs of Staff, could oversee world peacekeeping. The minister's hands shook as he typed into his computer the ideas that would become the platform of the Fundamentalist Party of God.

∽∾ৎ∾

While the others packed for India, Gina brooded over the two letters she had found in the back pocket of Kief's bloodied jeans when the hospital returned his clothes in a sealed plastic bag. One was from a New York senator, who agreed to push for states' rights and limits on the federal government, in return for Nazim's million-dollar contribution to his campaign. The senator made an obscure reference to similar activities of Nazim's counterparts in the Soviet Union. Gina guessed that the Arabs had also had a hand in the fall of the communist empire. With the Soviet Union fragmented, the United States would have no reason to maintain a strong central government, leaving the followers of Allah as the most powerful military force in the world.

This is my country they want to take over, Gina whispered to herself. They want us in chaos. Easy pickings for the jihad. She had written as much to Senator George Gage, demanding that he open an investigation in Washington, or she would warn the nation's realty organizations not to sell properties to rich Arabs.

The other letter in Kief's pocket was from the president of a television network, offering his controlling share to Nazim for 200 million dollars. His network had recently dropped to third place, and the president was trying to bail out. After the IRS deduction for charitable contributions was eliminated, it hadn't been long before public television was taken over by special interests, Gina reflected, sipping her rum and Coke on the front porch under the jacaranda trees. More and more often, PBS had been running "fake news" from the Middle East, short documentaries given free to the networks by Arab fundamentalists. The public seldom heard the Israeli side, that eight-hundred-thousand Jews had been driven from Arab countries when Israel was created, and that the Palestinians openly planned to wipe out the tiny Jewish democracy once Israel's guard was down.

She thought of old Aunt Hannah making halvah for her nephews and nieces, oblivious to the nuclear and biological weapons surrounding her from all sides. A chill ran through Gina, and she put down her icy drink. So the jihad was moving right along, she thought, absently tearing to shreds the purple jacaranda petals that landed on her lap.

A screech of worn brakes told her that Annie had pulled up, so Gina folded the letters and put them aside. Annie ran up the walk, her gray caftan billowing in the brisk morning breeze and her thin blonde hair flying around her head.

"Where's Jason?" Gina asked, trying to keep her tone friendly.

"Fatima and Yasmin are watching him. They're plain crazy about that baby." She plumped down in a chair across from Gina. "Fatima has five kids, but they're all girls. Yasmin hasn't got any kids, and she feels real bad about not being pregnant yet. So Jason's their baby, like." She beamed at Gina, who didn't smile back.

"I guess you're wondering how come those guys knew Kief was your son," Annie began tentatively, then picked up speed, her fingers nervously sliding back and forth across the tabletop. "David and me, we feel real bad about what happened."

"Kief said somebody recognized him. Yes, I've wondered about that." Gina rattled the cubes in her drink, then set the glass down hard.

"Well, it was David that knew who your son was, from the picture in the guest house. But all he said to the guy next to him was, 'That's Gina Hoffman's son.' He was surprised, y'know? Didn't think, actually. Then the other guy yelled, and the whole bunch went after your son. I'm real sorry. You gotta believe me." Annie tucked her flyaway hair behind her ears, awaiting forgiveness.

When Gina did not reply, Annie smiled brightly, looking down at the table. "Say, you think I could have a Coke, too? I'm so hot. It's hard getting used to this outfit. No rum or anything, though. Mr. Nazim says we can't drink alcohol." She fanned herself with her hand.

Gina was glad to go back in the house. A wave of nausea had come over her when Annie's bubbling voice touched Kief's name, conjuring up the men who had attacked her son. Sometimes in dreams she saw crude-faced, heavy-handed men falling upon Kief in the dark, and she would groan and cry aloud as she tried to pull them off. Jerry would shake her awake and hold her close until she stopped shivering. Then she would lie rigid, watching the branches by her bedroom window drop their petals on the sill. It was hard for her to sleep, thinking of what she had to do before leaving for India. Her tax forms must be finished. An agent must be hired to keep the business alive while they were gone. Her things would have to be put in storage so the little house could be sublet.

The trip was still unreal to her, and the preparations seemed slow, like wading through deep water. She was going only because Kief wanted her to go, and she wanted to help take care of him. Kori would have her hands full with the baby. Jerry's job would be to look after the bags and get the family into the right planes and buses. Travel books made ominous references to swarming crowds at the Bombay airport and slow lines at customs. Gina wished the voice that had dogged her for so many weeks would speak now to reassure her that she was on the right track. But she had not heard the voice since the night Kief was attacked.

She poured the last of the Coke into a glass and squeezed a little lemon over the cubes. When the phone rang, Gina answered, taking her time, not wanting to hear more of Annie's chatter. The ice cubes in the drink were half melted by the time she finished nailing down her new agent.

When Gina came back to the porch, Annie was gone and so were the letters. She swore as she dumped the drink over the porch rail. She hadn't bothered to photocopy the letters, and now Nazim would have them back. He would also know she was onto him. It was just as well the whole family was disappearing into the seething hordes of South India, she told herself. Even Nazim, with his army of fanatics, would be unable to find them there.

At Kief's suggestion, Gina took her money out of CDs and Ginnie Maes, putting them into land and municipals. The property she bought tripled the size of Kief and Kori's spread in the mountains above Santa Cruz. She signed the contracts just two days before they were scheduled to leave for their six-month stay in India.

Through most of the long plane ride to Bombay, John Philo slept or lay quietly, watching his mother's face as she read from the Shirdi Baba letters, which she had photocopied and brought along. Kori also had a Sanskrit grammar and was teaching herself to read the portions of Uncle

Philo's letters which were written in that ancient language. Gina had known her daughter-in-law was a scholar, but was not prepared for the intense, focused attention the young archeologist gave to her new task.

When Gina tried to ask about Kori's mother and why she had killed herself, Kori would give brief answers, then return to her Sanskrit study. Gina managed to learn only that Damaris Dahlquist had been a devoted but hovering mother, wanting more of her daughter's love than Kori was able to give. The girl had worked at being like her father, whose protegé she had been until his death. Gina hoped they could be friends but wondered now if she would be seen as another Damaris, anxious and interfering, lacking in the tools of intellect that Kori valued so highly.

"Listen to this," Kori said, as if to short-circuit another effort on Gina's part to become personal. "Little is known of Shirdi Sai Baba's childhood except that he was abandoned by his parents and adopted by a holy man. In 1859, he came to Shirdi, where he set up his ashram and spent the rest of his life. Your Uncle Philo believed he was not born in the usual way, but as an avatar, taking on a body. He willed himself into being."

John Philo hiccuped in his sleep and smiled.

Jerry put down his Bible and said, "You mean like Jesus? I believe that Jesus was the only Son of God." Gina was annoyed at Jerry's obsession with talking about his Savior whenever someone was willing to listen. She had learned to cut him off at the pass, but Kori seemed to suffer from the same mania and let Jerry talk. He explained to Kori that he had his doubt about a new divine incarnation. "Surely," Jerry said, "it was enough for God to come once to earth. Mankind could not bear any more generosity."

Gina sighed and looked out the window at the clouds below them, hoping the flight attendant would interrupt the sermon with an offer of drinks.

"Like you, I believe Jesus was the Son of God." Kori smiled gently at Jerry, with whom she seemed more at home than she did with Gina.

"But do you think God left the human race in ignorance of divinity for a hundred thousand years before the coming of Jesus?" She checked under the blanket to see if the baby's diaper was wet. "Ever since we flew over Hawaii, I've been trying to translate a Sanskrit verse that explains how divinity might come to earth. The words go something like this: 'A soul wishing to enter a body might do so with or without a normal birth or childhood, sometimes simply by creating a body fully grown or entering into a body already mature.'" She scratched out a few lines of her interlinear writing and frowned, biting her pencil. "When the people of Shirdi first saw Baba, he was entering town with a marriage party. His face shone like an angel's, and each person saw him as a reincarnation of his favorite deity."

"I suppose he sat on a pillar like a statue and never said a word," Gina said, trying to read over Kori's shoulder, but giving up, since the penciled remarks were in Swedish. "Much good that would do anyone."

"No." Kori kept her head bent over the text, writing as she spoke. "He talked and laughed with his friends. Muslim and Hindu friends, which is strange, given the hatred between the two groups. Uncle Philo says that Shirdi Baba dressed like a Muslim but wore the caste marks of a Hindu. No one knew what to think of him."

"Like Jesus," Jerry said, his face lighting up. "He loved even the Samaritan woman and the Roman soldier who killed him—so much that people ever since have been willing to die for him out of love."

If Jerry weren't derailed fast, Gina thought, they would be a captive audience for another one of his sermons. Not that Jerry didn't live what he preached, but she preferred being loved to hearing about it. "Yes, yes, but Jesus was a Jew," she objected. "He was a Jew first of all. He believed in the Law. You told me that, Jerry." She wanted to be sure of him, at least. One thing about Jerry, he was a Christian who knew where his religion came from. His father, a fundamentalist preacher, had raised Jerry to believe he was a "Jew by adoption," but Gina could not understand why anyone would want to be a Jew who wasn't stuck with it by birth.

Maybe being Jewish sounded romantic to Jerry, but drunken Cossacks hadn't ridden into *his* hometown spearing Jewish babies on their swords. Aunt Hannah's stories had become her own. She would not let Jerry's cheerful talk about carrying the joyous cross of redemption color her dark picture of the world.

"Yes, Jesus was a Jew, the Messiah of the Jews," Jerry said. "But he came to bring the Jewish message to everybody. Love God, love your neighbor as yourself. That was it."

"So the rabbis said, too," Gina murmured, "but no one listened."

"Jesus listened," Jerry said, putting his hand over hers. "You know, I always said that if someone were performing miracles like Jesus did, I'd go anywhere in the world to see him. Of course, Sai Baba's not Jesus, but his miracles are something I have to see."

"So you're going to India because Baba does miracles?" Kief spoke slowly, afraid he would dislodge his newly implanted front teeth.

"And because of the dream I had last month." Jerry closed his Bible and put it back in his stained canvas shoulder bag. "It's all I have to go on. I feel like the blind man in the scriptures. I don't know anything about God except what I've seen him do. Homer Healey's the theologian, not me."

"Thank God for that," Gina muttered. "I've heard all I need to hear of Homer's religion. I'd rather have been married by a Zulu medicine man than him."

The flight attendant's voice came crackling mechanically over the loudspeaker. "Ladies and gentlemen, we are beginning the descent into Bombay."

Turning bright red, John Philo arched his back and began screaming. "His ears," Kori said, as she patted his back, trying to make him burp. "The doctor warned me that the change in pressure drives babies crazy." She held John Philo's face close to hers and yawned until he imitated her and stopped crying.

As the plane lurched into a landing pattern, Gina took a few pages of

Uncle Philo's papers from Kori's lap. She had read the letters but had not yet looked into the diaries included in the package. "Do not demand or desire anything," Uncle Philo had written, quoting his master. "Give yourself in total trust. Cast all your burdens on me and I will bear them." She did not realize she was speaking aloud until Jerry answered her.

"Jesus said, 'Come to me, you who are weary and heavy-laden. I will give you rest.' It's what happens when you trust God, Gina. I wish you could know how that feels." He opened her tightly clenched fist and stroked her palm. "It feels like love. Like you were never loved before."

"When God stops kicking me and my people in the head, maybe I'll try trusting him," Gina retorted, looking out the window at the sprawling jumble of shacks and towers and brilliant greenery that was Bombay. She closed her eyes to avoid the exotic swamp of color and the alien thoughts rising to engulf her.

⁓ɔc⌐

Gina stood stiffly in line while her bags were being inspected. The others had been waved through and she could see them in the swarming crowd beyond the customs area, watching her. They were probably hoping she wouldn't blow up and chew out the customs official. Gina wished she could communicate with this slow little man, who acted as if he expected to find a bomb or a cache of drugs in her innocuous luggage. He held up her high-heeled black patent leather pumps and looked at them doubtfully.

"You are a disco lady?" He spoke so fast that she could hardly distinguish one word from another.

"I am an American woman," she snapped. "I wear what I choose."

"And you are in India for what?"

"I am going to visit Sai Baba of Puttaparthi, because my family is going." Gina had a strong urge to snatch her hairdryer out of his hand before he decided it was something Americans used to blow cocaine up their noses.

"Swami," he beamed. "You are going to see Swami." He put the hairdryer back in the bag and clicked it shut. "Sai Ram, madam."

Gina had no idea what he was talking about. Her visual image of a swami was from childhood cartoons showing men with turbans, playing flutes to make snakes dance in baskets. The very word made her feel suspicious. Whoever this swami was, he would not get hold of her or her money. Tossing the strap of her hand luggage over her shoulder, Gina passed through the customs gate to join the rest of the family.

"We have to find the plane to Puttaparthi," Kief said, consulting his travel papers. "From these directions, it looks like we go across town to the domestic terminal."

A well-dressed Indian came up to them and bowed, his fingertips together near his heart. "You are going to Swami," he said. "If you wish to stay overnight, we have a place for you. It costs very little. Our taxi will take you to the airport in the morning."

Gina stood in front of her little family, as if defending them from a firing squad. "I've seen a movie about crooks like you. You get poor, dumb people to move into an apartment that isn't theirs and steal all their money. You can take your free offer and shove it. We'll find a cab and get the hell out of here." Her heart was beating like a jackhammer, and Gina held her hand to her throat, feeling something bitter rising up. She shouldn't have eaten that strange, sugary thing that Jerry had bought for her. Probably she already had cholera, Gina thought, coughing as the sharp taste reached her mouth.

The little man shrugged and bowed, then backed away into the crowd. Unembarrassed, Kori gave a sobbing John Philo her breast in front of the milling people who were pressing against her. "You know," she said mildly, "some of Sai Baba's followers keep an inexpensive hostel where people traveling to see him may stay."

"Well, why didn't you tell me?" Gina anxiously looked around for a bathroom. Sharp pains were stirring her bowels, but she was too proud to double over. "I'm about to be sick, Jerry. Hang onto my bag."

Gina stumbled into a dark little restroom. At the last moment she realized that the next step forward would have put one foot into a hole that looked like a bad place for anyone's foot to go. Holding her nose with one hand, she tore off her underwear and positioned her feet on either side of what in these parts evidently passed for a toilet. After struggling to keep the sugary thing down, Gina exploded, vomiting into the hole. "Oh God," she sobbed, through her raw throat, "I wish I could die, except I'd fall into this stinking hole. Please help me. Please." She didn't know why she was praying, since the last time she had prayed was for Kief to be normal again. And God had thrown that prayer back in her face like spit in the wind.

The voice she had almost forgotten came back, whispering as if from a far place, *I want you empty, empty.*

"I am, I am," Gina whispered back as the pain receded. "I'm all wiped out. If that's what you want, you've got it."

Someone was pounding on the door, yelling at her in an incomprehensible tongue. Gina took her time, ignoring the pounding and the Indian words that sounded like a song, however angry they were.

"I'll never eat again," she announced to Jerry, who was standing outside the door, trying to calm down an old woman in a ragged sari who surged into the small toilet like a tsunami. "I am finished with eating."

"Well, being empty is okay," Jerry said, looking at her with concern, wiping the corner of her mouth with his crumpled handkerchief. "I won't eat either, until we get to the ashram. They say the ashram food is clean. We'll take a van, Gina, if you can make it. Think you can?"

"Don't know." Gina felt her voice fading, and for the first time in her life she didn't care if she made the van, the plane or the next meal. "We can try. If we don't make it, I guess there'll be another."

When the van pulled up, the driver wanted twenty dollars extra to drive them to the domestic airport. At this time of night, he said, the fare is more, because thieves might waylay them.

Kori put away her small white breast. Tucking John Philo under her arm, she stepped up to the driver, standing head and shoulders above him. "If there is a thief, it is you," she said in a deep voice that carried through the terminal. "You will take us to the domestic terminal for five American dollars, and if you do not, I will break your arms. Both."

The dark little man trembled, bowed his head and ushered them into his rickety van. Three American dollars would be fine for trip to terminal. The large madam would please not to harm him.

"You will receive five," Kori said, settling herself in the front seat. "Two extra dollars for the wheelchair." The man hurried to lift the chair into his bus, following Jerry who was carrying Kief. Kori smiled at Gina, "It is a different world from yours, one I am familiar with. Survival is the thing here, you understand."

The van moved off choking and shaking. As the driver entered the crowded street, he began to lean on his horn, which every other driver was also doing, regardless of need. The shriek and blare of horns did not seem to disturb the sea of sleeping people who overflowed the sidewalks, settling like waves on either side of the black-topped street, leaving a narrow isthmus for cars, cows, bicycles and other vehicles.

Gina covered her nose with a handkerchief and coughed as she breathed the smoke belched by a two-decker bus ahead of them. The air tasted of exhaust fumes and dust, setting her teeth on edge. Whenever they stopped, brown hands reached through the open windows. Behind the groping hands, Gina could see the faces of women and young girls holding babies. They were nodding in a strange, side-to-side motion. Gina supposed the gesture had some special meaning in this part of the world but couldn't guess what it might be.

She shrank back and closed her eyes, not wanting to see the open mouths with sores and rotting teeth. In her nightmares, Gina had seen herself like this, helpless, living on the street, begging for handouts. Kori believed that past lives often haunt the present one. Uncle Chaim said the Kaballah taught that human beings returned over and over again to earth until they learned their lessons. Gina had argued that once around was as much as anyone could take, but Uncle Chaim would only look at her with his small bright eyes and say, "How do you know, fortunate girl, what is the worst? You think you have suffered?" He would shake his head and go back to his calligraphy, usually for a ketuba, a wedding document, remarking that he hoped some day to write one for her.

For a moment, Gina wished they were pulling up to the small, clean airport near Tel Aviv, where Uncle Chaim would be waiting, the warm wind stirring his bushy gray beard. Instead, the van stopped in front of Bombay's dirty, sprawling domestic terminal, where no one would greet them with love. Too many people already and none of them cared about a handful of Westerners on some harebrained pilgrimage. In fact, Gina thought, some of these Indians would kill for a trip to California. They must wonder what temporary insanity had overtaken these Westerners to make them come so far to see so little.

Once inside the domestic terminal, the family sat for three hours waiting for the plane to Puttaparthi. Gina felt a strange peace rise within her, spreading from her feet, through her body and up into her head. The Third World, was it? Well, Kori and Kief knew what to expect of savages. Let them take care of everything. Her head fell back against the wall. She was grateful that her stomach seemed to have shrunk into a tiny, hard, undemanding ball and that the desire for sleep had swelled in her head, displacing every other thing. She watched the Indian women, their multicolored saris fluttering as they arranged their children and themselves on mats before settling into sleep, arms covering their broods as if to keep away all pains, attacks and the ever-present mosquitoes that were diving kamikaze-style into their skin.

"If the planes are delayed, these people may be here for days. It is the custom here to wait," Kori observed, feeding John Philo again when he stirred and fussed.

Kori will spoil that baby, thought Gina. She will turn him into a brat by feeding him whenever he wants. But, enervated by a touch of nausea and the hot, humid air, Gina said nothing, wishing only that she had a thin mat to lie on as the Indian women had. They looked prepared to stay in the airport indefinitely, seeming not to care if their planes were delayed. As she started to fall asleep, her body leaning uncomfortably against the plastic arm of the chair, Gina saw a young mother nursing one child while she cuddled another. The young woman's face was soft and gentle, and her little girl's arm curved naturally around her neck. Tears stung Gina's eyes as she watched the baby, whose eyes were closed peacefully despite the noise of the angry, demanding crowds.

Gina drifted off to sleep, no longer worrying if she were safe and in good hands. She hiccuped and her mouth fell inelegantly open. As Kori's fingers stroked her cheek, Gina heard sweet words she could not quite believe. "Sleep now," the soft voice said. "We are taking care."

❧

The plane to Puttaparthi was small and crowded. Gina was glad she had eaten nothing that day, as her head seemed to be hovering somewhere above her body. While the map of South India unfolded beneath the plane, she saw green fields planted between raw, brown, rocky stretches. Small hills rippled beyond the edge of a huge plain. Then she saw a bowl of mountains, holding a ribbon of river and a round valley. The plane circled over a small landing strip, near a few flat buildings. Adjacent to the airstrip was a huge ornate structure that Kief said was a hospital built by Sai Baba. A sprawling complex with twin spires, it looked to Gina more like a temple. Just beyond was a large block of apartments on the edge of a small village, most of whose residents worked at the hospital.

Physicians had been drawn from around the world to this three-hundred bed hospital to perform major operations. Free medical services were available to all, including penniless, desperate people. The hospital had been built in one year, and Sai Baba declared it would stand for a thousand more. Its two curving sections on either side of the great dome welcomed the sick with loving arms.

Gina hoped that Kief could talk to these surgeons. Perhaps they would be able to help him. Then she smiled bitterly at her fantasies. If nothing could be done in America, nothing could be done here. Kief was crippled, his life ruined. She was a fool to have any hope.

An old Mercedes, minus the driver's-side door, met the plane, and a slight, smiling man approached as they came down the metal steps. He was neatly dressed in white slacks and a long-sleeved white shirt.

"Namasté. I am Jayaramakrishna," he said, bowing slightly, his hands folded together pointing toward his chin. "You may call me Jay. Bring the wheelchair over here," he called to the baggage men who were unloading the belly of the little plane. "I am taking this party to the ashram."

"But how do you know about us?" Gina's head began to swim again, and she leaned against Jerry. "We didn't send word about a wheelchair. We never even said we were coming."

"It is not necessary to say anything for Swami to know what you need." Jay expertly slid the folded wheelchair into the trunk, then piled their luggage precariously on top of his car. "Nonetheless, it is considered proper to notify him when you are coming and to request his permission. Of course, no one is turned away, but here it is the custom to ask. On your next trip, you will remember what to do." Speaking rapidly in crisp, British English, he tied down the trunk with a frazzled piece of rope.

"Considering that the whole country seems to be run like an animal shelter, it's weird to hear these people talk about propriety," Gina whispered to Jerry, as they squeezed into the front seat, leaving the back for Kief's little family. She felt stronger now, able to breathe freely despite the still, hot air that reminded her of the Santa Ana winds back home in California. Maybe it was good to be "empty, empty," though she would not have said so back at that toilet in the Bombay airport.

"Kori says Sai Baba is big on propriety," Jerry whispered back. "He wants people to discipline themselves. Be on time, be clean, be honest, remember our duty to God."

Gina did not answer, remembering Annie's sudden transformation into a creature of duty who would steal to please her master. She smiled, thinking that by now Senator Gage had read her paraphrases of the stolen letters and would pass the information on to the governor and perhaps the president. Nazim wouldn't carry off his scheme to turn the United States back to the dark ages, not if she could help it.

On the narrow road into the ashram, they passed busloads of Indians packed together as tightly as nestled spoons, the open windows of their buses letting in blasts of scorching air. Feeling a sudden surge of empathy, Gina imagined a woman like herself, traveling with a crippled son, with no money or friends, with nothing but faith. Despite the gentle, reassuring touch of Jerry's arm over her shoulder, she felt a brief, choking loss of air as she stared out the window. Her eyes connected with those of a woman in a white, blue-trimmed cotton sari, a woman who was probably much younger than she, but whose hair was pure white and whose smile framed bare gums. Without thinking, Gina said "Namasté," and folded her hands in a gesture of prayer, nodding toward the woman, who smiled and returned the blessing.

"You know what namasté means?" Kori leaned forward, shifting the weight of the baby on her lap. "What is the meaning of this gesture?"

"No." Gina didn't know and didn't care. Remembering the woman's toothless smile, she was nursing a sweet feeling that warmed her like a blessing. "I suppose it means hello."

"It means that, yes, but also it means 'I salute the divinity within you,'" Kori replied.

Gina stared out the window. She did not believe people were divine. If anyone had asked her, she would have said people were much more likely to be possessed by the devil than by God. Yet old Aunt Hannah used to say that she waited with love for every person who came visiting on Shabbat, for in each person she saw God. Aunt Hannah didn't make any special gesture when people came in, only offered them a tray of food and a friendly nod. She had survived Auschwitz. To her, it was a blessing just to be alive, to make the Shabbat loaves, to cover her eyes and say the candle blessing, celebrating the sunset on one more week of life, one more week that saw no pogroms, no grenades, no missile attacks. "If you are alive," Aunt Hannah would say, with her slow, heavy Polish accent, "you are a miracle. If you should see what I have seen, you would know what you are."

Then she would set down the tray, arrange her hands under her apron, and tell the guests little stories about life in the Polish stetl where she had grown up. "We grew the wheat for our bread," she would say, her hands working under the apron. "When we were girls, we tossed trays of grain into the air and watched the chaff blow away like bad thoughts."

Having a lifetime of bad thoughts to exorcise, Gina could not help being curious about what Aunt Hannah's bad thoughts might have been. A long look into the lustful eyes of a village boy who danced in front of her, inviting her into his arms for a brief, public moment? Gina thought of her own teenaged, half-undressed tussles in the back seats of cars and wondered at Aunt Hannah's innocent chaff.

The ancient Mercedes passed under an arch that announced they had entered Prasanthi Nilayam, the Abode of Highest Peace, as Kori interpreted it, in her precise, cool voice. Sometimes Gina wished her daughter-in-law was as stupid as Annie, for Kori made her feel awkward and unlovable, like a girl with a pimple on her nose.

"The air feels different here." Jerry's voice was soft and slow. "I can't get enough of it." He closed his eyes, and Gina could see his chest expanding as he breathed deeply. "It's like breathing roses."

Kief was sitting straight up, his eyes wide. "Look at the elephant. Over to the right." As the car slowly passed, Gina caught a glimpse of a smallish elephant raising one front leg to rest its foot on the edge of a water trough.

"That's Gita," Kori said. "She belongs to Sai Baba. They say she cries whenever he leaves her."

Gina laid her head back on the frayed seat and refused to look. Spiritual elephants yet. These people were too much. Dimly, she heard the others talk about what they were passing. She looked only briefly as they drove through the narrow street. When the car pulled up to the registration building she felt a sudden quiet. For the first time since they had been in India, no insistent voices or honking horns assaulted her ears.

"If you register for a room in time," Jay said, "you can go to afternoon darshan. It will be at four o'clock." He opened the rear door for the backseat passengers and gestured toward a small office that looked like a general store. "I will wait while you are assigned a room."

"Darshan?" Gina turned to Kori for an explanation.

"It means a seeing. You go to darshan to see a holy being."

"Does he give a speech or what?"

"No, he is just there. People feel happy to be close to him, that is all." Kori seemed distracted, not her usual crisp, contained self. Her cheeks were pink and her eyes looked moist, as if she were about to cry. "No, I'm all right," she said, as Gina got out a packet of tissue. "It is not the sad kind of crying." Kori turned away and walked off by herself to stand under the roof that extended over the narrow street.

Gina felt too weak to go inside with Jerry and hoped he wouldn't blow their chances for a decent room. These crafty Indians would quickly detect Jerry's innocence and assign them to one of the crowded sheds that Kori said Westerners dreaded. Probably overcharge for it in the bargain. Gina imagined herself in a huge barracks with hundreds of Indians curtained off from each other by makeshift sari-tents, everyone sharing a single bathroom, with hole-in-the-floor toilets like the one in Bombay. She hoped Jerry would tell the officials that she couldn't use an Eastern toilet, that she would throw a public fit if they couldn't have a private room with a real toilet and shower.

Tears began to run down her cheeks, and she spoke inside herself as she did when answering the voice that had been hounding her. I need something to remind me of home, she cried silently. Please, please, don't make me sleep with all those people I saw on the buses. When the face of the smiling, toothless, woman suddenly appeared on her mental screen, Gina sighed. Okay. That woman, I wouldn't mind being near.

"We have roundhouse rooms," Jerry said, waving a paper over his head. "Kief and Kori and the baby have a place of their own. We're next door to them with an Indian woman and her son. Since they have the inside room, we need to go through their room to use the bathroom. But we do have a real toilet that flushes. The man at the desk said we're lucky. A couple of large groups are coming in tomorrow."

"How much does it cost?" Gina put down her shoulder bag and rubbed her sweaty palms with a handiwipe. "Too much, I bet."

"Three dollars a day." Jerry picked up her purse and smiled at her. "And that's only because we can afford it. If we couldn't, it would be free."

Well, Gina thought, Sai Baba's not after our money. What, then?

Jay unloaded their luggage and carried it into a cubicle in one of the many six-story round towers created especially for Westerners. Slowly and sadly, Gina looked around the tiny, bare room, with its slit of a window, that would be their home for the next six months. On the concrete floor were their beds—a pair of thin, pink-flowered mattresses, hastily purchased by Jay. No other furniture was in the room.

When the door of the inside room opened, Gina was glad to see that the toothless woman from the bus they had passed would be sharing their apartment. Her son was hanging over the arm of his wheelchair, drooling and smiling at no one in particular while his eyes rolled up to the high, cobwebbed ceiling.

"Namasté, madam," the woman said, going into the main room of the little apartment. "I am happy it is you who will be here. The bathroom is to be shared by all."

Gina was by no means sure she herself was happy to be in the empty room, though she was not sorry this gentle woman would be her companion.

"I am Lakshmi," the woman called over her shoulder. "In a little while we will go to darshan together and then I will take you to buy a sari. Swami likes women to wear saris or long skirts."

Gina tried to imagine how disorderly she must look in the long-sleeved, floor-length hippie dress, borrowed from Kori and shortened with safety pins. Gina had brought mostly slacks, not realizing until her arrival in Puttaparthi how out of place they would be. Although Kori had mentioned the custom of wearing long skirts, Gina had insisted that she would dress as she pleased. Now she felt less sure of herself and regretted not following Kori's advice.

She waited for Lakshmi and her son to come out of the inner room, then followed them down the sandy walk to the temple where Sai Baba had once lived in two small rooms. Now he lived in an apartment above the auditorium. He could have afforded a mansion, Gina thought, given the size of the ashram property. She guessed that it must be several hundred acres, but had no idea what land values were. If Baba could afford to build so many accommodations for his guests, he might have managed something better for himself than two little rooms.

At the last minute, Gina remembered to drape a long silk scarf over her chest, as she had seen other Western women do. Jerry walked beside her, not speaking, and she felt completely alone, except when Lakshmi turned and smiled at her. Ever since their arrival in Puttaparthi, Jerry had seemed far away, noticing her only when she needed him. And then he would go back inside himself and close the door. When she tried to talk, he shook his head and smiled, as if she were speaking in a foreign language. Sometimes Gina tried flirting with him, hoping to rouse the romantic adoration he had shown back home. But Jerry responded only with an absent smile, saying that had he known more about love, he would have realized that sex was the least of it. Gina bit her lip, wondering if her fierceness had finally driven him away, as it had all those who once had loved her. Yet the fierceness was a part of her being. She could not change it without destroying who she was. Nor could she change her need to criticize and set right whatever she saw that did not suit her. And in India she saw much that did not suit her.

Along one of the walkways that laced the ashram, a tiny old Indian woman, her back bent at a right angle, swept the ground in long, slow motions with a short-handled broom. Another old woman holding the same kind of broom hobbled over to the first. This one could not stand straight either, obviously having swept with short brooms for a long lifetime. You'd think that by the beginning of the twenty-first century these poor souls would have learned how to sweep standing up, Gina said to herself. But their men probably wanted to keep them humble. Just then, one of the women stopped sweeping and turned toward Gina, her black eyes gleaming. When she smiled, her face looked as innocently wise as John Philo's.

The great marble-floored courtyard in front of the temple was already filling up when they arrived. Jerry wheeled Kief's chair toward the men's side, facing the cream-colored structure with its blue and pink trim. Kori fell in beside Gina on their way to the women's section. Sevadals, stern-faced guides who kept order on the ashram premises, directed Kori to the section in the rear for women with babies. Not sure what she was supposed to do, Gina followed a sevadal to a seat under the pink and gray ceiling that covered the courtyard. Fanning herself with her hat, she sank onto a stone bench near one of the brown marble pillars which supported the ceiling. The worst heat of the day was past, but she was still sweating, and her heart was beating unaccountably fast. She watched Lakshmi find a place in the corner of the courtyard with the other wheelchair people. Lakshmi smiled and bowed to her, as if inviting her to come closer, but Gina was glad to be sitting in the shade. Other women had brought colorful cushions, and Gina made a mental note to ask where she could find one.

Throbbing Indian music with a high, thin melody started playing over a loudspeaker, so ancient and weak that it probably went back to the time of the Moguls. Gina found the music pleasant, like birdsong.

She closed her eyes and followed the strange, wavering melody, then felt a sudden surge inside, as if her heart had doubled in size. Her eyes opened wide.

The woman in the next seat nudged her. "He's coming out." She pointed toward the white temple that looked like a large, sugary wedding cake.

A slight, orange-robed figure with a head of bushy, black hair came through the high, carved doors. Lifting one hand, he made a small motion, more like a blessing than a greeting, then moved toward the women's side, his back to the chairs where the sick people sat. Poor Lakshmi, Gina thought. How much she would like a blessing for her son. Just then Sai Baba looked over his shoulder and Gina was sure he looked straight at Lakshmi, who raised her hands to her cheeks with a radiant smile.

Sai Baba slowly walked among the seated women, leaning over to take letters from outstretched hands, tolerant of the hands touching his feet. As unexpected tears spread to the corners of her eyes, Gina wiped them away, feeling foolish. She hadn't cried in public since a boy in her third-grade class had rammed his pencil point into her elbow because she wouldn't share her math answers.

When Baba passed by, he looked directly into her eyes. He did not smile, but Gina felt his glance pierce her heart. He knows, she thought with a sudden tightening of her throat, he knows I am a materialistic bitch who doesn't believe in him. He doesn't mind, but thinks it would be better for me if I could believe. In anything. She wiped her eyes, trying not to smear her mascara. As Baba turned down the narrow aisle toward the women with babies, Gina held her breath. Perhaps he would come close to Kori, she thought. Perhaps he would put his hand on John Philo's head, just as he had touched the Indian babies in the front row. Their mothers had lined up an hour earlier to have a chance in the lottery that determined who would sit in the front rows.

Sai Baba walked almost to the wall that surrounded the courtyard, then paused. Stopping near Kori, he raised his hand and beckoned to her. Kori rose, carrying John Philo close to her breast, and began stepping over the women in front of her. She came to the aisle, where Baba was waiting, then knelt and laid her forehead on his feet. When she stood up, stooping a bit, as if to apologize for being so much taller than he, Sai Baba said something to her before walking toward the men's section.

Kori went to the center of the courtyard and turned, one hand shielding her eyes from the bright sun. When she waved, heads turned and Gina realized they were looking at her. She put her hand to her throat and felt her breath grating harshly.

Gina's neighbor nudged her again. "It is you," she whispered. "Go, go."

"Where?" Gina stood up, wondering what to do. "Why should I go?"

"That woman is of your family? Yes? When he calls one, the whole family goes in." The nudger, who seemed to feel as great a joy as if she herself had been called, pushed Gina forward. "Go on. Climb over the other women. They will let you pass. The women on the temple verandah will tell you what to do. Hurry. It is an honor."

Gina held up her long skirt and awkwardly picked her way through the field of women who leaned aside to let her pass. What if Sai Baba wanted to see only Kori? Then Gina would have to pick her way back again, with these thousands of faces staring at her, knowing she had been rejected, as she probably would be. After all, she had no idea who Sai Baba was, and her spiritual life had about the profundity of a gnat's. Feeling lonely and uncertain, she walked across the courtyard and joined Kori, who was already sitting on the temple verandah, her long legs folded Indian-fashion. It was easy for Kori to sit cross-legged, Gina said to herself. Kori practiced yoga for two hours every day. Even though Gina's legs hurt when she crossed them, and one knee kept popping up toward her chin, she willed herself to sit still like the others, waiting for Sai Baba to complete his circuit of the men's section. Her heart leaped when she saw Jerry pushing Kief's wheelchair toward the verandah.

"An interview," Kori whispered, tears standing in her blue eyes. "He is giving us an interview. Out of twenty thousand people here, we have this blessing. Do you understand, Mother, how lucky we are? It is a miracle."

Maybe he did send us Jay and the Mercedes, Gina thought, watching Baba walk slowly back toward the temple, seeming to float over the sand. Perhaps, as Jay says, he does know us, knows everything about us. Suddenly a hard shell closed over her. Why then had he not stopped Kief's crippling? Why had he not stopped the slaughter of her people in the gas chambers of Europe? Some god, some love. Her heart felt frozen and she lowered her head.

Sai Baba's small, delicate feet had stopped in front of her. Did he want her to kiss them, as the others had? Gina's back stiffened and her lips tightened. "No," a light musical voice said above her. "Do not, if you do not want."

She looked up into a pair of deep brown eyes and full, smiling lips. Baba was laughing at her, seeing her thoughts. At first Gina started to get angry, then she smiled, too. He was laughing, not at her, but with her, as her mother had when Gina did funny, childish things long ago. Tears stung her eyes as she tried to speak over the sob in her throat. This person felt like a mother, Gina thought, astonished because she had forgotten what it was like to be loved for who she was, not for what she did. Leaning over, Baba swirled his empty hand in the air. The gray ash that fell from his fingertips landed first on her forehead then in her open mouth. It tasted sweet and powdery on her tongue. Where had he hidden this ash? she wondered. Maybe he keeps it up his sleeve. He must be some magician to have these tricks down so pat. Kief and Kori had said that he could materialize objects, but Gina had her doubts. For a scientist, she thought, Kori seemed to have pretty low credibility standards.

"Vibhuti," the woman next to her whispered reverently. "May I take some from your forehead?"

Gina looked down at the ashes falling into the woman's palm. Baba's hand had been empty. She was sure of that. *In emptiness, there is more than you think*, said the familiar inner voice. Finally certain whose voice it was, Gina felt her internal security system activate. How could Sai Baba, whoever he was and whether or not ash fell out of his hands, communicate around the earth like some kind of spiritual satellite? Such things were impossible in Gina's reasonable, tightly organized world.

Joining the others, she followed Baba into the small interview room, trying to sit as close as possible to his high-backed armchair in the corner of the room. One woman wept silently, hands covering her face as tears slid down between her fingers. Kori rocked back and forth, davening like the orthodox old men Gina remembered at the synagogue. Bending over, Baba touched John Philo's forehead, leaving a circle of ash.

"Welcome, old friend," he said softly to the baby, then looked at Gina across the room. "The ring you wear is for him. I will give you another."

Gina shifted uncomfortably, wondering if Kori could have told him about Uncle Philo's ring. She wasn't sure whether or not to reply and just nodded her head, keeping her eyes on Sai Baba as he turned to Jerry.

"You would like a ring, too?" He smiled down at Jerry, who knelt at his feet. "Whose face would you like?"

Jerry hesitated, then said, "Yours, Baba."

"No. For you it is Jesus." He pulled back his sleeve, with a quick look at Gina as if to say, "you see, no tricks." Then he made a circle in the air with his hand, and between his thumb and forefinger there suddenly appeared a heavy gold ring. Gina half-stood in order to see, but other women tugged on her skirt, pulling her down so they could see, too.

"And what do you want from me?" Baba's voice was gentle as he leaned closer to Jerry, who was trembling and almost dropped the ring. It seemed too small, so he finally forced it on his pinkie finger.

"Ask for Kief's healing," Gina muttered fiercely under her breath. "We may never get another chance."

"Freedom," was all Jerry said, his voice firm now. He had stopped trembling.

Damn, thought Gina. Selfish, selfish. Not at all like Jerry.

Sai Baba looked at her again, shaking his head. "Your turn will come. Wait." Baba's heavy, dark brows came together as he took Jerry's hands and looked directly into his eyes. "You know what is moksha? Liberation?"

"I know what it means." Jerry's voice sounded strong and deep, more certain than Gina had ever heard it. "Being with God. Letting go of everything but God. Yes, I want this. Now."

What are you saying, Gina raged inwardly, wanting to climb over the close-packed, sweating bodies so she could pound Jerry on the back, wake him up. You want to die or something? Not be with me? You were so hot to get married, make a life together. What's this about letting everything go but God? Maybe it was only a figure of speech, she hoped desperately. He might have meant that he wanted to be closer to God, that's all. She frowned, looking around the room from one face to the other.

"You want this now? Then you shall have it." Baba leaned forward again and blew lightly on Jerry's forehead. Jerry wavered a bit, then sat back on his heels, hands over his face, leaning against the man next to him.

Though Baba's voice was soft, Gina could hear it clearly. "Soon," he said to Jerry. "Soon."

Baba turned to answer questions from some Indian people who spoke in high, rapid voices, their language sounding like water running fast and shallow. Then he motioned for Gina to come and sit at his feet, the feet she had seen so many people touch and kiss that day. She knelt, but sat up straight.

"Not so fond of feet, are you?" He smiled. "You have many questions. Your head rattles like a bag of dried beans. Ask."

"Well for one thing," Gina said, "If you are God, I don't understand why you let so much bad stuff happen. Six million of my people died in the Nazi camps. Where were you then?"

Baba's face turned somber, and his voice sounded as if it came from far away. "Those great souls knew what would come upon humanity if they did not choose to return to the world in that form, at that time," he said. "As Jesus knew and came and suffered before them. You would not be here now if not for their sacrifice. No one would. Be grateful."

"He means that the martyrs were Bodhisattvas," Kori whispered into Gina's ear. "They chose to be reborn in order to serve some purpose that we cannot understand. It is a mystery."

"Yes, a mystery." Sai Baba nodded at Kori and then looked into Gina's eyes. "Have trust. In me or in whomever you wish, but if you do not learn to have trust, you will be unhappy all your life. You know this?"

Gina's eyes spilled over and she sniffed hard, feeling like the little girl sitting before her father, who had just replaced the tricycle she had care-lessly lost, using money saved for buying needed tools. Her father's gentle eyes seemed to be shining at her now, and she wept in a loud voice, as she had so long ago, wailing for her lost bike.

"How can I trust?" she cried, her voice so loud and angry that the devotees around her gasped and pulled away. "I called to you when my son was hurt, and you didn't save him. You could have, but you didn't."

"This is your son?" Baba asked calmly, as if she had not spoken. When Gina nodded, wiping her nose with the end of her silk shawl, Baba approached Kief's wheelchair. "You know that it was necessary for you to be hurt?" His voice was soft and clear, without emotion, without even sympathy. "Long ago, before coming into the world, you chose this, though you don't remember now. There is a reason you had to pay such a price."

"I'm sure there was." Kief's voice was barely audible. His head dropped, and he stared at his hands folded in his lap. "I accept what has happened."

"Do you want to be well again?" Sai Baba held Kief's large, callused hands between his own small, delicate ones.

"I want what is God's will for me," Kief said, his fingers curling around Baba's. "I want what you want."

"The price has been paid," Baba said. "Grace has done away with karma. You are free. Get up and take your mother outside," he smiled. "She is about to burst."

As Kief stood and slowly began moving his legs, the crowd separated to let him through. The blood throbbed so hard in Gina's head that she felt she was about to pass out. Kief seemed to be coming toward her from a great distance, as if he had started from halfway around the world. Perhaps he had, she thought. They had been separated for so many years that she had often felt no more a part of Kief's life than his high school prom date. Since returning from Egypt, he had spoken with two voices. For his mother there was only politeness, while for Kori there was a warmth that seemed to put them in a world of their own, where Gina had no place.

She opened and closed her lips, but no sound came. Suddenly Gina understood the depth of Baba's gift. After the healing, Kief glanced at Kori with a smile, but then walked directly to his mother, arms open, eyes shining. Her mind flashed back to the day he took his first steps, thirty years before, and she saw him now as she had then, as more important to her than her own life.

"Thank you," she whispered to Baba. "Thank you for making me remember how it feels to love." She saw now that it had been necessary to be emptied before she could be filled and was grateful for the pain that had brought her to this room, to this moment.

"Well, Mother, your prayer has been answered," Kief said, his eyes steadily on hers. It was as if they were alone in the room. "Do you have trust now?"

"I have you," Gina cried, opening her arms to hold her son. "He's given you back to me." Her heart beat so loudly she felt that blood would pour from her ears and songs from her mouth. Kief was whole, safe and hers again. Yes, she had trust. It was growing in her like a baby in the womb. If people back home asked how she had come to trust, Gina would say it was because of the miracle. But she knew that the greatest miracle was the trusting itself, which had finally broken the stiff back of her resistance to being loved. As warmth spread through Gina's body, her insides felt like they were melting, weakening her so that she could hardly stand.

"You see," Baba said, "the trust comes last. But it does come." Then he motioned to Kori and an Indian couple to follow him into the small room adjoining the main interview hall. "We must talk of this child," he said to Kori, closing the door behind them. "And of your next one. You will need to help them with their task."

Gina kept her arm around Kief's waist, afraid he might lose the strength Baba's presence had given him and fall crashing to the ground. *Your trust falters so soon? You are a hard case.* The words whirled through her head, which felt numb, as if it were full of Novocaine. A hard case, he had said. Well, that was true enough. The shell she had built around herself was harder than even she had realized. Long before Kief's father had left them, she was sure he would inevitably find someone younger and better looking. The armor was necessary, Gina explained to herself, and to the voice inside her head. Without it, people would stomp her into the ground as they had her gentle father. And as they did to Jerry. She suddenly realized how much Jerry was like her father. Too good for this world, people said of them both. When her father had died at age forty from a heart attack, Gina began to build her shell. The business world and her divorce had hardened it.

Gina stroked Kief's cheek, his shoulder, his hair. She could feel the trust filling her like a living thing. She wasn't sure what it looked like, or what it would do, but she knew it was Baba's gift. "I'll go back for Jerry," she said. Her capacity to plan was returning, though without the usual sense of needing to be in control. She would plan, and maybe the plans would shape up. Maybe not. It was all right with her in any case. "You want to sit here and wait for me?" Gina paused outside the high white wall.

"I don't want to sit. I've done enough sitting, thanks." Kief stretched and bent to touch his toes, then whirled around like a dancer. "This all seems quite natural, somehow. When we tell people about it, they'll think we're crazy. But just now, it seems almost ordinary. Funny how fast we get used to miracles."

"I'm not used to this one yet," Gina smiled up at him. "I'm stunned out of my mind. And what's with Jerry? What does he want liberation from, anyway?"

Kief stood still. "I think I know. Go get him. I'll wait here."

The sevadals would not let Gina back into the building but allowed her to wait on the verandah, shaded from the heavy sunshine. Finally Jerry came out, half-carried by an Indian man much smaller than he.

"I can walk okay," Jerry said, his voice slurred and sleepy. "Just let me lean on your shoulder."

"What happened in there?" Gina pulled his arm around her. "Why did you ask for freedom? Tired of marriage already?" Her smile faded when she saw his face.

Jerry breathed heavily and held one hand over his chest. "So happy, so happy," he whispered, closing his eyes.

"Kief," Gina shouted as they came out the gate. "Help me carry him."

Between the two of them, they got Jerry back to the roundhouse. After laying him on the flowered mat in the small, airless room, they waited for him to open his eyes.

"Sometimes people go into a state of bliss that lasts for days." Kief laid a cold, wet cloth over Jerry's hot forehead. "Maybe that's how the darshan hit him."

"I didn't like that stuff about liberation." Gina said, nervously fanning Jerry with her straw hat. "What a thing to ask for."

Opening his eyes, Jerry gripped her hand. "It's what I want," he said, his voice strong again for a moment. "Later you'll understand that freedom is what I've always wanted, Gina. Always." His head sank back on the jacket Gina had rolled up as a pillow.

"How is he?" Kori came in and knelt down next to Gina. "You must be very frightened. This is not a common thing."

"I am, I am." Gina absently patted the sleeping John Philo on his damp, pink cheek. Then she went back to fanning Jerry, who was breathing irregularly. His forehead felt flaming hot, even through the wet cloth. "I wish I'd asked Sai Baba what Jerry meant by liberation. He never said anything about it to me."

"I will tell you later," Kori murmured, setting the sleeping baby down on the other mat.

Gina pulled her gaze away from Jerry. "What did Baba say to you? Anything about Jerry?"

Sinking down with the grace of a flower in the wind, Kori shook her head and sat cross-legged on the floor. "Not about Jerry. About John Philo. And he said there would be another child. A daughter." She touched the baby lightly, her face wondering and uncertain. "That couple in the room with me will be the grandparents of Prema Sai."

"I don't understand." Gina held her hands to her head, which burned almost as hot as Jerry's. "Prema Sai? How can anyone know who their grandchild is going to be?"

"Prema Sai Baba will be the third and last incarnation of the one who came to Shirdi a hundred and forty years ago. Our Baba, Sathya Sai Baba, is the second." Kori clasped her hands tightly together. "John Philo and our daughter will help care for Prema Sai while he is young and in danger. Baba gave me instructions for them, and the Indian couple was told what to tell their daughter when she is old enough."

"He can't mean that, Kori," Gina choked on some phlegm building in her throat. "We're talking forty years in the future. It's nuts." She found her eyes drawn to the ring on Jerry's finger, from which the eyes of Jesus stared back at her.

Jerry opened his eyes and looked into Gina's face. "Trust," he said softly. "Remember. I've done what I came for. Brought us here." He would not say anything more, but kept his face toward the wall, smiling slightly whenever Gina tried talking to him.

4

All evening they sat beside Jerry's mat. Lakshmi brought them a pitcher of sweet lassi to drink and a tray of chapati bread with vegetable sauce, but only Kori ate. By midnight, Jerry's fever had risen even higher, and he hallucinated that Baba was in the room. Kori sat in the corner, bowing down as if Baba really was there. Gina shook Jerry, hoping he would speak to her. It was just a bad dream, she told herself, swaying a little as Jerry's fever seemed to surge from his body into hers. They would wake up back in the little house on Olive Street and never leave, ever again. She would take better care of him, not let him work so hard, not expect so much.

Did Jerry seek liberation because he knew she had not loved him as he had loved her? That was true. "But I do now," Gina whispered fiercely. "Please come back. I do love you. I love you as much as I can." She was hugging Jerry so hard that Kief had to pull her away. A movie scene flashed through her mind, and Gina remembered a monkey, crying aloud, carrying her dead baby until it began to rot, and she finally had to let go.

"We're taking him to the hospital, Mother," Kief said. "Jay is here with his car."

The two men carried Jerry outside into the car. Gina sat in the back seat, Jerry's head in her lap, blowing on his forehead, hoping to cool him.

off. "I should have married you sooner, the first time you asked," she said softly, not sure if he could hear. "It was my fault we've had such a short marriage. Baba, let him live, please let him live." She cried aloud, hoping her prayer would carry to Baba through the dark, silent night of the Indian countryside.

"Don't," Jerry opened his eyes and whispered, smiling faintly. It did not seem as if he were looking at her, but through her. "I am so happy."

When the orderlies at the ashram hospital took Jerry from her arms, he was dead. The doctors said the next morning that he had died of a heart attack, complicated by a swift, vicious virus that had struck a number of people at the ashram that week. Gina didn't say what she was thinking, that Jerry had left her for God and that she was almost too angry to grieve for him. Sai Baba had given Kief back to her, but he had taken Jerry away. Suddenly she remembered Aunt Hannah's words when her only child had died at birth, "The Lord giveth and the Lord taketh away. Blessed be the name of the Lord." How easy it is to trust when you are given what you want, Gina thought. And how hard it is when God's will, not your own, is done. If she had thought that once she put her faith in God, he would grant whatever she wanted, as her gentle father had done, she could think again.

She had overheard Kori telling Jerry that freedom lay in the breaking of all attachments, even the attachment to life itself. It was Kori who had led Jerry to long for liberation. Gina's heart burned with anger toward her daughter-in-law. But then she remembered that Kori's longing to see Sai Baba had brought Kief here for healing. As her thoughts swirled like a storm, Gina stepped back and watched, to avoid being blown apart. She was angry because Jerry had not wanted what she wanted, and that Jerry's will, not hers, had been done. Bowing her head, Gina wept and said the words she had heard so often from Jerry's lips. They came slowly, as if she were speaking a foreign language. "Lord, not my will but yours be done." After saying these words aloud, Gina felt her breath slow down and her heart stopped pounding. She was able, finally, to sleep.

❧❧❧

"Freedom," Gina muttered to herself as she slogged through the mud created by a brief, heavy downpour. She had always believed that freedom was control over her own life. Security. No hassles. Well, sure enough, Jerry had no hassles now. Had she burdened him too much with her nagging certainty that someone, somewhere was devoted to taking away her money as fast as she could make it? First it had been bills for Kief's schooling. Then it was loans to keep her business going. Then taxes, house payments and the unexpected jumps in health insurance premiums. All she ever got out of the insurance company was payment for her yearly gynecological exam. They wouldn't even pay for mammograms.

Numbers danced in her head, cluttering it with trash she wanted to be rid of. Whenever confronted with pain, Gina had always stuffed her head with ways to make and spend money. At least that was something she knew how to do, and it gave her the illusion of being in control of her life. But now the numbers seemed to be a trap that had sprung shut, gripping her head like a migraine.

Lakshmi hurried along behind Gina, carrying a basket of flower petals. Gentle Lakshmi, who made only a few hundred dollars a year stitching mattresses, lived fifteen miles from Puttaparthi. Her tiny shack had no electricity, just a gas lamp for which she could often not afford the fuel. She had no children but Naranjan, and when she was old there would be no one to take care of her. Gina had offered to pay for electricity so that Lakshmi could sew late at night, but the Indian woman had only laughed. "If Baba wants me to have electricity, he will give it to me. I am content."

People in India didn't seem to care if anything ever changed. No matter how many foreign armies swept through or who controlled the government, India just fell back into her familiar way of letting things take care of themselves. No one seemed to be in control of anything. Indians seemed to think their country would muddle along as she always had, while her people prayed to their gods and taught their children to care for nothing but their parents, their souls and their karma. The thought struck Gina that if reincarnation was actually true, the selfish life she had lived might cause her to wind up next time on the streets of Bombay.

She seldom talked to Lakshmi, but felt a sense of peace when the woman was nearby. Gina had not realized that tears were running down her face, merging with the raindrops, until Lakshmi wiped them away, whispering, "Don't cry. Pray to Baba." Fearing that since Jerry's death no one would be there to love her, Gina wondered if she could pray. She tried a tentative prayer, asking Baba to give her some sign, some hope that her mind would not always be such a rat's nest of dismal projections.

As usual, Gina was in a state of fear—fear of being alone, fear that she would wind up a bag lady in the street, unable to keep up with the stream of paperwork that kept her fragile financial operation afloat. Sure, she had the land up in Santa Cruz now, and a few hundred thousand in municipal bonds. She wouldn't starve, but she would never be rich enough to live as she pleased. This desire for power and security, she wondered, where did it come from? Her parents had always given her the freedom she needed. Jerry had never made demands. Why then was money so important to her? Why did she want so unreasonably much? Whatever Gina saw in catalogs or TV commercials, she wanted. It was as if there was a hole in her heart that could never be filled.

She looked back at Jerry's body on the stretcher and shuddered. That was what she feared most, total loss. No more hope of filling the hole in her heart, no more wants, no more Gina. Whatever she was would some day be gone as absolutely as Jerry was gone. She put her hands to her throat, which felt hot and swollen, as if unshed tears were being stored there.

Kief walked ahead with Jay and two Indian men, carrying Jerry's funeral stretcher. Reaching the narrow, shallow Chithravathi River, they began heaping scraps of wood and cow dung around the cloth-covered body. Kori had scattered flower petals and a perfect pink petal lay across Jerry's lips. Gina did not disturb it to kiss him goodbye. The women who were washing clothes in the river stopped their work out of respect and made their namasté to the mourners. The cows continued to wade and drink, without looking up.

Just as the first flames began to crackle in the kindling, Kori handed the baby to Kief and leaped forward to take the ring from Jerry's hand. "It is yours, Mother," she said. "I just remembered. Baba told me to exchange it for the one that will be John Philo's."

Silently, Gina removed her ring bearing the three sacred names and gave it to Kori. The baby laughed and tried to grab it from his mother's hand. Kori handed Jerry's ring to Gina, who gazed at it for a moment, wondering dully why the picture had changed from the face of Jesus to the face of Baba. Her head hurt too much to make any sense of it, so she didn't try. Gina put the new ring next to her wedding ring, where it fit perfectly. She watched the flames turn Jerry's body to ash, but did not stay to watch the ashes being thrown into the slow-moving brown river.

❧

When Kori returned to the roundhouse, Gina was lying on her mat, barely conscious and burning with fever. Kief sat beside her, anxiously replacing the warm compresses on her forehead with cold ones, brought in by Lakshmi. Standing at the door, Kori looked to Gina taller than a human being, more like an angel.

Dimly realizing that she was sick with whatever had killed Jerry, Gina called out in what she meant to be a loud voice, but which sounded like a whisper, "This fever is catching. Don't let Kori in with the baby." It's a good thing that Baba put Kori and the baby in a separate room, she reassured herself, trying to focus the muddled, directionless thoughts that squirmed like a tangle of snakes in her mind. But, no. Kori and the baby had been with Jerry last night and could already be carrying the infection.

"Take care of my family, Baba," she whispered. "Don't let the baby catch this sickness." From the burning pit of her mind, Gina could hear Baba's light, lilting voice. *You don't take care of the baby. I take care of him.*

Soothed by the laughter behind the words, she sank into sleep as the darkness closed over her like water over a drowning victim. In her dream, Jerry was flying in circles above her, his face dazzling. "Don't you care about me?" she cried. "You said you loved me." Here he was, dead, she scolded herself, and she was trying to lay a guilt trip on him. But his expression didn't change. He looked down at her, smiling his amazed, childlike smile, and continued to circle overhead in a ring of endless light.

Gina slept for two days, then woke up suddenly in a dark room to find Kief huddled asleep on the mat beside hers. Thinking she heard the door open, she tried to sit up, but her body felt like wet spaghetti. "Who is it?" Her lips moved, but no sound came out.

"It is I. Do not be afraid."

She could see Sai Baba's form, his face, but not clearly. He seemed to have drifted slowly into shape, like a cloud, his orange robe shining brighter than the sunset.

"Are you real or am I hallucinating?" Gina dragged herself to a sitting position and leaned against the wall, feeling the cool whitewashed cement against her back.

"What does it matter if you dream me or if I dream you?" Sai Baba glided closer to her, holding out his hand. "Do you want to come with me? Be with your husband?"

Gina shrank back, flattening herself against the wall. "No, no, I don't want to be dead." She had a vision of her flesh curling into black ribbons, then crumbling to ashes that would drift down the small, brown river. Wanting Sai Baba to understand that dying was not what she had in mind, Gina tried to tell him so, but her lips only flapped, making a sound that was hardly human.

He nodded. "Very well. You will live a while longer in this world. It is your choice." He leaned over and gently blew on her forehead, as he had Jerry's. Gina was surprised to feel her body cooling off, since she knew she was still dreaming. "I have a task for you," Baba said. "From now on, I want you to live as a Jew."

"What does that mean?" She had a general idea, but wanted to know how much it would take to satisfy him. Maybe no more bacon. Maybe just keeping Shabbat would be enough.

"Go to where your people are and live as they do," he said. "They will teach you."

"But I want to stay with Kief and Kori. I want to take care of the baby." Gina began to cry and leaned over close to him, so that her tears fell onto his feet.

"You yourself are a baby." His voice was gentle and seemed to smile, although his lips did not. "Leave your grandson to his parents and me. Go where you will be taken care of. I will be with you. Go in trust."

Gina could not explain the sudden sense of being loved so deeply, so absolutely that her molecules felt stretched, split apart by a force driving through her like a whirlwind. He knew her and loved her as she was. He understood her and did not judge. Gina crouched down and laid her hands and forehead on his feet, in the sign of respect and love that Indian children show their parents. As she did so, this ritual did not feel so strange. She remembered kissing her son's toes when he was a baby, and the feeling was not so different. She covered her eyes with her hands and stayed bent over on the floor. A sense of trust was growing in her, warm as the blood that brought life to every cell in her body. When she sat up, Sai Baba was gone. Or her dream was over. She could not be sure which.

"I will go. I will do as he says." Her words were loud enough to wake Kief.

"Mother?" Kief sat up, rubbing his eyes. "Are you feeling better? Do you need to go to the bathroom?"

"I think I'm well." Gina stood up cautiously and started to brace herself against the wall, then stopped. She would trust that she was strong enough to stand without help and found that she was.

The sound of women's voices floated into the room, coming first from far away, then closer. Kief opened the door and the voices were louder still, the gentle melody rising and falling like breath. "The nagarsankirtan. Look. People are up singing before dawn to welcome the sun."

Gina stood beside him, watching the shawl-wrapped women pass by on the dusty ashram lane. The dawn was just touching the encircling hills, turning the sky a light purple. A tiny, bright arc at the sun's rim shone above the tallest hill. As Gina breathed deeply, smelling jasmine in the air, she smiled, remembering that jasmine was the scent of Baba's feet.

An hour later, at morning darshan, she was sitting beside Lakshmi and her son, who trembled in his chair, drooling as he slid down in the seat. Lakshmi pulled the boy up and settled the blanket over his lap.

"Many new people are here," she whispered to Gina. "There is a large group from Delhi, so poor they had to walk all the way. Also some rich men from Europe. They want to present gifts to Swami."

"Hush, hush." A sevadal frowned and motioned at Lakshmi, who shrugged.

"Last night the light in Swami's room never went out. He was still working at his desk when the men came to get him for darshan."

"No talking, madam!" The sevadal glared at Lakshmi.

Gina sat silently, staring at the door where Baba would come out and wondered how he could have been in her room and his at the same time. A mystery, as Kori would say. Gina's capacity for trust was being tested.

Birds suddenly began to squawk and twitter, circling and diving over the roof of the temple. Several began to mate, noisily flapping on the roof. The women around her straightened up, craning their necks to see Baba as he came out and began his long walk through the courtyard. There was no talking now. All eyes were on Baba, and all ears were straining to hear any words he might speak to some fortunate person.

Gina's heart beat faster when she saw Baba diverge from his usual course and start down the row of wheelchairs lining the court. Lakshmi had said he almost never came to the chairs these days. After taking a few letters, he stopped near a white-haired Englishwoman.

"What shall I do, Baba?" she asked tearfully. "I cannot decide whether or not to have the operation. Tell me what to do."

Baba swirled his hand and touched her forehead with ash, then put the rest into the open hand in her lap. "The real guru is inside." He touched his chest. "Do not wait for me to tell you what to do. God speaks to you in your heart. Listen."

Suddenly Lakshmi's son sat up straight and cried out "Jai," in a loud voice. Hallelujah, was the closest Westerners could come to the meaning of jai, Kori had said. Heads turned, faces disapproving, until people saw that it was the crippled boy. Baba came close and stood by Naranjan's chair, then touched his forehead with ash. The boy leaned his head back, smiling.

Baba said something to Lakshmi in Telugu and she responded, her face full of surprise and joy. Maybe he was telling her Naranjan would be healed, Gina thought. But still Lakshmi's son sat in his chair and drooled, his hands twitching in his lap.

Turning to Gina, Baba said, "Trust and go. Remember."

Through blurred eyes, she watched his small form move down the line. Her dream had not been altogether a dream, unless he had dreamed it with her. He meant what he said. She was supposed to leave everything and go to Israel. Learn from Aunt Hannah and Uncle Chaim how to be a Jew. No way to squirm out of it. Gina sighed and tried to imagine herself doing the wash by hand in Zefat, standing for hours during the long prayers. It would be a miracle if she lasted a week. And Baba would be far away. *You still think so? Do you not see that we are friends? We will never be apart. Never.* The voice rang in her ears and she looked up. Baba had paused before reaching the men's section and looked over his shoulder directly at her. He pointed at his feet and smiled at her, as if they shared a secret, then moved on. A soft breeze blew by, and Gina smelled jasmine again, remembering the scent of his feet.

Before returning to the temple, Baba beckoned to the crowd of ragged visitors from Delhi, who followed him for an interview. Lakshmi explained that they were the ones who had walked a thousand miles to see him. The rich foreigners had asked for an interview, but Baba had chosen the Delhi group instead.

"They are his children," Lakshmi said. "He told them so. I think the rich men must be very mad."

"And how do you feel?" Gina laid her hand on Lakshmi's brown arm with its scars and knotted veins. "He did not heal your son."

"He blessed my Naranjan. Baba told me this is all Naranjan wants from him. And he said that in my next life, both you and I will be with Prema Sai. We will live together again in that lifetime. We do not always see as he sees. I trust him."

Gina left Lakshmi praying in the courtyard and walked by herself behind the temple, her hands folded to keep them from trembling. For a moment she imagined that Jerry was walking beside her. Then she was alone again, not knowing what to do with her rat's nest of a mind, her anger, her longing to be safe. She would not leave for Israel until she could learn to feel what Lakshmi felt and trust as Lakshmi trusted. It would likely take a long time.

∾⋐⋑∾

Whenever Kori did not need her to watch the baby, Gina would walk up the winding path toward the Museum of Mankind's Religions and spend a few hours in the basement reading room, which held a large collection of books in many languages, including English. She didn't bother with the scriptures, except for the Bhagavad-Gita, for they seemed impenetrably Hindu and made no more sense to her than had the Talmudic commentaries on Uncle Chaim's bookshelf. Instead, Gina studied the books about Baba—his life, his teachings, and stories of those who had been close to him.

For weeks before his birth, the strings of the family's tamboura twanged without being touched, and the maddala, the drum used for accompanying holy songs, beat as if under the hands of an inspired drummer. The village priests wagged their heads and said that some benevolent power was about to come into earthly form. Early one morning, the pious Easwaramma went into labor just after performing her puja, her daily prayer ritual.

As the sun rose over the mountains, she gave birth to a boy, who was laid on a bed of folded clothes by the village women. There was a sudden shifting under the pile, and a large cobra slithered out. These women had seen the snake as a most favorable omen, a sign of divine protection for the infant. But Gina shuddered, imagining how terrified she would have been for the life of her own newborn.

The baby, Sathyanarayana, was the attraction of the village, and visitors would come to sit by his bed, fondling his curls, smelling the sweet jasmine scent that filled the air around him. He was a gentle, uncomplaining child. Even as a small boy, he avoided places where animals were slaughtered and he would not eat meat, even though the rest of his family did. If a chicken was destined to be cooked for dinner, little Sathya would hold it in his arms and try to convince his parents that the bird should live. When a beggar came to the door, this three-year-old "brahmin child," as he was called, would insist that the person be fed. If they refused, he would weep until the beggar was fed. Finally, his mother shook her finger at him and said he would have to do without food himself if he insisted on feeding beggars. That was fine with Sathya, for he simply stayed away from lunch and dinner and went on giving out food. When his mother asked how he could bear to go hungry, he explained that Thatha, an old man, had been giving him balls of milk-rice. He held out his hand and his mother smelled the fragrance of butter, milk and curds of a quality she had never been able to afford. No one but Sathya ever saw this old man.

The children of the village referred to little Sathya as "guru." If one did not have a pencil or eraser, replacements could often be found in Sathya's bag. It was suspected among the students that he had a spirit working for him. Once when some boys were late to school and huddled under the schoolhouse eaves, fearing a beating from the master's sharp cane, Sathya brought them warm shirts and towels to keep them from being chilled by the rain and fog. He himself was a model student, and at the age of seven began composing holy songs that were performed for the community. At ten, Sathya organized a traveling musical troop of boys who presented sacred operas based on the ancient Vedic stories of the gods. Many of those who watched him dance thought they saw the god Krishna, leaping like a lion and singing as he defeated the powers of evil. Gina studied the illustrations of slim, blue-faced, flute-playing Krishna, but could see no resemblance to the Sathya Sai Baba she knew.

Manifestations of his inner powers continued to increase throughout his childhood. When valuable articles were lost, he could find them, even when they had been hidden. One servant had stolen his master's pen, and Sathya described exactly where it was, in the hands of the servant's son, miles away at school in Anantapur.

His fellow students admired Sathya as much for his gentle disposition and running ability as for his miracles. They even followed his leadership in prayer at the beginning of the school day. Gina tried to imagine a school where children would be admired for holiness, but could think only of the orthodox yeshivot in Israel. There, small boys wearing short black pants and side curls that bobbed over their ears as they rocked back and forth, chanted Hebrew prayers in high voices and were given prizes for their learning.

A sudden change occurred in Sathya when he was thirteen, and Gina thought of the bar mitzvah, when Jewish boys became men. But Sathya's ritual was much more of an ordeal than learning to read Hebrew. He was bitten by a scorpion and fell into an unconscious state that lasted for days. It was the first of a series of comas during which he would leave his body, often being seen in two places at once. Well, Gina considered, that might explain how he could have been in his room and mine at the same time.

After the scorpion bite, Sathya started to speak and sing in strange ways. When he began having visions of gods passing across the sky, his parents feared for his sanity. He said to them, "Why do you worry like this? There is no doctor who can cure me." His father would not listen, but summoned numerous priests and exorcists, including one witch doctor, a giant of a man with blood-red eyes, who was determined to cure the "wonder boy."

The would-be exorcist sacrificed animals and made Sathya sit in the center of a circle drawn with their blood. He chanted every curse he knew while the boy smiled at his failures. Desperate, he shaved the boy's head and with a knife carved three X marks on his scalp. On the open wounds he poured lime and garlic juices. When the evil spirit would still not leave, he beat on Sathya's joints, screaming curses and threats.

In frustration, the witch doctor used his strongest weapon, the kalikam, an acid which he rubbed into Sathya's eyes, causing his entire head to swell beyond recognition. The boy's body shook with the force of the pain, yet he said nothing and let the torture take its course. Astonished at Sathya's calm endurance, his parents finally gave up.

One day his father asked if he was a god, a ghost or a madman. Sathya answered, "I am Sai Baba, the same one who lived at Shirdi. I have come to end your sorrows. You prayed that I would be born to you, and so I came." He then threw a handful of jasmine petals on the floor and they mysteriously moved together, spelling "Sai Baba."

In 1940, at age fourteen, Sathya stopped going to school, saying, "I am no longer your little boy. I am called to do my work and cannot stay with you any more." He continued to live in his village of Puttaparthi, which until the 1960s would remain inaccessible, except by foot or bullock cart. There he performed an increasing variety of miracles and materializations, healing the sick, halting storms in their tracks, rescuing people in far away places and feeding the hungry.

Later, he began sending his followers, hundreds of thousands of them, into the villages of India to build schools, clinics and water systems. Graduates of the Sathya Sai universities had already started climbing the ranks of India's civil service, but Gina wondered if even they could hasten the heavy-footed pace of change in India. This miracle would be a greater one than any Baba had performed so far, she thought, but at least there was reason to hope.

At darshan, tears welled up in her eyes as row upon row of boys and girls dressed in white sat quietly at prayer in front of Baba's temple. She saw their faces brighten with joy when he walked among them, talking with them, blessing them. Following graduation, these students would not forget to carry Baba's message of truth, discipline and service into the marketplace.

One day, Gina asked Lakshmi what she remembered from Sathya Sai Baba's youth. Rubbing her stiff fingers, the woman sat back, glad to drop her mattress-stitching for a moment.

"I remember how he made fruits grow on the tamarind tree, the one you see as you go up the path to the university. All kinds of fruits, not just tamarind. And it didn't matter what time of year. That tree is still alive." She pointed up the hill. "People meditate under it every day." Lakshmi hunched up her narrow shoulders and laughed high in her head. "But never again has the tree borne foreign fruit." Twisting some thread, she squinted as she put it through the eye of the needle. "And there was the day back in 1950, Vijayadasami Day. We were making long, thick garlands from fresh tulsi leaves to decorate Baba's little ashram. Not the great one you see now, but the first one. He asked if we wanted two more baskets of tulsi, and of course we said yes. Then he touched our empty baskets, and when he stood up they were overflowing. He has often done the same with food to be given to the poor. Or with medicines."

"Why does he give so many gifts?" Gina asked. "Is it to win people over?"

"Perhaps," Lakshmi said, bending over her flowered mattress cover.

"He once said, 'I give you what you want so you will want what I have to give.'"

"And what did he mean by that?" Gina asked, rolling up a spool of thread that had escaped across the floor.

"Only that the real gift is a heart full of joy," Lakshmi smiled. "That is true liberation. A blessing that fills you so that you want nothing else."

"Like your Naranjan when he called out 'Jai' and was so happy just to have Baba's blessing?"

"Yes, like my son." Lakshmi pricked her finger, but went right on sewing without a murmur. "Naranjan has what he needs. We all do. The real miracle is to realize it, like he does. Then we do not need gifts materialized out of the air. Do you see, madam?"

Gina did not answer but walked outside across the sandy yard where the children at play were kicking a ball carefully, to avoid hitting her. They reminded her of the children playing politely in the square of Jerusalem's Old City under the watchful eyes of armed soldiers only a little older than themselves. Her mind traveled north to the mountains near Zefat, where it seemed that the sounds of playing children never stopped. Aunt Hannah said that the women of Zefat had such large families because they were trying to make up for all those who had been killed in the Holocaust. Perhaps, Gina thought, remembering Baba's words in the interview room, the women of Zefat were busy embodying great souls who would sacrifice themselves in their turn for the sake of a world needing redemption.

Gina shivered as the sun began to sink over the Indian mountains, recalling how it seemed to melt as it slid down behind the golden Galilean hills. Soon she would be in Zefat celebrating the Passover with her own people in Uncle Chaim's house. She would ask the question that was always asked by the youngest child in the family: "Why is this day different from all other days?" Because, she answered herself, Pesach is the day God saved his people from bondage in Egypt and promised to bring them into their own land, where they would be safe.

She walked over to the little temple of the elephant god, Ganesha, that aspect of God which removes obstacles. A man wearing only a white dhoti stood in front of the brilliantly painted elephant statue, breaking coconuts until streams of white milk ran down the steps.

"He made a vow," said one of the bystanders, seeing Gina shake her head at the waste of food. "Baba healed his child and this man promised twenty coconuts to Ganesha."

Here, vows were taken seriously, like the vows Abraham made to God and God made to Abraham. *You shall be my people and I shall be your God.* After hearing these words, Abraham had left the safest, richest place in the known world, searching for the land promised to him and his children forever. As she herself would soon be doing, leaving America for Israel.

A crowd of children closed in on the broken coconuts, laughing and pushing as they salvaged the white meat, eating some and taking the rest home to their families. Gina held the silk shawl tightly around herself, wishing she had listened to Lakshmi and brought along the wool one. Walking around the Ganesha temple, she saw a little cage with a scrawny monkey in it. Were they keeping this poor thing to eat? Should I let it go? she wondered. A little girl came at that moment and gave the monkey a piece of coconut. She looked up at Gina with a smile, showing gleaming white teeth that were too big for such a tiny mouth. "We feed him every day, Auntie," she said in careful English. "He fell out of a tree and broke his arm. We will feed him until he is strong enough to go back up the tree."

Why, Gina asked herself, do I always think the worst? Why do I assume that people are savages just because they're poor? Often, in her business, she had carelessly relied on first impressions, looking no deeper than the surface. All her life she had lived in a world of shadows and illusion, like someone stuck so long in a movie theater that the images on the screen were mistaken for reality. The scenario of imminent poverty had become so real she believed in it like some primitive peoples believed in bloody human sacrifices. Perhaps she was afraid that if she ever became poor, she herself would turn into a savage who would do anything rather than starve.

Maybe it was true that everyone kept returning to this world to learn new lessons. Maybe life on earth was all the hell anyone needed as payment for past sins. Maybe she herself would come back as an Indian woman with arms thin as sticks and a back bent from sweeping with a short broom. She would learn then, if she could not learn now, how to live without needing total control over her life.

Give it up, said the voice inside, as she looked up to the windows over the auditorium where Baba lived. *Sooner or later you must. Someday, yes, you will come back and your name will be Radha. You will have little wealth, but your joy will be great. You will serve Prema Sai. Be happy, not afraid.*

Gina saw a stirring at Baba's window and for a moment thought she saw him looking back at her. Just in case he was watching, she bowed, and the bowing felt good, like the completion of an examination. Then she went back to the Ganesha statue to see if she could find a few fragments of coconut meat to feed the monkey.

5

Senator George ("Gas") Gage, who technically represented California but, in fact, represented the interests of domestic oil producers, sat in his Washington office looking at Gina Hoffman's letter. Attached to it was a note saying that Ms. Hoffman had contributed five hundred dollars to his campaign fund last year. The senator ran his hand through his white mane, noting that it did not feel so thick as it had before his hairdresser started dying it white-white. A pity, since the mane, enhanced by his firm, square jaw and thin, elegant lips, was his trademark, standing as it did for virility, strength and statesmanship. Senator Gage thought that he looked much more presidential than the president and hoped voters would agree. The nominating convention was coming up in less than two years.

Gina's letter contained news he did not want to hear. Nazim had assured him that the Arabs' activities would be kept secret, and now this nosy woman was threatening to tell the entire real estate community that properties were being bought up by foreigners who planned to subvert the federal government. It wasn't just foreigners. Some highly placed members of the government, including Gage himself, were also secretly scheming to Balkanize North America and take over the fragments for God and fundamentalism, which were one and the same in Gage's book.

The senator had his own role figured out. If nominated for president, he would expose the plot and secure the election. If not, he would throw in his lot with Nazim and with Homer Healey's Fundamentalist Party of God, becoming president of the new country of California, which would be the eighth richest nation in the world. Gage looked across the room at the mirror, which was placed far away from his desk. He didn't want to see the lines that were turning his California-tanned face into a road map. This was one road map that led nowhere. He was seventy years old and looked it. Not much time left to get a leg up.

Senator Gage put on his tiny reading glasses, over which he stared so effectively into television cameras. After scanning Gina Hoffman's letter again, he placed a phone call to Yusuf Nazim. The Hoffman woman had a big mouth and friends in high places. She would have to go. Gage's friends in the Federal Emergency Management Agency had well-trained hit men who would take her out if she was still in the country. It was a good thing, he reflected, that most of the fourteen thousand men in FEMA were loyal to him. They were trained to combat emergencies. But the emergency they were most prepared to fight was a civil uprising by Californians who might not want Gas Gage as their new president.

⁓◦⌡⌠◦⁓

Even before hearing from Senator Gage, Nazim had put two of his men on Gina's trail. But they had drawn a blank. Homer Healey was no help, for Jerry had disappeared without a word to him. She might be in Israel, Nazim surmised, where his informants said she had relatives. He notified Gage that a small but reliable band of Lebanese terrorists was already looking for Gina Hoffman. Since FEMA's arm did not reach outside the U.S., Gage was glad to let Nazim's terrorists take care of the problem. And much less chance of murder being traced to the senator's holy hands, Nazim thought sourly, as he hung up the phone.

He lit his own cigarette, not bothering to call the valet. These Americans were too quick to murder, he thought, perhaps because they saw so many of their own filthy films. Neither Nazim nor his extended family watched movies. The screening room in the right wing of his oceanfront mansion had been turned into a little mosque. If Al-Hallaj could have visited Santa Barbara, he would be pleased, Nazim thought, as he pulled his picture of the old Sufi across the desk, staring into the deep, dark eyes that still held him from beyond the grave. He wished the master were beside him, making the way clear and straight, for Nazim was in need of comfort.

Words from the Koran rang in his ears. "Intrigue is the work of Satan. . . . In Allah let the faithful put their trust." And did he not trust Allah to do what was necessary to bring the world back to purity? Nazim coughed, then stubbed out the cigarette before it was a third gone. He had been smoking too much lately and often woke in the middle of the night, his heart beating fast. He must stay strong for the jihad. "The aggressors, the enemies of Allah, must be slain wherever you find them," taught the Koran. These words gave Nazim the right to order Gina Hoffman's death. Yet master Al-Hallaj had said the Koran meant you should slay only the enemy of Allah within your own heart. Nazim held his head in his hands, digging the heels of his palms into his eyes until he saw light. It should be simple to follow the will of Allah, he thought. But it was not, and for him it never had been. His beloved imam had sent him to the university to study the infidels and their Western ways, so as to destroy them more effectively. Nazim had his orders. He was to be a destroyer, but he was a destroyer who found it hard to sleep.

Homer Healey slept well, Nazim knew, for he had asked the minister how his nights were. Homer was elated that his country was falling into the hands of hard-liners, as the minister proudly called them. Into the hands of men who saw no gray, only the black and white of evil and good. The party of God had racked up 55 percent of the vote in the state elections. With the presidential primary campaigns approaching, the Healies, as newspaper headlines called them, were doing their job, and he must do his. Already hate crimes against intellectuals, homosexuals,

New Agers and Jews were increasing. Full-scale persecutions would proceed on schedule once the elections were over. Nazim had no doubt that the Party of God would win. When he prayed, the voice of the imam seemed to roar in his ears, and the word he heard was "victory," over and over.

"Yusuf?" Fatima was at the study door, knocking discreetly.

"You may come in." He was pleased to see his wife. Fatima always knew when he was unable to sleep, even when it was not her bed he had left.

She sat on the other side of the desk and reached out her hands. "Do you want me to make some tea?" Her soft voice always sounded to him like music.

"No. My stomach is a bit upset." Nazim took one of her hands and stroked it absentmindedly. "You know that the Koran says we should not kill the innocent, but should do good and let Allah take care of the world?"

"I remember." Fatima kept her eyes on her husband's face. "You are finding it hard to take a middle way between what the Koran says and what the leaders in Lebanon say you must do?"

"Yes. Very hard." Nazim withdrew his hand and brushed it across his damp forehead. "Please, Fatima, open the door to the terrace. I would like to feel the wind from the sea."

With the cool air sweeping across him, Nazim shivered, but felt more comfortable. Before coming to the United States, he had never lived by the sea. His notion of infinity had always been the vast, empty stretches of burning sand. Now he often stood on the terrace watching the ocean waves break on the crags below, foam tossing above the rocks like wet lace in the moonlight. Who was he, or Senator Gage, or even the master Al-Hallaj in the face of these timeless tides that turned hard rock to sand? Would it not be better to give up the killing and the scheming, and take his wives back home, where the word of Allah sounded in his ears without contradiction?

"Tell me one of your stories, Fatima," he said, wanting to hear some other voice than the one that made his head ache.

Fatima leaned back in the chair, hands linked behind her neck, and looked at the beamed ceiling. "Once a man went to the Land of Fools and saw people running in terror from a field. They told him a monster was there, waiting to kill them. When he looked, all he saw was a watermelon, which he offered to kill for them. They became afraid of him, for if he could kill the monster, he could kill them, too. So they drove him away with pitchforks."

Fatima stood behind Nazim, rubbing his forehead gently with her cool, plump fingers. "Then another man came, and the people told him what they had told the first. But instead of offering to kill the monster, the second man tiptoed away from it, agreeing that it was dangerous. He spent many months with the foolish people, teaching them truth and wisdom, until they were no longer fools and knew a watermelon from a monster."

She bent over and kissed his forehead. "Come to bed, Husband. I think you will be able to sleep now. Remember, the holy teachings are spreading throughout the world. You are doing your duty."

But Nazim stayed in his study long after she retired, staring at the moonlight as it moved across the sea. He could hear the voice of his master under the roar of the waves, "If you cannot stand the sting, do not put your hand in a scorpion's nest." Perhaps Fatima was right, that example and patience alone would show the people of this childish, demented country their own demons. But he had no time. The foolish ones still had great power in the world, and their power must be broken if Allah's will were to be done.

As he looked into the crashing surf, Nazim imagined a paradise rising up into the moonlight, a gentle land where each man obeyed the will of God and sought nothing for himself. His master had once told him that obedience was always right, whether it gave pleasure or not. He would obey.

Yusuf Nazim felt no pleasure when he placed the call to Damascus, giving orders for Gina Hoffman to be hunted down and killed. He remembered that her eyes slanted like Fatima's when she smiled, and that it was his men who had crippled her son. He also remembered that when he left the university for service in Al Fatah, his master had told him, "All men, except for the wise, are dead." Nazim took two pills from a bottle of Western medicine for pain. Then he went upstairs to bed, and spent the hours till dawn holding Fatima as she slept.

❧

Kamal Al-Essa lay on his cot in the Lebanese refugee camp where he had grown up. He was having a vision. All the previous day he had fasted and prayed, hoping that Allah himself would confirm the order to kill Gina Hoffman. It was not enough that Sheikh Omar, ruler of the refugee camp since before Kamal's birth, had ordered him to do it. Kamal had doubted the sheikh's sanity ever since the old man, cursing and crying, had tried to shoot down high-flying Israeli jets with his rusty carbine. The sheikh had once owned two thousand acres near Tiberias and a fine house from where he could see Jordan across the water. For many years after the Partition of Palestine, he had beseeched his Jordanian neighbors to accept his people, but they had refused. Now he lived in a tent behind barbed wire, with four hundred adults and more children than anyone could count. Few of them could read or write.

Kamal was one of the few, since his mother had been an English teacher in the old days when there was still a school. She had taught Kamal English as well as Arabic, for she was the daughter of a rich importer, and had been raised by an English nanny. Kamal had a talent for art and often sketched the barren landscape spreading beyond the compound, his fingers aching to include the graceful figures of long-robed men and women. But he would not break the tenets of his faith by making an idol of the human form. He had often been tempted to draw his own face, which was fine of feature and light-skinned, from the long hours spent indoors. But that would be even more sinful than drawing the forms of others. So he drew rocks and shadows cast by the rocks in the savage light of the sun.

Now that his mother's eyes had gone bad from glaucoma, which the camp doctor could not treat, she had him read the Koran to her for hours every day. Kamal suspected she kept him indoors so that he would not hang around the compound with the restless young men who were often recruited by the Syrians for commando missions against the Israelis. But when the sheikh summoned Kamal, his mother had no reason to be afraid and sent him with her blessing.

"You are a good boy, they tell me," Sheikh Omar said, wheezing through his water pipe, his narrow eyes almost swallowed in fat. "You stay with your mother in her need, yes?"

Kamal nodded and wiped the sweat from under his eyes, hoping the sheikh would not think it was tears.

"You weep easily. Too much time with women." The sheikh frowned and blew smoke in Kamal's face. "It is time you become a man. You must leave the world of women and join the world of men. You are eager, yes?"

The boy nodded again, though he had his doubts about how he would get along in the world of men. Since most of his time had been spent in prayer or with his mother, Kamal lived largely in his imagination. Remembering his dreams of paradise, he would awaken at night and write love songs to God. In these dreams, he lay beside crystal fountains in the loving arms of houris. He knew they were only symbols of the invisible light that was God, the one behind all manifestations, whether the dust and garbage of the camp or the red silk dresses of the houris.

Kamal had a fine tenor voice and had even hoped to become a muezzin. Only there was no tower in the camp from which to call the faithful to prayer, and the dust would choke the voice of anyone who tried to sing outside. Kamal preferred waiting until he could sing to

Allah face to face. He did not want a long, dreary life like his mother's, but a quick entry into the light of Allah, where he would paint the splendors of heaven and sing his songs aloud.

Sheikh Omar leaned forward, placing his hand on Kamal's thick brown hair. "I have heard that you are a good young man," he said. "I have also heard that you know your duty to obey Allah, to do His will above your own."

"I have always obeyed," Kamal answered, his voice faint. The smoke was making him sick.

"Then I will tell you the important task Allah has given to you, through me," the sheikh said, arranging the faded brown caftan over his swollen legs as he shifted his bulk uncomfortably on the flat cushions. "You are willing to die for Allah, yes?"

"I am," said Kamal. "To me, death is not a terrible thing."

"Nor to me," the sheikh replied. "If I were young, I would do what must be done, but I cannot." He held up a picture and tapped it with one stubby, stained finger. "This woman we have been ordered to kill." His dark eyes blazed under heavy brows. "The order comes from our leader in America."

"Can it be so?" Kamal's heart thudded in his chest. "What sin has the woman committed?"

"She is a blasphemer, like all her kind," the sheikh went on, his voice wheezing. "If Nazim and the others say she is our enemy, it must be because of some sacrilege. They say she worships strange gods. That is enough. The order has been given."

Kamal bowed his head. Perhaps this killing would be his avenue into Allah's presence. If so, he must thank Allah for it. As always, he found a way to be grateful, regardless of what happened, good or bad, thus keeping both his faith and his sanity intact.

Though he seemed calm to others, Kamal was full of fear. During prayer, his fear seemed to go away, but when he became his small self again, it returned. He remembered it beginning when he was a little boy and the school next door exploded in the night, showering flames and chunks of concrete on the Al-Essa shack. Over the years he had formed the habit of keeping cotton in his ears, dreading the next explosion. Neighbors thought he was somewhat deaf, but his mother never noticed. Except when he was reading to her, she did most of the talking in the family. No one knew about Kamal's fear of loud noises, and he meant never to show how small and frightened he felt.

"I must obey Allah's voice," Kamal said. "But I hardly remember how to use a gun. It has been so long since my training." Like all the boys in the village, he had been taught by Syrian military visitors, as they were called, to use the Russian weapons smuggled into the camp under piles of food and clothing. But that was years ago, and his military skills were rustier than the sheikh's old carbine.

"I will train you myself," said Sheikh Omar. "Every day you will come here and we will pray together, then practice marksmanship. In a few weeks time, you will be sent on your mission. If you are killed, we will take care of your mother as our own. Your honor before Allah will be great."

Kamal felt a haze drop over his eyes, and the sheikh seemed to vanish, replaced by a golden light that was shaped like a human being, but with no limbs or features. He could hear a voice that sounded curiously like his own, and the voice said only one word over and over again: "Obey." Kamal knew it was a sign that divinity had at last touched his life, as he had always prayed would happen. His prayers were being answered in a way that he had never dared to hope. Kamal had no doubt that he would pay with his life for this assignment. Allah would take him young and he would enter paradise as a martyr. He had been chosen, and for that, as for everything, Kamal was grateful.

The sheikh placed his hands on Kamal's shoulders, gripping him tightly. "You understand what you are to do?" He was used to questions, fears, doubts on the part of young recruits, and wondered that Kamal had none. Perhaps it was true, as people said, that the boy was almost deaf.

Kamal studied the picture of the smiling woman. Standing by a large blond man, she looked very small and harmless. He hoped he would be able to kill her without having to look into her eyes.

"Study the picture," said the sheikh. "You must know that face well. You will receive instructions from our agents about where to find her."

One month later, on the night before starting his mission, Kamal lay on his cot with the picture of Gina Hoffman face down over his chest. Suddenly, he had a vision of a golden light rising over him as if his soul were floating out of his body, and again the voice repeated one word, "Obey." Behind the light appeared an indistinct form, and Kamal sat up, struggling to see it better. When the image came into focus, he fell onto the bare floor, gasping. It was the woman in the picture, and she was smiling at him. Then another figure floated forward and merged with the woman. When that face displaced hers, he saw it was his own.

6

During the hot, dry summer, the scruffy chaparral bushes kept encroaching on the garden no matter how often Kori cut them back. She stood up, hands on her aching back. This pregnancy was harder than her first. Now that she was over forty, her swollen body was even more bloated and waterlogged than when she had carried John Philo. She was too old to bear children, Kori told herself. This child would be the last. Too bad she had not started earlier, but she had chosen to do a man's work in a man's world. And now that the world was breaking down, as gangs roamed city streets and old women needed guns to protect themselves, who cared how many copies of her books the publisher had sold, or whether or not Mary was an incarnation of the mother goddess?

As her pregnancy was coming to an end, the rumblings from below felt as if within the depths of her body, lava was rolling and rocks grinding on rocks, the way the earth turns in its sleep before a quake. Kori felt like a bystander at an insurrection, watching with wonder and terror as civil war raged within her. Fat, featureless goddesses haunted her dreams, and sometimes in the mirror the face she saw seemed one of theirs and not her own.

Over the months she had tried to visualize the little being that was growing within her, remembering *in utero* photos of large-headed, smiling tadpoles, their astonishingly human hands spread, as if practicing to catch the breast when their time came. She thought of the little swimmer moving inside her, as she herself moved through the air and the earth moved through space. Kori had always been terrified of water and had never even tried to swim, sure that she would sink. Kief said it was simply a matter of letting go and spreading out, a trick he would gladly teach her.

She wondered if the baby would have curly dark hairs sticking out of her ears like Kief. Would she have his chin? Whose eyes? Without any planning on their part, their united chromosomes had been multiplying and swelling like balloons at the secret party going on beneath her heart for the past eight months.

Kori bent over the horse trough, then pumped cold water on herself. The water trickled down her rough cotton shirt, staining it in dark rivers to match the circles under her arms. Kori's proper, elegant mother would have wept to see her daughter with sweaty, unironed clothes, fingers rough and red from hours of hard work. Kori often imagined Damaris calling futile, inaudible advice from whatever celestial realms suicides inhabited.

"This entire generation has fallen on evil days," Damaris would have said. The last of the women of quality, gently bred to pour tea and direct the polishing of their silver, were now moldering in nursing homes, while their granddaughters studied law, waited on tables, hustled real estate and raised a child or two in their few hours of free time.

Kori turned her mind quickly away from real estate, for it made her think of Gina. The thought of her mother-in-law made Kori's throat tighten until it hurt to swallow. During their time in India, Kief had just begun to know his mother as a friend. Making up for his years of indifference, he had spent many hours sitting with her under Sai Baba's magical tree, the one that had borne many kinds of fruit. Kief had not talked about Gina since her death. At least he had come closer to his mother before the end, Kori had told him, trying to be of comfort, but he would not answer.

She heard voices below and wondered if Kief was back from his trip to the village. Combing her damp hair with her fingers, she tried to make herself presentable. Kori had not felt pretty for some time and was afraid her husband must be disenchanted by the circles under her eyes and the thickness of her ankles.

Baba had said that he had given her a good, faithful husband, whom she must work with, not try to control. Fortunately, that had proved an easy task, since Kief wanted whatever she wanted. If she asked, he gave, perhaps because she made her requests in an offhand way and never pushed him as his mother had. Would you mind feeding John Philo, she would ask, while I chop the beets? Or, you might think about having Juan show us how to grow soybeans. Whatever it was, Kief followed more often than he led. It had been a good year, except for the silence about his mother and his leaving the house when Kori said her prayers at their altar.

The men's voices grew louder, and Kori realized that a number of strangers were coming up the hill. Her heart pounding so hard she could hear the blood beating in her ears, she blew her whistle to summon the people from the farm. But they were too far down in the bean fields to reach her before the strangers arrived. It was impossible for Kori to run, but she managed to waddle back to the cottage, praying she could remember how to load the shotgun. But first, she hid the jewels Gina had given her under a loose floorboard and dragged the dresser over it.

With an axe in one hand and shotgun shells in the other, Candelaria, a tough young Indian woman, stationed herself by the front door. Maybe she should be the one to face the strangers, Kori thought, for Candelaria seemed afraid of nothing. The Indian woman had delivered many babies, so Kief had insisted she stay close to Kori during this last month. That was fine with Candelaria, for she adored Kori, who had found her when she was wandering in the mountains, pregnant and starving. Her family had turned her out for having a baby with a white man, and she would have died except for Kori.

Candelaria had a gruff way of speaking that put some people off, but with Kori she spoke easily and rapidly, like a child trying to finish a story before the mother runs out of time to listen. She loved to sit by Kori's feet at night, nursing Consuelo, her three-month-old daughter, while Kori combed and braided her thick black hair, telling stories of ancient goddesses in lands the other woman had never heard of.

Perhaps afraid of Candelaria's temper, Kief had taught only Kori how to load and fire the gun, and now she would have to protect them both. Kori's fingers shook so much that she dropped the box of ammunition and stood frozen for a moment, unsure if it might blow up. For all she knew, the gun itself might explode. It hadn't been used for nearly a year, when Kief had scared off a mountain lion. She hoped he had cleaned it since then. Probably he had, because Kief was a stickler for security, especially after the news had come about his mother.

"Don't forget to take the safety catch off," Candelaria said calmly.

Flicking the catch, Kori aimed the gun down the hill toward where the strangers' voices could be heard. Candelaria held the axe with both hands. They waited on the porch while the men came up the steep path from the valley. At first, only their heads could be seen, and Kori noticed that some had heavy beards. Maybe they were mountain men who had banded together to steal from the more prosperous farms.

Kori's damp fingers slid on the steel as her grip tightened on the gun. "No farther," she called out in a hoarse, deep-throated voice. "We are armed and will fire."

One of the men spoke. "Perhaps you would let me come closer, alone? We have no weapons but our walking staves."

"All right," Kori said reluctantly. "Just one, and only close enough that I can see you from head to foot."

The one who had spoken was a bearded giant of a man, at least six-and-a-half feet tall. He wore blue jeans and carried a tall, curved walking stick in one hand, steadying his overladen backpack with the other.

"My name is Father Gregory," he called out. "We are monks."

"You look like no monk I ever saw," Kori said, keeping the shotgun pointed at him. "Why should I believe you?"

The one who called himself Father Gregory put down his backpack, squatted on the ground, and began to rummage through his belongings.

"Better not be any weapon in there," Kori warned.

"Not to worry," the man stood up, holding a rumpled white robe. He threw it over his head and let it drop around him like a tent. "Is this proof enough?"

"Anyone could carry a monk's robe to put people off guard." Kori silently prayed the words, Om Sai Ram, over and over, so that they beat in her mind like the sound of her heart. They were words that brought Baba close and made her feel safer.

The man pulled out a chalice from his bag and a flat, gold-colored paten that glinted in the sun. He held them up as if celebrating a Mass. "And these? They're not so grand, but they are what they seem to be."

"And what do you want here?" Kori clicked the safety switch on and leaned back against the porch railing, suddenly feeling very weak.

"We've heard you have a big spread," Father Gregory said, putting his paten and chalice away, wrapping them first in a red velvet cloth. "Our monastery down in Santa Cruz was sold and the money given to the poor. Most of it, anyway. We felt embarrassed, having a big, fancy mansion while other people were sleeping on the sidewalks. So here we are, looking for a few acres to build a simple place to live and grow our vegetables."

"Why should we do this for you? We're not even Catholics," said Kori, sitting down wearily on the porch steps. When she laid the gun beside her, Candelaria snatched it up, staring fiercely at the priest.

"His kind always comes to take, not give," the Indian woman said. "I say shoot them. Drive them off."

"No, no," Kori waved her hand tiredly. "They will do no harm. Look, they are just a few. How many, Father?"

"Only six. The rest decided to quit when we sold the fine house."

"You can tell them to come forward, one by one and stand with you," Kori said. "We will talk."

At his call, five other men climbed up over the crest of the ridge. Three were bearded, as he was, and two were so young they looked like teenagers. He told all their names, but Kori could only remember Brother Elijah, a slender, bald man with a pointed nose and bright, happy eyes that crinkled when he smiled. "We're Benedictines," Brother Elijah said. "Our job is to pray and study, but we also do farm work. We could help during your harvest, since we'd be neighbors."

Brother Elijah walked with a light step, and his voice was a lilting baritone. A singer, Kori thought. How pleasant it would be to hear a man sing again. Kief had not sung since the attack on his mother. Relaxing a bit, she smiled back at him. There was no guile in this priest. She knew it as surely as if Baba had whispered in her ear. "And we could come to your services if we wish?" she asked.

"You would be welcome," Father Gregory said. "May I come closer, please? I'm a doctor, as well as a priest, and I see you are near your time. I could be of help."

Kori allowed him to check her pulse and blood pressure.

"Not so good," he said, leaning down to inspect her ankles. "You have toxemia. Did you know that?"

"I suspected it." Kori leaned back against the banister, closing her eyes. "There was a bit of it with my first baby."

"Well, I'll be on hand," said the priest, as he packed the stethoscope back into his bag. "If you want me, just call."

"We will do fine," Candelaria burst out, glowering at him. "We need none of your kind. It is a woman's business, this."

Father Gregory smiled at Kori, shrugged and stepped back beside Brother Elijah. "We have nowhere to go until we find a place for the monastery," he said. "Could we stay in your barn? We'll gladly work for our keep."

"I would tell you yes right now," Kori said, "but we must wait until my husband comes home. He will decide. Until then you can wait in the barn. We will have dinner in the hall over there." She pointed to the low, flat structure with a tin roof that Kief had finished building three weeks before. "About six."

"Thank you," said Father Gregory. "Perhaps you will allow us to say vespers before dinner?"

"Of course." Kori rather hoped Kief wouldn't be back in time to hear the monks singing their evening prayers. He was not fond of the Catholic Church, since Gina had raised him on stories of priests ordering their people to slaughter Jews. Kief might feel that allowing the monks to stay on the land would be a slap in his mother's face. It would take some doing to convince him, and Candelaria would vote against their presence, for sure.

Kori sent the Indian woman out to the barn with a pitcher of water and some homemade bread. The monks had not asked for food, but she could see that they were thin and pale. Brother Elijah's eyes had brightened when he spied the loaves rising on the porch railing. He would probably be the one who would sing the grace, Kori thought, wishing she had the energy to go out to the barn and listen. She would have taken the food herself, but Candelaria had insisted that she stay quiet. With a grim, skeptical look, the Indian woman had set the tray of bread on her head and stomped off to the barn, hoping aloud that the monks would choke on it.

Kori felt hot again and went down to wash her face at the horse trough. She loved feeling the cold mountain water as it splashed over her head like a baptism. At the sound of hoof beats, she raised her hands to protect her eyes from the sinking sun.

Kief was just topping the ridge above the soybean field. Kori waved down at him, hoping he had stopped to see old McCaver, who brought their milk twice a week from the farm next door. She could see Juan Herrera, one of their first community members, riding behind Kief with a milk can balanced between them. God bless Shay, she thought, grateful for the sturdy, thick-bellied Icelandic mare that could easily carry their whole family on her back. Since the price of gasoline had risen so sharply, thanks to Governor Gas Gage and his oil partners, they now used the horse more than the pickup truck. Money and conveniences were in increasingly short supply.

This was indeed the Kali Yuga, Kori thought, the age of iron, when men were worse than animals to each other. Baba had called the Kali Yuga a state of mind, turning the world dark and grim just before the Golden Age, when God would return, bringing an unimaginable, irresistible love. Weighed down by a heaviness of spirit that pressed on her far more than the heaviness of her body, Kori murmured a prayer, asking Baba to fill her mind with light. The words came to her in Sanskrit, *"Om bhur buvah suva'a . . ."* As she chanted, she imagined Baba in brilliant color behind her closed eyes, enfolding her and her unborn child in his arms.

"You okay, Kori?" Kief came riding up to the trough and tossed his reins over the post.

She didn't answer, but reached up to her husband as he slid off his horse. Kief hugged her carefully, to avoid crowding the baby in her belly. The dark curly hair was beginning to recede from his temples, and his face was heavily creased from many hours in the sun.

"Thanks, Juan, you can put the milk can in the stream for now. The fridge is down again." Kori smiled at the dark, stocky man who was shuffling his feet, as he always did when she spoke to him. Juan was still unsure of her acceptance. After all, Kori had first seen him as a wounded bandito, and six months of good behavior was hardly enough to live down that initial encounter.

In his pre-Candelaria days, Juan Herrera had been a gang member in Santa Cruz. They had met when he tried to steal the community's weekly purchase of dry goods from Candelaria, who was riding home from the general store in the valley. Her mule, trained to kick anyone who threatened her, had danced sideways, then sent Juan flying with a kick to his rear. He had landed headfirst in a pile of rocks and was knocked unconscious.

Under her gruffness, Candelaria had a kind heart, as well as sturdy arms, so she loaded the bleeding bandito onto her mule and brought him back to her cottage. After prudently tying the young man up, she and Kori waited for Kief to decide what to do with him. It was the first time a gang member had gotten this far into their mountains, but would probably not be the last.

The blow on his head seemed to have done Juan some good, for he settled down with Candelaria and never returned to his gang. He was a skilled guitarist and quickly became the main attraction at the community's weekly meetings. The two were married when she was well along in her pregnancy. At their wedding, Juan played while Candelaria did her traditional Indian dances to a Spanish beat. Dancing along with her, Kief had even laughed a little, something he had not done since hearing the news about his mother.

The ex-bandito also turned out to be a good farmer, having been taught by his Mexican grandfather how to grow beans. Before Juan came along, Kief had had no luck with beans and was considering a change to tomatoes.

"Another generator failure?" Kief pushed back his stained leather hat. "Eddie still hasn't finished building the new back-up system." He wiped down the mare with the saddle blanket and laid the blanket out in the sun to dry.

"Eddie's been trying to fix the tractor." Kori sometimes worried that Kief's pressure would drive Eddie Szu, their soft-spoken Chinese machinist, back to Los Angeles. Letters from his family came often, begging him to return. They still hoped he would marry and settle down, but Eddie preferred his quiet, solitary life on the mountain. Sometimes Kori would see him at dawn in the clearing near the community kitchen, practicing his slow, ballet-like t'ai chi movements to the music of the wind.

"I know, I know." Kief wiped the back of his hand across his forehead. "It's my fault our parts supply is down. But I didn't want to drive as far as San Francisco until after the baby comes."

"Now we will have help with the baby." Looking away, Kori began scraping at a patch of green algae that was discoloring the trough. "Some men are here. We need to talk about it."

"Who?" Kief's eyes narrowed. "They came while I was away? God, Kori, I told you to shoot any stranger who sticks his head over that ridge. You know the danger."

"They are monks, Kief." Kori decided to get it out quickly, feeling too tired to make a story of it. "Six Benedictine monks. They sold their monastery in Santa Cruz and gave most of the money to the poor. Now they want to buy a few acres from us. They seem like good men to me, and I would like them to stay."

"Monks?" Kief snorted incredulously. "Men who sit around all day and pray? I suppose we'd have to feed them and clean their latrines. Damn it, Kori, I hope you didn't tell them they could stay."

"I told them I would ask you," Kori's voice was low and even. "They do have a little money to pay for their land and are willing to help with the farm. Perhaps you could give them a try."

Folding his arms tightly against his chest, Kief turned his back. She could see his fingers nervously tapping his biceps. "Monks, yet. We haven't enough mouths to feed. Are they old? Young?"

"Mostly young, I would say. And strong. If they don't suit you after a time of trial, they could be asked to leave. Besides, one is a doctor who could take care of me."

"Well, I can't say no to that." Kief pumped hard and stuck his face into the sudden stream of water. "But after the baby comes, we'll have to talk again about letting them stay."

"Thanks, Kief." She took the corner of her long apron and wiped his face. "I hoped you would say yes."

Kief took her hands and looked into her face. "Those dark circles under your eyes make you look like a refugee. Let's get you inside and put your feet up for awhile."

"We are all refugees." Kori smiled and let herself be helped into the house, where Kief propped her legs up with pillows and brought her a cup of cold water. Installing a pump in the kitchen had been a good idea, since the county water system couldn't be counted on if there was another drought.

Kori put the water supply out of her head, remembering what she needed to do. She must focus her thoughts and breathe deeply, clearing her mind of useless worry. She thought of India and the face of Sai Baba telling her to be at peace. "Do your duty and keep your heart fixed on me," he had said to her. "Put your life in my hands, and I will guard you as the eyelids guard the eyes." Kori often wished she could hear Baba's voice in her head, the way Gina had. But perhaps that had been because he knew what was going to happen and was giving Gina a special, necessary grace. Closing her eyes and leaning back on the pillow, Kori tried not to think about her mother-in-law.

"There's a bit of news," Kief said, pumping a glass of water, his muscular arms glistening with sweat. "Nazim's guys are beginning to tangle with Homer's Healies. Actually, public sentiment seems to be more with Nazim. At least his Muslim Peace Corps is providing schools and work. Now that the public schools are falling apart, Nazim's a hero."

"But the Healies have the middle class." Kori sipped the water, then dipped her kerchief and laid it across her warm forehead.

"Which is sinking fast," Kief said, pacing the room. "So Healey's got nothing solid except Gage's troops backing him up. Nazim was smart to bet on numbers. There are a lot more poor people now than middle class."

"Numbers and discipline," Kori murmured. "That's something new for the poor in your country."

"Looks to me like we can expect civil unrest, as the media hygienically calls blood in the streets." Kief lit a fire in the stove.

"Between the Healies and Nazim's people?" Kori shook her head. "Nazim is too smart for that. He needs Healey's Party of God. And Gage needs them both."

"Let's hope. But at the next community meeting, I'm still going to push for an earthen wall around our main complex. Eddie says he could rig wires at the top so we could electrify the fence after dark."

"We already have an armed guard out every night," Kori objected. "I think weapons attract trouble. It's as if they want to be used. God will protect us. We have to believe that." She hoped he would remember how Baba had healed him and that Baba could be trusted, but Kief no longer seemed to trust anyone, especially God.

"Did he protect my mother?" Kief's voice was low and cool, without feeling.

It was the first time he had mentioned his mother since Uncle Chaim's call from Zefat. Kori held her breath, hoping he would continue, but he went outside, slamming the door behind him. She could hear him calling for John Philo. When Kief was in a bad mood, the child's presence comforted him. He would take John Philo up, nuzzle his neck, and ask if he had picked berries with his mother that day. After trudging back to the house behind Kori, bloody scratches on his arms, the boy loved to feed his father the berries he had picked. Kori studied her son's absurdly grown-up face, with its full jaw and straight-lipped mouth. He would become a tall man, she thought, given the genes he had inherited.

Kori wished their next child would also be a boy, for a six-foot daughter, though useful on the farm, might not find a husband. Sai Baba, however, had said to expect a daughter and that she would have a special task. Don't worry. Peace. Breathe and remember. With Baba's face in her mind, Kori's tight shoulders relaxed. How little it took for her mind to hit the ground running, to forget who was in charge of her life. She was more like Gina than she cared to admit, Kori reflected. She began to re-read the letters from Israel, searching her mother-in-law's words for signs that her last days had been blessed with peace.

෴

When Gina landed in Israel, she felt like kissing the ground, except that the oily tarmac was not especially inviting. The lights from the long, low airport buildings twinkled for miles in the desert night, and the antiseptic white terminal welcomed her with a crisp, neat familiarity so unlike India that she could have wept with gratitude. Surrounding her were dark-faced immigrants from Ethiopia, their heads heavily wrapped as if wounded in action. They had come with nothing, fleeing starvation and bullets, their heads covered against the African sun and out of honor to God.

Feeling foolish with her tinted hair and long red fingernails, Gina began to chip away at the polish. By the time she reached Zefat, her nails would be a plain, virtuous pink. In Tiberias, where she changed buses, she bought a hand-painted head scarf. Thinking twice about her sleeveless dress, she also bought a cotton shawl. She paid too much for it, fearing to miss her bus if she wandered from the station. The tourist prices made her wonder how long the monthly check from her stockbroker would last in this bare, spartan, expensive country. Maybe she should not have followed the impulse to leave her jewels with Kori. It seemed as though the Israelis were spending everything on defense. They certainly weren't wasting money on over-priced consumer goods. With its dingy station and overcrowded buses, Tiberias wasn't so different from India.

As the bus wound its way up the mountain, zigzagging along the edges of steep cliffs, Gina noticed two young soldiers, a boy and a girl, dozing opposite her. Each time the bus stopped to pick up passengers, they would open their eyes and lift their Uzis. Then they would relax again, hands still resting on their guns. At the same age, her Kief would have been lying on the beach, reading his physics textbook or daydreaming about ancient civilizations. *They know that death can come at any minute*, the voice inside her said gently. *Do you?*

Well, to be honest, I don't think about death, Gina answered, glad for Baba's momentary companionship.

Life is what you should be thinking about. Are you so sure you know what life is? Your body is just a garment worn for a little while.

I know, I know, Gina replied, thinking of Jerry's body turning into streaks of flame and charred bone. I was there, I saw.

Well, remember. You are not your body.

"I do remember," she said out loud. "I will." Gina blushed when the soldiers woke up and stared at her. After what I have seen, she said to herself, death is only a little thing anyway. She smiled, because the words sounded like Uncle Chaim's.

They met her at the bus station, Uncle Chaim and Aunt Hannah, then walked with her up to their little house. From her bedroom window, Gina could see all the way across the rocky, barren valley to where the great rabbi, Ari the Lion, was buried. Because it was the day before Shabbat, many men had already come to the mikvah above the tomb, towels and clean shirts in hand. Aunt Hannah had promised her that before Shabbat began, when the men were busy in the shul, the women would go down to the ancient pool and bathe in its cold, pure water.

Before the mikvah, Gina, known as Gilah to her Hebrew relatives, had to wash every part of her body, down to her toenails. Aunt Hannah checked her over before allowing her to step into the icy, blue-green water of the Ari mikvah. For a moment, Gina stood naked above the swirling water, shivering in the cool wind from the darkening mountain. *Purify, purify,* she heard Baba's voice as she jumped in, gasping at the shock. Obeying Hannah's instructions, she held her breath and crouched under the water so that she was immersed to the ends of her hair.

Abraham, Isaac and Jacob, she said to herself. Take me home. She bobbed up, red-faced and smiling as the cold receded into numbness. "Om Sai Ram," she cried out. "Jai."

Aunt Hannah shook her finger for silence, then cloaked her shivering niece with a towel. "The men will hear," she said. "Come along."

Her head thrown back, Gina watched the setting sun as she followed
her aunt up the steep, rocky path. When they reached the little house,
Aunt Hannah covered her face to say the Shabbat candle blessing.
Wrapped in her shawl, Gina said nothing for several hours. Her heart
was pounding and her eyes were closed, as if in the presence of too much
light. For this little while, it was easy to believe that she was not her body.

❧

As she put the letter down, Kori felt her belly harden drum-tight and
wondered if it was time to wake Kief. She knew this feeling, life struggling to escape, to roll away the stone from the tomb. For a few minutes
she lay still, thinking of Gina's last hours, so different from this moment
when life was waiting to be born. She thought of Uncle Chaim's call,
which had turned Kief silent and remote.

The attack had been a complete surprise, Uncle Chaim told them. At
dawn, an Arab had slipped over the new border of the Golan, only eight
kilometers from the Sea of Galilee. He had followed the shore toward the
Tabgha, that place of seven springs where Jesus and other prophets had
spoken to the multitudes.

As she often did, Gina had brought a group of grammar school students to see the Tabgha and have a breakfast picnic on the gently sloping grounds of the deserted Franciscan monastery. The sound of
splashing water made music in the morning, as she recited the
Mourners' Kaddish. It was her father's death day. She had just come to
the words, "He who makes peace in his high heavens, may he make
peace for us, and for all Israel," when the young Arab jumped out of a
battered truck and covered them with his assault rifle.

His hands shaking, he started to shoot wildly, as if trying to drop the
birds from the trees. Most of the schoolchildren fell to the ground, wrapping their heads with their arms, but one boy stood frozen beside Gina.
As the rifle swung their way, she stepped in front of the boy, knocking
him safely to the ground. Holding up her hands, she said something that

sounded to the children like, "Oh sy ra." When the bullets hit her chest, Gina fell face forward and lay on the grass, arms still stretched out toward the killer. The boy was unhurt, as were the other children. Later, some reported hearing what sounded like crying as the Arab ran back to his truck. But others said he was probably laughing. No one could be sure, since the young assassin had not been caught.

Kief had immediately left for Israel, but when he returned, said nothing about Gina's funeral. Kori wanted to know, but never asked if he had said the Kaddish for his mother. Although Kief did not believe in such rituals, she thought he would feel better if he did and wondered if she should say it herself. Feeling guilty that she had not shown Gina much love, Kori was glad her mother-in-law had called out "Om Sai Ram" before she died. That meant Baba had been with her.

∾ↄc∾

As Kori put Gina's last letter back in the drawer, a pain stabbed down her legs from her lower back. Although the baby had not been expected for two more weeks, it was time to call Kief and Candelaria. She shuffled over to her bed, and covered it with a rubber sheet just before her water broke, running down the inside of her thighs.

Long black braids flying behind her, Candelaria rushed through the door. She insisted on walking Kori around, not letting her go to bed yet. When Kori was tired of walking around the room, the Indian woman took her outside. They walked down the gravel path, and Kori leaned over to smell a blossom as big as an open hand. She watched a long-legged spider spinning a web between two branches of an olive tree, while the sun lit the wet, intricate threads of the web. For a moment, it seemed as though the glistening web were being woven inside her, connecting every part of her to Kief.

"And to you, my dear friend," Kori whispered aloud to Baba, for it was his face she saw at the center of the web.

Her first thought was to send Candelaria for Father Gregory, but she knew the doctor-priest had not returned from Santa Cruz, where he was trying to find antibiotics for her toxemia.

The contractions had become a single, endless pain bending her knees so that only Candelaria's strong arms kept Kori from falling. Kief carried her to the bed and sat beside her, his face tense and baffled. He was used to being helpful, and suddenly there was nothing he could do.

"Shouldn't this baby be coming out pretty soon?" Kief anxiously asked Candelaria, who was rubbing Kori's enormous belly with herbs. "I read somewhere that it doesn't take long after the baby drops into the birth canal."

"That is true," said Candelaria, "but this baby is very large." She was frowning and sweating, as if she herself were in labor. "I would like to have the doctor here. My skill is not enough."

Kori tossed and groaned, holding Kief's hand, then flinging it away. "It's harder than last time," she whispered. "Much harder."

"She is bleeding too much," Candelaria said to Kief. "A bad sign. The herbs do no good."

"Pray," Kori said to Kief, suddenly reaching up and holding his head between her hands. "Mary, Jesus, Baba. I can't. Too tired." Her voice faded and she fell back on the sweat-soaked pillow.

Resting his face against Kori's shoulder, Kief began murmuring in a desperate voice. She listened from far away, her lips moving, repeating his words silently.

"God, I've been ungrateful. You give and you take away, but don't, please don't take away my Kori. Baba, be here for her now, and for me. Never again will I forget you."

Kori drifted back enough to hear a soft knock at the door, and Candelaria ran to open it.

"I felt you were in trouble." Brother Elijah's clear, gentle voice brought Kori fully back to consciousness. "Not that I can do much, but sometimes I've assisted Father Gregory at births. May I come in?"

Candelaria grudgingly stepped back from the door to let him enter.

"She is very bad. I can do nothing for her. Where is that doctor-priest of yours, now that we need him?" Candelaria's voice broke and Kori knew things must be very bad indeed.

"Yes," she said, trying to call out, though her voice came as a whisper, "I would like you to be here, Elijah. I would like your blessing. Please."

Kori thought of the times Elijah would come to sit on the porch as she peeled potatoes, reading aloud to her from the book he was writing on prayer. Whenever they talked, he always kept his eyes on the book, but still his cheeks would turn red. Once she had caught him staring at her face during Mass. Then he turned redder than usual, and his gentle brown eyes closed tightly, as if in a sudden attack of prayer or pain. Candelaria had noticed, too, and warned Kori that priests who admired women too much were trouble. Kori only laughed. What man could fall in love with a woman as swollen and shapeless as she, with fat ankles and dark smudges under her eyes?

"Just wait." Candalaria slowly nodded her head, heavy with the knowledge of this world and its sins. "When you are thin again, he will make his move. Be warned." The Indian woman sat tensely at the bedside, looking from Elijah's face to Kori's, her lips locked in a grim disapproving line.

Brother Elijah came to the bed and touched Kori's forehead lightly. Looking up, she could see his large Adam's apple throbbing as he spoke the words of absolution. "Would you like me to do the laying on of hands?" he asked, his eyes bright and tender.

Kori felt tears rolling down her cheeks. Brother Elijah's presence gave her permission to cry, since he never judged anyone for weakness. "Do whatever is right to do," she tried to smile, but groaned as another pain shook her.

As soon as Brother Elijah laid his hands on Kori's belly, her whole body softened and became still for a moment. When the next pain shook her, it was more of a relief, a hard driving urge to push. Her body was engrossed in pushing and growling, while her angry, screaming head wanted to be somewhere else. The body was in a world of its own, where only grunting and pushing made any sense. While the head was screaming for the help of God, the body was busy bringing bloody, helpless life down between the reluctant bones, finally twisting out the breathless baby, head dented and body covered with a white cheesy substance that made her look to Kori like the experiment of some ambitious gourmet.

Candelaria held up the baby, whose plump pink arms swung freely as her body spread to fill the great void in which she suddenly found herself. Watching the eager hands grasping as though in search of her breast, Kori sang out loud, her voice not so far off pitch as usual, welcoming this child to the world, to the gracious, giving God who so blessed them all. The baby seemed at once part of her, of Kief and of Baba who was holding them all as they danced in the circle of his arms. The face of her dead mother shone in Baba's face, and Kori knew she would never grieve for Damaris again.

Candelaria waited before cutting the cord, letting the baby take her first tentative breaths under no pressure to survive. Her fat little cheeks working like a bellows, the infant's one-track will focused on filling her small lungs, bringing oxygen to every cell. It was work, and she did it with ferocious attention.

After gently cleaning the baby, Candelaria brought her to Kori's breast, where the tiny mouth continued to work. The baby seemed aware, even from the beginning, that life was hard, but not nearly so dry and joyless as Kori had once thought, laboring over her books and intent on taking all she could from the world.

Kori wondered, *Can I make the milk flow? Can I breathe air into the baby's lungs?* She knew she was no more in charge than the rain falling from the sky and this thought made her glad. For so long she had felt responsible for everything that happened around her, and now the responsibility had dropped away like the blood and water from her tired body. Her own mother, Damaris, must have felt just this way after Kori's birth, and her mother before, and so on back, forever. She was one of a long chain of daughters, back to the beginning, and she in her turn had given herself to the redeeming process of birth. No longer was her mother's death on her head. Nor did she feel guilt at having kept her distance from Gina. They were both in God's hands, held in life or released from it at God's will, like the leaves of a tree.

"The baby will be called Gilah Damaris, after both our mothers," Kori said softly, before falling asleep. "But her real mother is the Mother of us all."

The door burst open and Father Gregory rushed in, cracking his head sharply against the door frame. "Something told me to hurry back," he said. "Let me see that baby." He leaned over and checked the infant's eyes and heart. "Kori, you probably need a shot to stop the bleeding."

"Yes, the bleeding needs to stop. I'm glad you came." Kori kept her eyes on Brother Elijah, who had withdrawn a few steps and stood with his head bowed.

"You guys can stay," Kief said. "Stay as long as you want. I owe you."

Father Gregory sterilized the needle. "Thanks. I kind of hoped you'd say that. By the way, the beans down at the foot of the hill are getting too much run-off water. We'll lose 'em if we don't dig a trench."

"We'll do it tomorrow morning if you can spare a few men," Kief said, hugging Elijah.

Kief stroked his daughter's cheek, then walked out into the night, leaving Candelaria and Father Gregory in charge. The new moon was as pale and white as his little girl's hands. She will be alive, this child of mine, he thought, when Prema, the God who is love, returns to mother his people back to the ways of peace. Jesus the Messiah, Moshiach, Prema. Whatever name they chose, it was God who heard and God who would come. Who had always come. Kief stood looking over the valley where his beans grew. With uncertain lips, since the ancient prayer for the dead was rusty in his mind, he began to say the Mourner's Kaddish for his mother.

PART II

Awakenings

PROLOGUE

Early twenty-first century Ladakh, the Himalayas—Dhattu was still a child when eleven Indian monks, wearing nothing but white dhotis and light wool shawls, came up the steep, winding road from Fatula Pass. They must be cold, he thought, pulling his blanket tightly around him. The full moon was bright in the clear sky, and the stars seemed near enough to touch. Both moon and stars looked as crystalline as ice, their light turning the snow a pale, luminous blue. In the distance, white mountain peaks chewed the horizon.

More than five years ago, Dhattu had come to Lamayaru, Ladakh's oldest monastery. Now, standing on the parapet overlooking the road, he stared down as the odd group of travelers passed through the tiny village which was huddled below the monastery wall. Then he scampered inside and down the steps, wanting to be at the gate when the visitors were greeted.

His heart beating fast, Dhattu peeped out at the men from behind the tall iron gate. For a moment, their calm, remote faces dissolved in brilliant light, and he wanted to sing out loud. Now he knew what the lama meant when he said that all is maya, a passing and changing of the forces that drive all things, even the great mountains that seemed so solid and immovable. These, too, the lama had said, would someday be ground to dust by the force of wind and the fall of snow.

Dhattu tried to imagine gentle snowflakes wearing away a mountain like Mount Kailas, the source of purest divinity, where he had been taken the year before. He had made the *kora*, a twelve-mile walk around the peak, then immersed himself in Lake Manasarovar, even to the little knot of hair on top of his head, so that in his next life he might be reincarnated as a god.

Seeing these strangers made him feel like bowing down, as he had to the great icy dome of Kailas. In this stone temple, the heart of the earth beat so loudly he could hear it roaring in his ears. The self-effacing lama was pleased that Dhattu had seen the world dissolve in white light, for it confirmed his belief that the boy was the previous lama of the monastery, reincarnated. However, the child had no memory of any previous life or of this place which he had come to love.

Dhattu especially enjoyed the breathing exercises that would someday allow him to utter the deep, reverberating chants that sent shivers up his back and caused the world to shimmer before his eyes. He did not even mind his regular duties of throwing ashes down the toilet chute or packing yak dung into the stove.

He breathed deeply now, determined to calm himself so that he would be allowed to meet the Indian visitors along with the senior monks. Dhattu told the head lama that he would like to serve the guests hot buttered tea after dinner and listen to them talk. So it was that, after he had poured the tea, he found himself sitting cross-legged by the big brass pot, not an arm's length away from the head of the monks from the Gufa Ashram in Nepal.

They were not pilgrims, as Dhattu had first thought, but intended to settle above Lamayaru. Some years ago, the two well-respected older gurus, together with ten young men in their thirties, had been sent by their master, Sathya Sai Baba, to a certain cave in Nepal. Sai Baba had created for them the *Akshakya Patra*, a divine vessel which would provide their food and drink. At that time they were twelve in number. One, an arrogant fellow who had insisted on carrying the divine vessel, became lost and thought the others had deliberately abandoned him.

As the room grew colder with the approach of evening, Dhattu inched closer to the brass teapot. He giggled, wondering how the fellow could be stupid enough to think such foolishness, since the other monks knew he was carrying the food supply.

The leader of the monks went on to explain that the lost man finally reached the gorge at Urvashi Kund. When he found the little cave where the eleven had taken refuge from the cold night, they were already seated in a circle, enjoying the bliss of samadhi. At first he thought they were tricking him, so he tried to tease them, poking the ribs of one and tickling the soles of another's feet. But they did not move, and he could find no pulse.

"They are all dead!" he wept, wondering how he would bear the terrible solitude of this lonely cave. "Surely, Sai Baba has deceived us and sent us here to die." In a fit of rage, he threw the divine vessel into the gorge of Urvashi Kund, where it fell to the bottom of a deep lake. Then he walked back to the village and began telling people that his companions were dead.

When the eleven monks rose from their divine contemplation after eighteen days, they were very hungry. They looked around for the twelfth man and for their *Akshakya Patra*, but saw no sign of either. At first they stared at each other fearfully, wondering, "How can we live without food so high in these mountains?" But they finally calmed down, for they were very holy men and had managed so far with nothing to eat. They agreed that Sai Baba had looked after them well till now and they would go on leaving everything to him.

The monks set out to find a better place to live, and after walking a few miles, discovered a spacious cave with a clear stream of water running through the back corner. Their new home was big enough to make a small room for each of them and a temple in the back. Now all they needed was food. They felt it was their fault, not Baba's, that the divine vessel had been lost, and they should not bother their master with prayers to bring it back. They would have to manage by themselves.

In meditation, two of the monks had a vision of the vessel lying on the bottom of the deep, clear lake. So they all climbed down to the water's edge where they could see it. One monk had learned through breathing exercises to hold his breath as long as an hour, so he dove to retrieve the vessel. He succeeded, but nearly froze to death in the cold water.

Dhattu was very impressed by this feat and determined to work even harder at his pranayama exercises. The story reminded him of how the Buddha had sat for forty-nine days under the Bodhi tree, determined to stay until he had seen to the depths of human life and understood its mystery. He returned to the world holding the vessel of truth that releases man from his suffering, emptying him of ego so he can be filled with wisdom. "Sit in stillness and trace your pain, your misdeeds, to their source," the Buddha taught, "and finally you will enter the sweet emptiness of peace." Dhattu's teachers had explained that by breathing with complete concentration on the one thing needed for life, all needs will be met. When Dhattu breathed in this way, he felt the unreal world around him disappear like a dream. He would wake into a gentle, breathless darkness where his soul would sing within him.

Wanting to fill his own bodily vessel with sacred prana, Dhattu began practicing as he listened to the visitors, becoming so engrossed in his breathing that he missed part of their story. But he did not miss what they said at the end.

Because their ashram had become widely known as the place where Sai Baba sent the monks to pray for the world, they were besieged by visitors. Therefore, they finally left to seek a new home. For a number of years they had wandered. Then, in meditation, they saw Lamaryaru and a large cave not more than an hour's walk up the mountain. There, they planned to live until Prema, the third and last Sai avatar, came to bless the world. They would require nothing of the Lamaryaru monks, since they had the *Akshakya Patra.*

Dhattu could not contain himself and leaned over the shoulder of one visitor. "Oh please, may we see it?" he whispered.

None of the Lamaryaru monks corrected his boldness, since they also wanted to see the *Akshakya Patra*. The visitors looked at each other, then were silent for a moment, their eyes closed. After several of them nodded, the head monk took the shining vessel from an embroidered drawstring bag. The vessel's bright surface reflected the flickering light from the yak butter lamps, mirroring Dhattu's round face and large dark eyes.

He thought of the moments of illusion that every day he took for solid truth and then relinquished, knowing that behind the swirling, shifting appearances that pass for reality there is only the great unifying darkness. Out of this gentle darkness, as from a mother, all things come and will return—darkness so intense that it becomes its own opposite, as when the soul plunges to its depths, finally turning into that light to which the sun is shade.

"Hold out your cups," said the Indian monk. "And we will see what comes from the *Akshakya Patra*."

The first to hold out his cup, Dhattu was amazed to see an amber-colored liquid flowing from the empty vessel. When it touched his lips, he tasted a sweet nectar which warmed his whole body. This must be the soma of the ancient gods, he thought, feeling as though his soul were drifting above his body in a dance with the other souls around him. In this moment he decided that when he was grown, he would devote his life to serving Prema, the god named Love, whose sacred feet would tread the snowy mountain peaks, and who would take the whole world in his arms.

Suddenly the head lama dropped his cup and put his hands to his face, rocking from side to side as if his head hurt him.

"What is it that disturbs you, Father?" The monks gathered around their leader.

"The Evil One has taken human form. Much suffering will come to the world because of this incarnation."

A chill came over Dhattu as he sat still on the stone floor, his hands clasped together in the mudra of grief.

The lama spoke slowly, his eyes closed as if looking inward. The boy whose body the Evil One had entered lived in northern Europe. His name was Brom. Though only twelve years old, he was a boy of great strength and great beauty. His family was rich and powerful, but under their restrictions, light though they were, young Brom had fretted and complained. He had recently begun to realize that his parents' wealth and position would be his if they were dead. The boy began to think of ways they might die and leave him free to do as he pleased. Their death became such an obsession that he prayed to the devil for an end to them. It was at that moment that the spirit of the Evil One entered and possessed him.

The lama stood, raising his hands in the mudra of prophecy. That very day, he said, Brom's parents would be killed in a bizarre automobile accident, and the child would rejoice that he was now his own man. For some time he would not know whose man he really was, but even had he known, it would make no difference. The soul that had been Brom's was now crushed under the dark entity that squatted in his mind and spread like a toad, leaving no room for what had once been human. "The Evil One," said the lama, "will take this form into the final battle with Prema Sai."

"And who will win?" Dhattu's high voice carried over the murmurs of the monks. "Surely you must know."

"I do not want to know, my boy. When gods battle, men had best make themselves scarce."

Dhattu stared into the fire, sensing the invisible forces that clashed around and above him. The air was thick with demons and angels, though he could not see them. Flitting among endless, incorporeal planes, they fought unceasingly over that small precipitate of spirit that humans call the universe.

That night Dhattu dreamed of a man tall as a god, whose face shone coldly, like metal, and who turned the earth to ice where he walked.

7

On the night of her fifteenth birthday, Gilah woke in the middle of a bad dream. A man in a dark robe wearing a towel on his head, was shooting at her while she was trying to protect a flock of frightened sheep. In the distance, she could hear the sound of a waterfall. When she turned toward the sheep, she saw a hillside sloping gently to a lake that sparkled in the bright sunlight. She held out her arms and begged the man not to shoot, telling him that this place, where pure water flowed between the rocks, was too sacred to stain with blood. A sudden roar filled her ears as pain exploded in her chest. When her eyes flew open she was not sure she was in her parents' farmhouse, high in the Santa Cruz mountains.

Gilah sat up in bed and swallowed the sour-tasting fluid that rose in her throat. Being careful not to wake Consuelo, who shared her room, Gilah threw back the covers and tiptoed to the window. She resisted the urge to wake her mother. Kori and Kief were too worried about protecting the farm from armed marauders to be burdened with their children's bad dreams.

Her brother, Philo, who was seventeen, never had such dreams, and Gilah supposed that was because he was a boy. Or perhaps bad dreams stopped when a person reached a certain age. Maybe she had to suffer only a little while longer through these long, bloody nights and pains that shot through her body like electric shocks. Her dreams were like the movies her parents had described. She herself had never seen a movie. The television set had broken down when she was very young, and replacement parts were impossible to find.

Not even the McCaver kids, whose folks had lived in these mountains for a hundred years, had television anymore. City people had telecons, which served as computers, television sets and telephones all in one. Her father said they were linked up directly to satellites, but Gilah wasn't even sure what a satellite looked like. Her parents often referred to things that seemed familiar to them but not to her. Terms like microwave and video flew by her, and no one stopped to explain them. They were discussed in a somber tone of voice, as if people were talking about the dead. Rather than disturb any ghosts, Gilah chose not to ask questions about the old days.

Gilah was often told that she talked too much, that she should think before speaking. "If I did that," she explained impatiently, "I would lose my train of thought." She had to talk fast, hoping to finish before a new surge of ideas washed through her brain, flooding out all that had been there before. Kori would sigh and try to listen, but Gilah knew her mother was thinking about grownup things, like a recipe for soup or a page of indecipherable text in some language that looked like curly hair stuck to the page.

Gilah looked out the window toward the small clearing, which was framed by an irregular line of pine trees, black against the moonlit sky. When a light flared from the electric fence, she froze, waiting for the guard's piercing whistle. But she heard nothing. Maybe a deer or coyote had brushed against the fence. Once a deer had been electrocuted, and Gilah found its body the next day. Lying nearby was a dead fawn that did not have the sense to avoid its mother's fate. Maybe there was a fawn this time, too, and maybe it was still alive. Gilah had always hoped to find one to raise as a pet. Eddie Szu would be happy, too, for he loved animals. Maybe they could raise it together.

She was always hunting for excuses to spend time with Eddie. In the past, Gilah had been able to talk with him about whatever came into her head. As he worked on motors, the parts spread neatly across a table in the barn, Eddie had never said she talked too much. He had seemed to like her bold gestures and cascading words. But now that she was nearly a woman, Eddie had grown silent and elusive, even doing his t'ai chi movements in the dark, before she woke up. Gilah had loved to shadow him as he did the exercises, and had learned her lessons well. But lately she had stopped practicing the t'ai chi and "push-hands" forms, because it wasn't as much fun without Eddie.

Gilah put on a sweatshirt and pulled blue jeans over her cold, bare legs. Carrying her boots, she tiptoed through the living room, where the last of the woodstove fire still crackled and smoked. As she opened the front door, Philo joined her.

"Did you see it? The light from the fence?" Philo zipped up his sweatshirt, swearing as his wiry chest hairs caught in the zipper. They were so new to his body that he often forgot about them, as he did the low lintel of the workshop, where he regularly hit his head. If Philo kept growing at this rate, he would soon be as tall as Father Gregory.

"Yes, and I didn't hear the alarm. Do you think Brother Elijah went to sleep? He was supposed to be guarding tonight."

"Could be." Shivering in the cold, damp wind that blew in from the ocean, Philo pulled up his hood. "If Elijah was praying on the job, he probably flipped out." Philo walked just ahead of her, swinging his ever-present sling shot beside his leg. He was even better with the sling shot than he was with a rifle. His keen, deep-set blue eyes were always darting around, hunting for the right stone for his next shot.

Gilah rubbed her hands together, wishing she had remembered her gloves. "At least Elijah makes great spinach pies. When he's not enjoying samadhi." Gilah giggled, thinking of the time Brother Elijah had been praying his brains out and one little push had sent him backward into the water trough.

"Not samadhi. That's for Hindus and Buddhists. Catholics do contemplation. I know because I asked him."

Philo was always asking personal questions, Gilah thought. "Why didn't you ask him about his sex life, while you were at it, for heaven's sake? You'd pitch a fit if he asked about yours. Don't think everybody hasn't noticed how you sneak around after Consuelo."

Gilah hadn't meant to bring up Philo's crush but heard her tongue running off like a horse stuck with a burr. Her brother had no business pestering Consuelo, who clearly wanted to spend her free time poring over Kori's spiritual books. First it was Kori who had time only for Consuelo, and now Philo. Gilah had lost two of the three people she loved best in the world to this small, nut-brown girl, whose dark eyes shone like an owl's and whose black braids were so thick and long she could wrap them once around a tree branch and swing by them. Since Gilah couldn't help loving gentle Consuelo herself, she grieved her losses in silence.

Even in the semidarkness, she could see the taut skin over Philo's high cheekbones flush. "At least I don't go drooling after a person twice my age, like somebody I know. Eddie's just about got asthma, running away from you."

Tears stung Gilah's eyes as she picked her way through the prickly, waist-high chaparral. "I certainly don't drool. I don't get all hot and bothered the way Consuelo says you do."

"She said that? I don't believe it." Philo stood still, staring over her head. It annoyed Gilah that he had a ten-inch height advantage over her.

"Wait." He seized Gilah's arm, pulling her down behind an oleander bush. "I hear someone."

"Three men." She moved her head to look between the branches. "One has a rifle." Her body grew cold and her stomach knotted in a familiar pain. Even the sight of a rifle made her heart pound.

"Blow your whistle," Philo said. "It's no good me trying to take them alone, with a girl and no gun."

Gilah was indignant. "I know how to fight. Haven't I done t'ai chi with Eddie for the last seven years? I'm one up on you, Schwarzenegger." She didn't know what the strange word meant, but it was what one of the monks called Father Gregory after he lifted a fallen tree off a dying dog.

"You haven't practiced in two months," her brother retorted. "You think I haven't noticed? Ever since Eddie disappeared on you."

She punched his arm and was glad to see him wince. Seven years of t'ai chi had armored her fist. "Eddie said I could take out two men, as long as they didn't know what I know."

"Okay. You're on." Philo's voice hissed in her ear. "Blow the whistle and I'll hit the one with the gun. When the gunman's down, go for the other two. I'll back you up as soon as I've got the rifle." He took a stone from his pocket and began spinning the sling around his head.

When the whistle shrieked, the three men stopped in their tracks. The one with the rifle whirled around, running face first into Philo's speeding stone. Gilah sprang between the other two, crouching as she swung the side of her flattened hand into the solar plexus of one man and kicked the legs out from under the other. By the time both men hit the ground, Philo had them covered with the rifle. His man was laid out cold with a blue egg swelling on his forehead.

"You're from the city?" Philo's new baritone cracked a little.

"Maybe." One man stood up slowly, his hands barely lifted, as if he didn't take Philo seriously. He was young and just a little shorter than Philo. His thinning crewcut hair was a muddy blond, and his face looked pale in the moonlight. "If the girl asks me real nice, I might say." He grinned at Gilah, licking his lips, as if he planned to have her for dinner.

"Okay," Gilah said, hands on her hips. "Who are you? Why shouldn't we just shoot you?" Her heart began pounding again, and she knew she could never shoot anyone. Hitting a person was one thing, but shooting she could never do. The idea of hard, vicious metal cutting into living tissue even kept her from going fishing with her father.

"Well, aren't you just a piece of cake," the young man said, stepping closer, until Philo warned him back with the rifle. "All that pretty hair. And blue eyes, like my momma's. I sure would like to take you home with me."

"Just your name." Gilah's voice was flat as she moved behind Philo. "And why you snuck in here."

"The name's Jason, honey." The lanky young man rolled a cigarette and lit it with agile, delicate hands. "And just so's you don't think I mean to fool around, let me say I'm a good Muslim. I don't mess with women. If you came home with me, we'd be married real quick. How'd you like that?"

As Gilah turned away, an unfamiliar tingle ran through her body. The cocky young man was what Eddie would call a low-life, but she felt drawn to him, even as she wanted to run the other way. He had the confidence she had always wanted, even if it would only have masked the fear that made her soft inside.

"You don't even know me." Her dark gold hair bounced on her shoulders as she shrugged. "What a silly idea, asking someone you don't know to marry you."

"I know you look real good," Jason insisted. "And you can fight like a man. I'm a fighter myself, and I like your style, girl. The offer stands."

"Leave my sister alone." Philo prodded Jason in the side with the rifle while Gilah blew her whistle again. "Tell us what you're here for. To steal horses?"

"That, yes." Jason smoked insolently, jerking his chin up when he inhaled, then blowing the smoke straight at Philo. Gusts of wind spoiled the intended effect, and the smoke blew backward, swirling around Jason's head. The moon turned the smoke into a bright nimbus, illuminating his pale face with its thin, straight mouth and wide, lop-sided nose. "We're scouts for the Party of God, checking out this territory. Anything happens to us, and there'll be a hundred armed men up here turning you into fertilizer."

Gilah shivered in the damp, cold air and clasped her arms around herself, whispering "Om Sai Ram," as her mother did in bad moments. This hard young man with his knowing eyes made her feel uneasy, as if she were fighting her way out of a bad dream. It was a relief to hear the sound of her father and the other men running toward them. Their voices carried in the wind, as Father Gregory's deep basso played under the others like a drum roll.

Father Gregory reached them first, carrying the long stave he had once used to stun a man-sized bear. Since they were in their middle-of-the-night prayer session when the whistle was blown, the monks were wearing long white robes that floated in the moonlight, making them look like ghosts. Clutching his rifle, Kief followed Father Gregory. Eddie and the others came from the direction of the house to surround the three intruders.

"You okay?" Eddie circled the group and stood at Gilah's side, brushing away the heavy black hair that fell raggedly over his forehead. "We were afraid for you when your father said you weren't in the house." He paused, looking down at the polished toes of his boots. "*I* was afraid."

Gilah's heart leapt as she looked into Eddie's finely featured face. "I'm glad you came to look for me." Her voice shook a little, and she smiled so he would not think she was nervous. She liked to show off the dimples on either side of her full mouth. Except for her dark-lashed blue eyes, she was sure the dimples were her best feature. Gilah was pleased when people said her eyes and dimples reminded them of her grandmother, Gina, who had been a great beauty, by all accounts.

Eddie's voice was even softer than usual, and he kept looking down at the ground as he talked. "I heard your whistle and figured you were in trouble." Since each member of the community carried a whistle with a different pitch, he had known who was calling for help.

At first Eddie didn't move when Gilah squeezed his hand. Then he pulled away and rejoined the others, still not looking at her. Why was he so afraid to touch her? Gilah wondered. When she was a child, he often hugged her, as everyone did, and sometimes would carry her around the farm as he went from chore to chore. Only six months ago, she had thrown her arms around Eddie one day and kissed him, just because she was happy to be close to him. But his body had stiffened and he pushed her away, as if she had tried to stab him. After that, he had never again allowed her to get close.

Father Gregory squatted beside the injured intruder, who was trying to sit up. Touching the egg-sized bump on the young man's forehead, the priest shone a flashlight into his eyes.

"Thanks, Father," the boy said. "We didn't know you guys up here was monks. Geez, what kind of bomb went off in my head?"

"No concussion, anyway." Father Gregory said, lifting the young man to his feet. "You can get back home all right, with a little help from your friends."

"The question is, should we let them go," Kief said. "Philo tells me they're scouts sent by the Party of God to look us over, to see if we're ripe for picking."

"You're not suggesting we kill them?" Brother Elijah's gentle voice trembled. "Surely not. They're only boys."

"That depends." Kief turned to Philo. "You caught them when they were just inside the fence?"

Gilah glared at her father, who talked as if Philo had captured the marauders alone. Her low, husky voice strained to carry over Philo's. "They were about a hundred yards inside the enclosure when we hit them. I got two of them myself."

"They didn't see much of anything," Philo observed quietly, as if she hadn't spoken.

That, of course, had been the point of her father's question, Gilah realized, clenching her teeth. She had run off at the mouth as usual, wanting to be noticed and admired. Sighing, she stared across the moon-lit circle of faces at Eddie, who looked away. His mouth was tight at the corners, as it had been when he buried the dog that had been crushed by a falling tree. Eddie probably knew what she was thinking and felt sorry for her. Gilah swallowed hard, trying to hold back a sob, as well as the bad tasting stuff rising in her throat.

Rubbing her eyes with the back of her hands, she turned and ran back to the house. Her nose had started to run and she was sobbing. At least Eddie didn't see her sniffling and splotchy-faced as she stumbled across the irregular pine door sill into the house.

"What happened?" Kori was standing in the living room, her arms wrapped around Consuelo, her hand pale against the girl's brown cheek.

Candelaria stood beside them with a rifle, which Kief finally trusted her to use. Kori had vowed never to touch one again, after that day she had almost shot Father Gregory. Now Candelaria guarded the women. Knowing that her mother didn't approve of her fighting, Gilah didn't mention knocking down the two intruders. It seemed strange to her that one minute she sought approval for doing something and the next feared disapproval for the same act. Always her mind seemed to bounce from one extreme to the other. Once Eddie had gently suggested that Gilah try to follow each thought, just observing where it went, but she always lost track of one thought when the next came storming in.

"Three guys broke through the fence." She sat on the floor and leaned against the rough pine wall, pulling off her boots. Kori liked people to take off their shoes at the door, a preference picked up in India. She had other preferences Gilah did not understand, like sitting in front of Sai Baba's picture for an hour every morning before doing yoga exercises. Gilah would become bored after a little while and wander off, but Consuelo would sit as long as Kori did. Consuelo copied the way Kori did yoga exercises, as she copied everything about Kori. Like Gilah, Candelaria often frowned at seeing the other two alone together. The Indian woman's baffled, angry face mirrored what Gilah herself felt when her mother and Consuelo withdrew into their alien world.

Gilah wished her mother would hold her the way she was holding Consuelo, but maybe Kori didn't realize how afraid she really was. Gilah thought her mother should have known, should have seen through her brave front. But she shrugged off the feeling, hardening her heart.

Kori's face was still. "The Party of God. I knew they would find us eventually. They raided the Mount Madonna ashram last month and burned the synagogue in Santa Cruz. I'd hoped they would think we were part of the monastery and leave us alone."

Gilah warmed her hands over the wood stove, which Kori had recently stoked. The flames leapt high, comforting the room with warmth. "Maybe it's just as well they saw the monks tonight," she said. "If Dad doesn't shoot them, they'll go back to wherever they came from and say we're religious folks up here. The Party of God shouldn't object to us."

Too bad they saw me, Gilah thought. They'll wonder why a girl is living with a bunch of monks. Maybe they'll forget about me. Please, Sai Baba, she prayed, glancing at his picture over the altar in the corner of the living room, let them forget. But she had a feeling that young Jason would not forget. She could still feel his cool, insolent eyes on her.

After Candelaria had returned to her cottage, still clutching the rifle, Kori went to the altar and lit a candle beside her ancient, cracked icon of Mary and the infant Jesus. "If you want to, you can join me. I am praying for the three young men, that they come to no harm and that they leave us alone."

Gilah and Consuelo sat on either side of her, both girls easily falling into the half-lotus posture they had used since childhood. A peace came over Gilah as she gazed at the picture of the dark-faced holy man with his gentle smile and hand raised in blessing. Sometimes she thought Sai Baba's hand was raised directly to her, as a warning to shut up, but tonight she felt only his blessing, and relaxed into the long, slow breathing pattern she had learned from her mother even before she could talk.

The candlelight flickered and Gilah's breath stopped for a moment. She seemed to see Sai Baba's lips moving, and at the back of her mind, she heard words spoken in a light, musical voice, one she vaguely remembered hearing before. *Time to wake up, little friend,* the voice said. *You have a great task to do and soon a new name. There is no time to waste. I want you to prepare now.*

Gilah leaned forward, straining to see the picture better. But his lips were now still, and it was just a picture of Sai Baba, blessing or warning or whatever the upraised hand meant. She was left wondering how she was supposed to prepare and for what. Should she ask Kori? Suddenly she felt shy, not wanting anyone to know about the voice. She had something to tell, but for the first time, didn't want to share it. Only to Eddie would she confide her secret, but Eddie wouldn't listen to her anymore.

Gilah's body was numb. For a few moments she had felt like a bird flying toward the sun, but now there was a cold sadness deep inside her, as if the voice had taken a vital piece of her when it left. It was bad enough to lose Eddie, but when this voice went away, the sadness was worse. Sadness is the ordinary state of people who are out of touch with God, Gilah said to herself. They just get used to it, like amputees adjust to getting around without a leg. She would get used to it, too. That night Gilah lay down and closed her eyes, wondering what her new name would be.

❧

The next morning Gilah was waiting for Eddie in the repair shed when he came back from the monks' morning prayers. He stopped at the door, watching warily as she walked toward him. Apparently not wanting to look into her eyes, Eddie stared at the red hibiscus flower in her hair.

"What happened to those three guys last night?" She figured it was best to start on neutral ground.

"Your father gave them a tough talk about sneaking into monasteries. Some of us took them down the road a ways, but we kept their rifle." Eddie's eyes were still fixed on the hibiscus.

"I need to tell you something," Gilah said firmly, surprised that she felt no fear.

"It's not a good idea." He backed into the sunlight and put his hands behind him. "Silence is best, as your mother says."

"No one else will do." Gilah followed him and closed the gap between them. "I have to talk."

"Maybe you should talk to Kori." Eddie looked around, sighing when he saw that no one was near.

"No, it has to be you." Gilah looked straight into the deep brown eyes that crinkled to slits when he smiled. He was not smiling now. "Shall we talk in the shed or somewhere else?"

"Okay." Eddie's shoulders slumped as he walked toward the community kitchen. "We can sit on the bench outside. It would be all right to talk there."

"Eddie, what's the matter with you? We used to be friends."

"I can't explain." Eddie turned away. "Years ago, before I came here, I was accused of something . . ." his voice broke off. "It's not for you to hear. Go ahead. Tell me what's on your mind."

"Last night, after we caught those men, I was meditating with Mom in front of Sai Baba's picture. The one that hangs over her altar."

"Yes, go on." Eddie seemed more at ease now that he was no longer the topic of conversation.

Gilah could still feel the small, musical voice from last night dancing in her mind. "Well, you won't believe this, Eddie, but the picture talked to me. I mean, I saw his lips move and heard words in my head."

"Your grandmother Gina heard his voice, too," Eddie said. "Kori told me about it. She herself has never experienced anything like that."

"Have you, Eddie?" Gilah leaned forward, scarcely noticing when the delicate hibiscus blossom fell from her hair onto her lap. "Heard such a thing, I mean?"

"No. Well, maybe a little. Sometimes when I'm out under the pine trees, I think I hear music, and thoughts come to me that don't seem like my own. I want to cry when that happens, but not because I'm sad."

"Yes, yes, that's exactly how I felt." Gilah paced up and down in front

of him, clasping her hands tightly behind her back as she had often seen
him do. She had adopted many of Eddie's gestures without even noticing that they were his.

"So, what did he say to you?" Eddie picked up the flower, lightly
caressing the petals.

Seeing how gently Eddie touched natural things, Gilah caught her
breath. She remembered the look of ecstasy on his face when he walked
on the moss-covered stones in the creek, and wished she could feel whatever it was he felt. Gilah took the flower from him and touched it lightly.
But to her, the petals were just petals.

"He said I had a job to do and to get myself ready." She held the red
hibiscus loosely at her side. "He said I would have a new name soon.
Maybe you can help me think of one. I'd like you to give me my name."

Eddie shook his head. "That's not for me to do. When the right name
comes, you'll know. Talk to your mother."

"Okay. I guess I knew you'd say that." Gilah sighed. "Here. You can
keep the flower. It seems to be yours." She dropped it in his lap and went
to find her mother.

Kori was explaining a Sanskrit phrase to Consuelo, who leaned over
the book, her long black braids brushing the page. "It means 'the gods
entered man.'" Kori's voice was cool and clear. This was her teacher voice,
the one that seemed to be coming from far away. "Or, 'all the gods are
seated in him.' Of course, the many gods were really just manifestations
of the One. The important point is that God lives in each one of us."

"I thought it was only men that God lives in." Gilah hated the ornery
tone in her voice, but lately she had heard it often when she walked in
on conversations between Consuelo and her mother. "In those stories,
women just serve up the chapatis."

Kori took her daughter's hand. "We are all part of the body of God.
Look at Radha, the consort of Krishna. Since she was always thinking of
him, she became part of him. You might say that Radha was Krishna, as
much a manifestation of God as he was."

When her mother said the name of the Hindu goddess, Gilah's heart leapt and tears came to her eyes. "That's my name," she said, so astonished that she swallowed wrong and started to cough. "That's it," she choked out the words between coughs. "Radha is my name."

The other two stared at her. "But you were named for your grandmothers," Kori said.

"It doesn't matter. I'm not them. I can't be them for you. My name is Radha, and I won't answer to anything else."

She ran outside and up the hill behind the house, where she could see across the valley to the blue haze hanging over the ocean. "Radha!" she shouted, wishing everyone in the valley could hear her. "That's my name." Sitting down on the damp earth, she hugged her knees to her chest. "Radha, the bride of God." She shivered a little, wondering how a bride of God was supposed to behave. Would she have to act sweet and quiet, like Consuelo? What was a Radha like?

As she leaned back and closed her eyes, the sun made bright cartwheels inside her eyelids. She was Radha. God would simply have to make the best of it. With a stick, she wrote her old name in the dirt, then rubbed it out with the metal toe of her boot. Now she wanted to know what her task was. Maybe the answer would come as fast and unexpectedly as her new name.

She walked back to the house, humming a tune her mother had learned in India. Her name was in the song, and for the first time Radha felt a part of her mother's inner world. Consuelo might know Sanskrit, might be able to read stories about the gods, but she, Radha, was part of the story, woven into it like threads into whole cloth. Her brother had chosen to be called not John, but Philo. If he could choose his name, so could she.

"Radha?" Consuelo's voice was tentative. "I've been hunting all over for you. Can we talk?"

"Okay," Radha said, falling into step beside her friend. She pushed up the sleeve of her sweater, allowing the cool, late afternoon air to touch her skin. "What about?"

"I just want to say that I've been taking up a lot of your mother's time. Maybe you don't want me to?"

"Well, I guess I don't," Radha said frankly, as she set a brisk pace. With her shorter legs the older girl had to take two steps to Radha's one. "But I don't much want to learn Sanskrit, and Mom wants to teach it. So, better you than me."

"Could we sit down?" Consuelo motioned to a log lying about five feet from the electric fence. "I want to talk about Philo."

"I wondered when you'd get around to that," Radha said, sitting on the log and stretching out her legs. "I'd kind of like to talk about somebody, too."

"Eddie?"

"You guessed."

"I've seen him look at you. He does that more often than you know." Consuelo twisted one black braid around her fist. "The same way Philo looks at me. One night he kissed me. I just wanted to tell you that. It was a week ago."

"Eddie's never kissed me." Radha felt the old jealousy sweeping over her and then stopped, reminding herself that she had been given a new name. At least in that she was special.

"I know he'd like to." Consuelo picked a few daisies and began stringing them together. "Eddie thinks he's too old for you. He told me so."

"But I'm precocious," Radha protested. "That's what Dad tells Mom. I *feel* as old as Eddie."

Consuelo concentrated on weaving her daisy chain. "I heard Eddie tell your mother something. Maybe you should know."

"Tell me." Radha held her breath.

"When Eddie was down in Los Angeles, a fifteen-year-old girl said he'd attacked her. Some guys beat him up and told him not to come back unless he would marry her. Eddie said he didn't do anything to the girl, but nobody believed him."

The sun had begun to set, leaving them in shadow. Radha released her breath slowly, watching a cloud of steam roll from her mouth in the cool evening air. "He couldn't have done that," she said. "Not Eddie."

"Of course not. But that's what they thought."

"So he's scared of me. Like I'm going to say something bad about him." Radha stood up, with her back to the fence, looking up at the narrow, rising moon. "I would never, never, say anything bad about Eddie." She turned toward Consuelo and spoke so softly she could hardly hear her own words. "I love him. I want to marry him."

"I think that's how I feel about Philo," Consuelo said, slipping the daisy chain around her neck. "But I'm not sure. Sometimes I think it's only my body wanting something. I don't know what to think."

Suddenly there was a loud, crackling sound and an arc of blue fire leapt from where the fence wires had been cut. Six men in black forced their way through the break and surrounded the two girls.

"Don't blow that whistle, honey," said one of them, pulling down the black kerchief that had covered his mouth and nose. "And don't try any of those moves you did last time."

It was Jason. Radha stood still, staring him down. "If you think you're going to steal our horses, you're dead wrong," she said. "They're well guarded. You won't get anything."

"I'll get what I came for," Jason moved so fast she had no time to raise her arm against him. "I came for you."

Two other men tied Radha's hands behind her back with a rope that cut sharply into her wrists.

"Don't yell." Jason held his revolver close to her throat. "Guys, bring the other one, too. She's too good-looking to leave up here with a bunch of monks. We'll take 'em both."

Radha opened her mouth to scream, ignoring the revolver. She didn't believe Jason would use it. But one man closed his hand over her mouth as the barrel of Jason's gun jammed up under her chin. They carried the two girls through the break in the fence and down to the road, where a truck was waiting.

"You'll be sitting in my lap all the way home," Jason whispered into Radha's ear as they settled on the hard metal floor of the pick-up truck. "I aim to make you like it."

Radha closed her eyes, not wanting to see his face next to hers. She tried to call Eddie with her mind, wishing she could come into people's heads the way Sai Baba did. But Eddie was probably singing vespers with the monks and had no idea she was bumping down the rocky road, falling against Jason, unable to keep his arms from closing around her.

Om Sai Ram, she cried inside her head, hoping that Sai Baba could hear her from so far away. I need you. If they take me away, I can't do the task you were talking about. She knew she was trying to bribe God and didn't care. As the voice returned, it seemed to come through static and then slowly faded away. *You will do your task. It has begun.*

8

For the third time that day, Yusef Nazim wished he had not given up cigarettes, but felt he had no choice after the doctor's warning that smoke was aggravating Fatima's heart arrhythmia. Fatima probably had told the doctor to scare him, knowing he would be more likely to quit for her sake than his own.

"Was not Healey supposed to be here ten minutes ago?" Nazim glared at Kamal, snapping his empty cigarette box shut.

"Perhaps he was delayed by the crowds. You know how they always want to touch him after his television message." Kamal smiled timidly, hoping to coax a smile from his patron. Nazim had been grim lately, ever since Jason brought Radha to the compound. He wanted permission to marry the girl, but Nazim, who had become a second father to the head-strong young man, had other plans. He wanted Jason to marry his youngest daughter, Ayesha.

Suppressing a momentary pang of jealousy, Kamal wished that it was himself Nazim wanted as a son, for he had regarded the older man as a father ever since Nazim had whisked him out of southern Lebanon. The police investigating Gina Hoffman's murder had been just an hour too late to find him in the refugee camp. Kamal shifted uneasily on the plush floor cushion. It made him nervous to think about the presence of his victim's granddaughter here in this house. So far, he had managed to avoid seeing her, since his duties as secretary kept him busy, even though Nazim's English was now nearly perfect.

"Healey thinks he is God himself," Nazim muttered, pacing before the open terrace doors as he pulled up the collar of his satin smoking jacket. "How quick men are to think well of themselves when the world congratulates them. Is it not so? Or did your old sheikh never tell you such things?" He stopped to stare into Kamal's wide eyes, then resumed his pacing.

"My old master was a limited man," Kamal said, feeling disloyal even as he told the truth. "I don't think he ever read the blessed writings of Rumi or Al-Hallaj. It is only because of you that I have had a chance to discover them." He wanted to use Rumi's words, saying that he had longed to wake up and look at his life with eyes clear as water, from the time Nazim had first introduced him to the ancient Sufi masters.

Kamal blushed and lowered his head over a letter, which tomorrow would be sent by courier to the heads of the four subgovernments into which the U.S. had recently been divided. Although a president remained in Washington, D.C., the federal government was now a shadow of what it had been before the collapse. The downward spiral had begun soon after the first fundamentalist president was elected. Massive tax cuts and reductions in the size of the federal government had crippled his administration. After a small flat tax had broken the power of the IRS, more and more people stopped paying taxes altogether. For a while the government had stayed afloat by selling off the national park system and other federal properties. Weighed down by the burgeoning national debt, however, America had become the first world power to declare bankruptcy.

Nazim picked up another letter and scanned it before throwing it onto Kamal's desk. "To think, Gas Gage has been dead for ten years, and now his son has the premiership the old man wanted. Though he is a greater fool than his father, I keep my word. But this is the territory I intend for Jason to have after Gage becomes expendable."

The door opened and a liveried butler showed Homer Healey into the room. The minister was angry, though he was too thoroughly in Nazim's debt to show it. He tried to keep his voice calm and deep, as he did on his telecasts. "I've just learned that you and Gage have agreed to partition California above San Francisco, not below Santa Barbara as you promised."

Hands behind his back, Nazim stared up at the brilliant chandelier, which scattered tiny rainbows across the ceiling. "We were forced to make the division according to demographics. You know that. Most of the people from San Francisco to San Diego are now black or Hispanic. A majority of these have become Muslim. Your Christian fundamentalists will be generously helped to resettle in the north."

"So we get nothing but Sacramento and Fresno?" Homer's voice quavered, and he clutched his throat in a gesture he often used to show television audiences how deeply moved he was. "The rest, with all the foreign money and taxes, belongs to you? I can't believe you would deceive me this way. God will punish—"

Nazim interrupted him coolly. "God's will has been perfectly honored in this as in all things, Healey. Accept what is. Does your religion not teach you that? Mine does. Inshallah. You should study the Koran, my friend."

"And my glass temple?" Homer wrung his hands, looking wildly from the Arab's cold face to the chandelier, on which Nazim's eyes were intently focused.

"It is no longer necessary. The Party of God has conquered. We will turn your temple into a mosque. Money will be set aside for you to build a smaller church in the north."

The minister took a step backward, lurching into a tall folding screen enameled with red and gold triangles. It collapsed against the wall and he went down with it. His face flushed and his voice quivering, Homer scrambled to his feet. "I've taken your Judas money long enough. No more. I will shake the dust of this house from my feet and go where the

Lord calls me." He turned and ran out the door.

Nazim made no effort to stop him. "I am weary of this place and these people," he said, half to himself and half to Kamal. "My role here is finished. It is time to go home. With his father's help, Jason will take charge of our operations. You will leave first to prepare my house in Lebanon. Take any passport that suits you from the supply. It would be unwise for you to use your own name. The Israelis have long memories."

"You will bring all your household home? Including your daughter?" Kamal blushed and looked down, hoping that his master had decided to change his plans.

"No. Ayesha will stay here to marry Jason as she desires. I will bring the others as soon as Fatima is able to travel. Or as soon as she . . ." He stopped in front of the fireplace. After a few moments of silence, Nazim held out a check. "Follow Healey and give him this. His principles will no doubt desert him at the front gate, and he will be glad to take the money after all."

When he was finally alone, Nazim carefully shaved his face and checked its smoothness before going to see Fatima on her sickbed. She was so fragile now, he knew she would be pleased that the cheek laid against hers would not scratch her skin. Fatima was too weak to make love anymore, but Nazim often went to her bed just to lie close and talk. Tonight he wanted to talk about Jason, whom they both loved as if he were the son they never had.

"Is that you, my love?" Although Fatima spoke faintly, Nazim could still be moved by the music in her voice. "I just had a dream. In it you went far away from me." As he sat down, she smiled and laid her head against his shoulder. "Though it is more likely I shall go far away from you."

Stroking her soft gray hair, Nazim sighed, "I cannot bear that yet. How often I have told others to accept what is, but now I am unable to do it myself."

"You have come to talk about Jason's desire to marry that girl. Yes?"

"I know it disturbs you," he said, "but we must decide. The boy is besotted. He will be good for nothing unless he has this girl, and there will soon be much work for him to do."

"But does she want him?" Fatima's voice was a little stronger, though her breath came in gasps. "Want him as our daughter does? Ayesha has done nothing but weep since Jason returned from the north with his concubine."

Nazim laid his hand gently over her pale lips. "She is not that, Fatima. I have talked with Radha, and she is a virtuous girl, though more forward than I would like. Jason is an American, after all, and such women are common here."

"Common, indeed. And what of Ayesha? Would you break her heart?"

"Annie and David have proposed a solution. Jason must agree to marry Ayesha first, so that she will bear his heirs. Afterward, he can marry Radha."

"But Radha is underage, and besides, American laws do not allow two wives." Fatima's breath was shallow and her forehead soaked with sweat.

"We will soon make our own laws here," Nazim reassured her. "Meanwhile, I have arranged a legal marriage for Ayesha and Jason tomorrow morning. Our imam will seal a private marriage later with the other girl."

"Will she consent to such a marriage? You say she is virtuous. Surely she will know it is a fraud." Fatima lay back, closing her eyes.

"She will not be told of the first ceremony. After the marriage is consummated, Jason can tell her when he likes. Do you agree, Fatima?"

"I feel sorry for this girl," she whispered. "Perhaps we are doing her wrong."

"She is being brought to Islam," Nazim said, turning off the light. "What wrong is there in that? And our Jason will be happy again."

Homer Healey did not realize he was driving too fast until he heard the siren behind him. His hands shook as he pulled over onto the shoulder of Highway 101. Fumbling for his wallet, Homer glanced into the back seat where the box of dynamite lay covered by a plaid blanket. "Please God," he prayed, "don't let them find it. Give me time to purify your sanctuary. Let it not be defiled by the heathen."

"Mister, did you know you were hitting eighty-five back at the Garden Street interchange? Let's see your registration." The tall highway patrolman managed to lean his head and broad shoulders all the way into the black Mercedes.

"Here you are, officer. I have no excuse." Homer bowed his head, hoping his humility would discourage the patrolman from checking the back seat.

"Oh, it's you, Reverend." The patrolman's voice softened and he handed back the papers. "Me and my wife, we came to Jesus in your church just last summer. She's been off the sauce ever since. Saved our marriage, you did. Gotta thank you for that."

Slowly releasing his breath, Homer whispered, "Thank the Lord, not me. God bless you both."

"I'd feel downright sinful giving a man like you a speeding ticket," the patrolman said, backing away. "You just take better care of yourself, y'hear?"

The minister sat trembling until the patrolman had driven away. Maybe God was rewarding him because he had torn up Nazim's check and thrown it at the young Arab's feet. If only he had done that with Nazim's first check seventeen years ago, Homer told himself. He had sinned against God, against his own country and against Israel, for whose shrunken borders and terrorized people he was as much responsible as any man.

Homer stopped his car just outside the front entrance to the church and looked up at the shining steeple. The moonlight reflecting from every surface made it appear to radiate light. At least, he thought, from this holy place the world has heard the message of the Parousia. Because of my preaching, many more souls will be prepared to welcome Christ when he comes again.

As he left the car, a bright beam flashed and the minister blinked. A voice shouted from behind the light, "Who's there? Oh, it's you Reverend. Don't get to see you around here this late at night."

"I've come to pray, Jesse," he told the guard. "There's a burden on my heart to pray for the coming of the Lord. I'll be here the rest of the night, so you can go on home."

The guard touched his hat and smiled, then drove off in a hurry, before Homer could change his mind. Unlocking the front door, the minister entered his church. It was so dark inside he could see the stars through panels of glass in the high roof. Touching a pew here and there as he walked, he said good-bye to the shining wood and to the carved pedestal that held God's Holy Word. For the last time, he stood behind the pulpit from which he had taught so many people to serve the Lord, to keep the wicks on their candles trimmed in case the Bridegroom would come soon. His people must not be found carousing like the heathen.

"For me, the Bridegroom will come tonight," Homer cried out from the pulpit as if millions could hear. "Hallelujah, I hear the wind of the Holy Spirit singing in my ears. *Maranatha*! Come Lord Jesus."

Without an audience, the minister suddenly felt weak, and the long stretch of empty pews reproached him for all the souls he would never reach. He deserved to be punished, purified by fire before the Bridegroom would receive him. But he would need to hurry, for he did not want to risk the police catching him again, this time for arson. Jesse, the guard, had seen him. Everyone would soon know who had done it, and his message could be tainted. If caught, he would be tried, imprisoned, mocked. It would be a bitter end. There was no other way, Homer Healey told himself, tasting the tears that rolled into the corners of his mouth.

He laid the dynamite sticks up the main aisle, carefully untwisting the wires between them. Over and over, again he repeated the words from the Book of Revelation, "Whoever did not have his name written in the Book of Life was thrown into the lake of fire."

Standing before the carved pedestal, he threw back his head and cried out, "Then I saw a new heaven and a new earth, and I heard a loud voice speaking from the throne, 'Now God's home is with mankind! He will live with them, and they shall be his people. God himself will be with them, and he will be their God.'"

Homer looked up through the great windows at the moon and stars, whispering as he lit the fuse, "'He will wipe away the tears from their eyes. The old things have disappeared, and now I make all things new.'" For him, the Parousia had begun.

The explosion threw the minister backwards into the pedestal, and he was killed instantly when the huge, metalbound Bible came crashing down on his head. He did not see the slow, sifting rain of glass that fell on him and on the flames that engulfed what was left of Homer Healey and his glass temple.

❧

Kamal Al-Essa was one of the few people within fifty miles who did not hear the destruction of Homer's monument. He was lost in prayer, his face pressed to the floor. As always, he prayed to be forgiven for killing Gina Hoffman, who still forced her way into his dreams. The memory of her murder made his hands tremble so much he couldn't pick up a rifle, even when his new master demanded it.

Suddenly Kamal's whole body began to shake, and an intense humming filled his ears, as if a swarm of bees had flown into his head. A piercing light blasted his eyes, and the unearthly voice he had known since childhood spoke again. *When you go to Israel tonight, you must take the girl, Radha. Jason must not have her. Bring clothes for her and Ayesha's passport. I will provide everything else.*

Kamal groaned. "And will I then be free of my sin?"

The voice was gentle. *You were always free. But you shall not truly know it until you join me in your next life. You will meet me then as Prema Sai.*

Although his eyes were closed, Kamal could see a brilliant light as it faded into rainbow colors and then fell like glittering rain all around him. He wondered who this Prema Sai could be, but his mind was as blank as a desert. Out of the void, the figure of Radha's grandmother floated toward him, and Kamal shrank back. He did not want to see those blazing eyes again. *Look*, the voice said. *Do not be afraid. You are loved beyond measure.* When he dared to look, Kamal saw that the woman was smiling.

⌒◡⌒

Thinking it was an earthquake, Radha jumped out of bed when she heard the explosion. She had been dreaming of home, and her face was still wet with tears. The door was locked from the outside to prevent her from running away, so Radha curled up under the heavy table that served as her desk. She had always dreaded being trapped in an earthquake and preferred to die outdoors, rather than slowly starve, buried under tons of rubble.

When the shock of the explosion was over, Radha rushed to the barred window and saw flames leaping through a cloud of black smoke, somewhere in downtown Santa Barbara. Sirens cut through the stillness of the night. Probably another bandit raid, Radha thought. And who knew where they would hit next? Maybe even this luxurious, walled compound, with its private police. Thieves always seemed to know where the money was. Nazim's original compound was now under water, and he had fortified a huge estate up in the Montecito foothills, from where he could look down at Santa Barbara. Near the shore, the city streets had become shallow waterways which shone at night, reflecting the moon. It was just like Jason to forget she was trapped and alone, Radha thought. Rattling the bars furiously, she decided not to wait any longer to put her escape plan into action. As she took a deep breath, the words, Om Sai Ram, came easily to her mind, and her heart stopped pounding.

Preparing to move fast, Radha quickly exchanged the long, flowing robe for her jeans, black turtleneck and boots. As an afterthought, she put the robe on over her traveling clothes. Then she punched Jason's three-digit code into the intercom, leaving a message that she had something important to tell him. Staring at the heavy Chinese vase that Jason filled with roses every day, Radha sat at the table and waited.

Two hours later, Jason unlocked the door and entered her room. His clothes were singed and blackened, but his face and hands had obviously been scrubbed.

"I got your message," he said, trying to slick back his long, wet hair. "Came as soon as I could."

Radha figured she would start off friendly, remembering Eddie's warning that she would catch more flies with honey than with vinegar. "Looks like you've been to a fire," she observed, caressing the smooth surface of the glass paperweight on her desk. She did not want Jason to notice that her fingers were trembling.

"I'm with the volunteer firefighters," Jason said. "Somebody blew up Healey's glass temple. Hell of a mess." He strode around the room, looking grim. "Too many fires these days for the fire department to handle alone."

He had copied the striding from Nazim, Radha thought, remembering how the Arab had paced in front of the barred windows, questioning her about her morals. "You said that when I was ready, we'd talk. Well I'm ready. What do you want to talk about?"

Jason stopped pacing and hung over the back of her chair, grasping her shoulders. "I want to get married," he said. "Being a strict Muslim is hard for a guy like me. I need a woman, and I want it to be you."

His hands tightened until her shoulders ached, but Radha didn't move. "Why not some sweet little Muslim girl?" Radha asked with more of an edge to her voice than she meant him to hear. "I'm not your type. I don't give in easy, the way you'd want."

"That's just it. Making you give in would be my idea of a good time." Jason leaned over her neck, sucking up a painful amount of skin between his teeth.

Radha gripped the crystal paperweight even harder. "I'd run away as soon as I got a chance. You know that."

"Not before you were all mine, honey," Jason laughed, then swung her chair around until their faces nearly touched. His hands clutched both arms of the chair. "And I'd find you, no matter where you'd run to, just like I did before. I don't let go of what's mine."

Radha felt a trickle of blood run down her neck and hoped he didn't have some filthy disease. She'd heard that many city men were carrying the new AIDS virus. "I don't intend to be yours or anybody else's. I told your Mr. Nazim that."

"Honey, you've got no choice," Jason's voice was soft as he bent over to nibble her ear. Biting was what he liked best, since he wasn't allowed to do much more to a woman until he was married. Biting made him feel as if he'd taken charge. "We're getting married tomorrow afternoon. Nazim says it's a done deal."

Radha brought the heavy glass ball up so hard under Jason's chin that his teeth crunched. When she hit him again, in the temple, he fell heavily on top of her, pinning her to the chair. After tipping the chair forward, sliding them both onto the floor, Radha took the keys from Jason's pocket. Pausing to check his pulse, she was relieved to find him still alive. Good. Her karma was still intact. With luck, he would be unconscious long enough for her to escape down the driveway.

She had just locked the door behind her and put the keys in her pocket when a voice behind her said, "I know who you are and I'm here to help you. My name is Kamal."

Radha raised her arm, prepared to strike the man's throat. He looked familiar, but she couldn't remember where she might have seen this tanned, oval face, with its high, flat cheekbones. He had slanting brown eyes and narrow lips with dimples on either side. His hand shook as he pushed back the lock of hair that fell over his high forehead. Something about him reminded her of Eddie Szu, and Radha almost relaxed, though she felt a faint thrill of fear when she looked into his eyes. Perhaps she was being tricked. No one in this house could be her friend.

"I will explain as we walk," he said. "There is little time. Here, you must wear this to cover your face." He handed her a long gray shawl. "Quick. I hear footsteps just around the corner."

"This thing is good for camouflage, at least," Radha whispered, hurrying to wrap the shawl around her face. She hung onto Kamal's arm, hardly able to see with the shawl so low over her eyes.

Two young women passed by, giggling as they stared at Radha. "Good evening, Ayesha." Kamal bowed, his hand over his heart. "I congratulate you on your marriage to Jason tomorrow."

"It is to be?" The taller girl clapped her hands. She was about Radha's height, and her eyes were large and dark-lashed like Radha's. "I was not sure. You will come to the ceremony, Kamal?"

"I leave for Palestine tonight," he said, bowing again. "Your father's orders. I do not think we will meet again, Ayesha."

"Then I am glad for you that you have found another woman so quickly," Ayesha said. "Allah's blessings on you, Kamal."

"And on you." His eyes followed the two women for a moment, then he hurried Radha around the corner.

"That rat," Radha muttered when they were alone. "He was going to marry her and me both. Where are you taking me, anyway?"

"My room," Kamal said, opening the door. "Here is your bag." He pulled out a passport and glanced from the picture to her face. "Ayesha's height and features are close enough to yours," he said. "You will cover the hair, but your blue eyes might be noticed. Keep them lowered when we go through the passport check."

"What's in the bag?" Radha asked, pulling the strap over one shoulder.

"All I could find to make you look like a legitimate traveler." He blushed. "I do not know much about women's apparel."

Radha stood still. "You haven't explained why you're helping me."

"I owe a debt to your grandmother," Kamal said, turning his face away. "Besides, you were to marry Jason after his marriage to Ayesha. She didn't want another woman in his life and asked me to help. What else could I do?"

"I see. You love her yourself. Is that it?" Radha followed him down the hall, trying to keep up with his long stride. "Did you tell her?"

"She knows and has made her choice." Kamal kept his eyes straight ahead. "I accept what is. Allah may do with me what he wishes."

His words reminded her again of Eddie, who often said that placing his life in Christ's hands was what gave him the peace she so envied. For her, it was different. Until she received a direct message from Baba, she would go her own way. Kori had often told Radha that her mind was so full of what she wanted, only a lightning bolt from the hand of God could get her attention. She sighed, struggling to settle the thoughts that swarmed in her head. One at a time, she reminded herself, trying to follow Eddie's practice. One at a time.

Unused to the flowing robe, Radha almost tripped as she entered the garage. "I've got Jason's keys. Can't we take Consuelo with us?"

"I saw her earlier," Kamal replied. "She said she cannot leave, that she has a task to do here."

Radha bit her lip and tears came to her eyes. "I'll have to send a message to my family. At least I can tell them where she is."

"Hush." Kamal pulled her down behind a pick-up truck parked next to a black Mercedes. "I hear voices." He held Radha close, his hand over her mouth. "When Nazim can't sleep, he sometimes goes out for a drive at night."

Radha watched as Nazim's tall figure passed by, his shadow crossing over them. The chauffeur was just ahead, opening the back door of the Mercedes.

"We just heard about your missus, sir," the black man said. "I sure thought a lot of her. We all did."

"Find Ayesha and tell her to meet me at the gate. I must tell her myself that her mother is dead," Nazim said to the man who had come with him. "We will stop to pick up the imam on the way to the mosque." He paused before closing the door, his face distant. "Did you hear something?"

The burly chauffeur stepped out of the car. "Want me to look around?"

Radha held her breath and leaned against Kamal, trying to shrink any shadow they might be casting from the strong blue light overhead. Oh Baba, she prayed silently. Don't let Nazim catch me. Don't make me marry Jason, and I promise never to be a blabbermouth again. I just want to go home.

As the chauffeur moved forward, Radha heard the inner voice again. *Go with Kamal to Israel. For now, that is to be your home and where your task lies. Do not be afraid. You are working with me, little friend.* Radha's tears overflowed, running down Kamal's hand, which still covered her mouth. Gently wiping the corners of her eyes with the end of her shawl, he shook his head for silence.

At the sound of Nazim's voice, the chauffeur stopped walking toward them. "We will go now. No time to waste. I shall alert the men at the gate to watch for strangers." The car backed out and the automatic door closed.

"Jason's keys?" Kamal whispered.

Radha fumbled under her robe, reaching for her jeans pocket. "Here. But what about those guards at the gate?"

"You must lie down," he said, lifting her into the back of the pickup. "Curl up very small between the crates. When we are clear of the compound, you can sit in front." He covered her with a musty, damp tarpaulin. "Remember. Not a word."

As the truck bounced along the pebbled driveway, Radha thought about her ride with Jason and shivered. How perverse it had been to enjoy the touch of his hands even though she hated him. Sometimes her body seemed to have a will of its own, shedding tears and quivering inside with sick desires her head wanted nothing to do with. *Think of me,* the voice entered her mind like a ray of light through dark clouds. *When desires come that you do not want, think of me. And your heart will remember only the desire for God.* Radha cupped her face in her hands and tried to stop trembling as the truck slowed to a stop at the gate keeper's order. "Om Sai Ram," she repeated, silently moving her lips. "Om Sai Ram." Baba, help.

A guard was beside the truck. "I'll need to check the back. The boss said not to let anyone through tonight without inspection."

The truck door opened and Kamal got out, his shoes crunching on the stones as he joined the guard by the truckbed. "I have a girl back here," he whispered. "My sweetheart. No one knows about her. Please, let us through."

"You, Kamal? And everybody thinks you are pure as a saint." The man snickered. "Well, go along and have your fun with her. I'll keep your secret."

Her eyes closed, Radha lay still as the guard pulled off the cover and leaned his face close to hers. His breath stank of garlic and she shrank back. After looking his fill, he whistled. "A beauty, she is. When you get tired of her, let me know."

The man tossed the tarpaulin over her, and Radha drew a shaky breath as the truck started up. Only after Santa Barbara was far behind them did Kamal stop so she could sit beside him in the cab. He hardly spoke on the way to the airport, and for once the silence suited Radha. Her mind was noisy with plans. She could almost hear Eddie's voice saying, "First let your family know where Consuelo is. Then ask them where to find the Hoffman family in Israel." She decided not to tell her parents about Kamal.

The truck turned off at Santa Monica for the elevated highway leading to the airport. The ocean covered Highway One, once called the Camino Real, the Royal Road. Now the desolate coastline was infested by beggars and bandits. Because of looting in the area, armed guards were stationed all along the route to the airport. Radha had never seen a big city in her life and was startled by the dark, crumbling buildings and the trash-strewn streets. Most of the parked cars were missing tires and had broken windshields, as they stood rusting in the swirling, dirty water that had begun to fill the Los Angeles Basin.

Not liking what she saw, Radha closed her eyes and fell asleep. Long before they reached the airport, she was dreaming of being in India at Sai Baba's ashram. Baba stood before her in the darshan and took from her arms a small child with radiant eyes, then held the child close to his heart.

9

After spending nearly two years in Zefat, Radha was still not sure why Baba had wanted her to come to Israel. And what was her big, important task, she wondered. Except for strong leg muscles developed by climbing hundreds of stone steps in the small mountain city, she could not see what had been gained. After helping the family bury Uncle Chaim, she had taken over the care of her aunt, who was expected to die any day, the doctor said. Radha's time was spent feeding and bathing ancient Aunt Hannah and listening to stories about the old days. Her aunt didn't recognize her anymore and had started calling her Gilah. The cousins explained that Aunt Hannah thought Radha was her niece who had been killed saving children from an Arab gunman.

Sometimes Radha had the eerie feeling that she *was* her grandmother, unsure where her identity left off and Gina Hoffman's began. Aunt Hannah had even given her the ring Gina was wearing at her death. Radha wore it always on a chain around her neck. Owning this ring, with its enamel image of Sathya Sai Baba, had soothed her longtime jealousy over the Tasmanian shaman's ring that Philo wore.

Radha often wandered in the Ben-Ari cemetery, looking out at the Galilean hills. She could see across to where Syrian troops were guarding the newly drawn border that, along with the rising sea level, had shrunk Israel to half its former size.

Arabs had begun moving back into the little hilltop city of Zefat, from which they had fled nearly a century before. Kamal was among them, and he sometimes joined Radha for walks through the artists' quarter. On these occasions, he didn't wear his Arab headdress in case members of her family should see them. Whenever their hands touched as they walked, he would thrust his hands into his pockets and look away.

Often Kamal's face looked as remote and tranquil as Eddie's. He seemed to possess a special quality, something she sought in herself, but had never found. She tried to give it a name, but the closest she could come was "peace." A person who had learned to live entirely within himself, demanding nothing from the outside world, would be at peace. Radha knew she could never feel indifferent to pleasure or pain, but perhaps she would someday marry a man with that perfect, peaceful detachment.

Gradually she had come to think of Kamal as hers, though he said nothing to indicate he belonged to her or anyone else. A little push might bring him closer. She decided to disturb his peace long enough for him to realize that he loved her.

The day she turned seventeen, Kamal surprised Radha with a malachite and silver ring. She had admired the ring in a little shop next to the Kosov synagogue, where she went for Shabbat services every Friday night. Kamal first tried the ring on the third finger of her right hand. When it was too tight, he slid it easily on the third finger of her left.

"I thought someday I'd have an engagement ring there," Radha smiled. "But this suits me better. Thank you." As she kissed his cheek, an elderly woman passed by, frowning and shaking her finger.

Kamal let her hand fall. "I must tell you something," he said. "All this time we have known each other, talked as friends, there is a shadow between us. I've been keeping a secret from you, Radha."

"Do you want to talk about it now?" She walked beside him, wishing he wouldn't avert his eyes like the Orthodox men did whenever they passed a woman in the street. "We can go up to the castle park. No one will see us there." Radha hoped he would say that he didn't love Ayesha anymore. Then, maybe he would say how much he loved her. She was sure he did, but wanted to hear him say it.

They climbed the wide stone staircase to the ruins of an old crusader castle overlooking the city. It was from here that the defenders of Zefat had held back Muslim armies in past centuries. Kamal stood for a moment looking at the hills beyond the city, where Arab militiamen, backed by Syrian troops, were now based. "Our people are enemies," he began, still avoiding her eyes. "They have always hated each other. When I was a boy, my hatred made me do a terrible thing."

Radha hugged Kamal, forcing him to look at her. "You are one of the purest, best men I've ever known. Don't beat yourself up for throwing rocks at soldiers or whatever it was you did. Jesus said to love your ene-mies, right? And if you love someone, he's not your enemy anymore. I'm Jewish, at least half Jewish, and I forgive you. I even love you." She kissed him gently on the mouth.

"You love me?" Kamal stammered. "But you cannot know what I am. We have been friends. Is it not a friend's love you feel?"

"No," Radha whispered. "A lover's love. Tell me you feel it, too." Her eyes filled with tears and she wondered if she had made an awful mis-take. Perhaps she would lose Kamal's friendship the way she had Eddie's.

Kamal said nothing for a moment, gazing into her eyes while his lips moved silently, as if in prayer. Then he embraced her clumsily and held her close, swaying back and forth.

"I do love you, Radha, even more than truth, God help me." He held his face against hers. "It has been so hard to see you day after day and not tell you. So hard."

"Then why didn't you?" She pulled away from him, smiling into his serious face. "Come on, smile. Is it so terrible to be in love?"

"Terrible, yes, when it is with . . ." Kamal broke off and started to walk up the path again, his hands shoved into his pockets. "How can we marry, a Jew and an Arab? Your family will not permit it."

"Is that all?" Radha felt suddenly light. "Your imam can marry us. Or a judge. The new laws allow it. As for my family, Uncle Chaim is gone, and Aunt Hannah doesn't know who I am anymore. Their house has already been put in my name. It will be our house, Kamal."

"You understand that my people will consider me a traitor," Kamal said, standing at the crest of the ridge, where he looked out over the city and beyond. "And yours will not accept me."

"Then we'll go to Jerusalem," Radha said. "Now that it's an open city, anyone can live anywhere. No one will know us."

"That is what we must do, for I cannot give you up." Kamal embraced her again, then withdrew. "What is it you are wearing under your sweater?"

"If I show you, I want your word that you will take what I tell you very seriously," Radha said. When he nodded, she pulled out the gold ring that hung on a chain around her neck.

"Who is this man? Someone you once loved?" Kamal tried unconvincingly to smile.

"Still do," Radha said. "He's ninety years old, so don't worry. This is Sai Baba, the Holy One of India. The one who teaches that all religions must learn to live together in love. He gave this ring to my grandmother."

For a moment Kamal looked away and said nothing. Then he touched the ring tentatively, with one finger. "I know of Sai Baba. Many Muslims say our scriptures foretold him. In *Medhi Moud*, the Prophet described the coming savior as a man in flame-colored robes, a small man with thick hair, front teeth spaced apart, and a mole on his cheek. Perhaps Sai Baba is the prophet who was predicted."

"More than a prophet. He knows everything about us, yet he loves us unconditionally." Radha glanced down, suddenly feeling shy. "He talks to me, Kamal. I hear his voice in my head. Now you'll think I'm crazy."

Kamal turned the ring in his palm as if he did not want to let it go. "Just touching his picture makes me think of the times Allah has spoken to me," he said, "the times when I have been the sanest. I want to know more. Whatever you can tell me."

"Radha!" A child's voice came from down the path. "Radha! I've been looking all over for you. My mother says to come quick. Your aunt is dying."

~⌁~

Kamal was right about what people in Zefat would think when he and Radha married. "Have you heard?" voices whispered. "The niece from America sold Hannah's house to a stranger when the old woman was hardly cold in the ground. And only two months after her poor aunt's passing she married that Arab boyfriend of hers."

Radha and Kamal did not hear the gossip. They had moved to Jerusalem, into a condo in the King David Commons, a fashionable but somewhat worn development just outside the city walls. Jerusalem was one of the new pollution-free cities, powered at very high cost by fusion energy. Only electric cars and buses were allowed in the Old City, in order to protect the monuments and walls from the same kind of damage that had crumbled the Sphinx and the Parthenon. If there was an eternal city anywhere, Radha mused to Kamal, Jerusalem was it.

Jerusalem was to Paris as Paris was to New York, a place of ancient origins that made newer cities look like they were made of mere tin and plastic. So Kori said when she and Kief came to visit after Radha and Kamal's son, Ibrahim, was born. It had been a difficult journey. After the great earthquake, flooding and threats of violence had closed the coastal airports in California. Kori and Kief had traveled by ship to the new province of Washington-Columbia, where international flights could still leave safely.

"Since it's fused with what used to be Western Canada, the northern province is still in pretty good shape," Kief said, wrapping his long legs awkwardly around a hassock. It was the only furniture in the room, which was scattered with cushions, Arab-style. "Hard to get in at the port though. If Father Gregory hadn't come with us, we might not have made it past the border guards. They don't much like Californians.

Home of the howlers, is what they call California. And they're right. The neo-punk howlers started in Los Angeles, but when the Muslims took over after the great earthquake, the howlers left for other parts. Not the Santa Cruz Mountains yet, thank God."

Sometimes Radha thought it might be better to raise Ibrahim back at the farm where the twenty-first century had not yet intruded. If her task, whatever it might be, did not lie in Israel, she would insist that Kamal take them back to California. Her parents were still managing, as Kori had put it, to hold back the rising tide of barbarism. There were some signs of hope, Kief said, for millions of black Americans, now called "Africamers," whether Christian or Muslim, had become followers of Sai Baba. Some said it was Baba's brown skin and Afro hair that first attracted them, but they were finally won over by his teaching that all people are united in love and by his success in breaking up India's caste system.

Dressed in an electric-blue caftan, Radha curled up against Kamal's chest and propped a cushion under her knees. "We hear terrible stories about gangs taking over whole cities and the persecution of Asians. Is Eddie all right? I've been worried."

She kept her eyes on the baby sleeping in Kori's arms. What kind of a world was little Ibrahim going to grow up in, she wondered, where neo-punks howled on TV, pounding empty oil drums and blasting steam whistles in their caricature of music? The howlers she had seen on the telecon wore red contact lenses and painted their lips black. They shaved their heads down the middle, letting the back and sides grow long. After greasing their hair with foul-smelling pig fat, they twisted it into snake-like locks. The more extreme howlers braided in live snakes for their performances. Kamal had a select-lock put on the music video channels so his family would not accidentally come upon one of the orgy or torture clips that accompanied the howlers' music.

"Eddie's the same as ever." Kori smiled down at her grandson, adjusting the blanket around his chubby body. "The man never ages, perhaps because of those exercises he does. You would think he was taking the anti-aging drug, as most people do these days. Even Philo."

Radha decided not to tell her mother that she too was taking Melody, the new drug that combined melatonin, DHEA and Oriental herbs. One doctor had said if she started now, she would not begin to age until she was seventy. Since Kori needed no drug to look beautiful at any age, Radha was ashamed to admit her own vanity.

"We all think Eddie should marry," Kief added, "but he hasn't yet. Probably never will, since he spends most of his free time with the monks."

Radha glanced guiltily back at Kamal, hoping he wouldn't see how glad she was that Eddie had not married. Still that selfish streak, she admonished herself silently. "Is the farm still safe?" she blurted out, wanting to shift the conversation away from Eddie. She preferred that Kamal not guess her thoughts with his occasional prescience, which frightened her with its accuracy.

"As safe as anywhere in Mexical, except the underwater part that used to be the Baja peninsula," Kief answered. "Which isn't saying much. The Muslim majority doesn't bother us, as long as we avoid drugs and dirty videos. I guess you've heard they've cleaned house on the movie industry. No more smut in Muslim-controlled areas. But it seems that no one, not even the militiamen, can stop the violence, now that everyone has guns."

"We have fundamentalists here, too, and violence." A question hung heavily on Radha's tongue, and she paused before continuing. "You wrote me that Philo went to see Consuelo. I can't believe she wanted to stay with Jason."

"Neither could her mother." Kori sighed, laying the baby back in his crib. "Consuelo said she had a task to do. I can't imagine what."

"Candelaria and Philo stormed down to Santa Barbara," Kief said, shifting from the hopelessly uncomfortable hassock to a gas-filled, fluorescent green cushion that instantly molded to the shape of his body. "But by then, Consuelo and Jason were married."

"Did Consuelo tell you that Jason has a Muslim wife?"

"No." Kori winced. "This is the first I've heard of it. I suppose such marriages are legal now, since Muslims have the right to practice polygamy."

"Odd that most of them don't," Kief laughed and bent over Kori, kissing her neck.

"Probably too expensive." As usual, Kori could not be teased.

Radha looked at her mother fondly, wondering how she could ever have thought Kori was cold. She imagined her parents years before, taking the same infinite pains to make her comfortable that they both took now with little Ibrahim.

"It's Thursday evening," Kori said. "We like to sing a few bhajans and pray together on Baba's night. Would you mind, Kamal, if we hold our service here?"

Kamal said they could do as they wished, but Radha looked down, embarrassed. She had not gone to a regular Thursday service since leaving home and hoped Baba was not disappointed in her. "The cleaning woman comes tonight," she said. "I'll leave the door unlocked for her and a note so we won't be disturbed. She's a fundamentalist fanatic, like so many here. I don't want to scandalize her."

Kamal set out one of Aunt Hannah's Shabbat candlesticks on the makeshift altar, and Kori laid a rose in front of her photograph of Sai Baba. Tears stung Radha's eyes, as Kief's voice began leading them through the *Gayatri*. It had been too long since she had said the words, "O light pure and holy, Flow from God to humanity, Shine through the face of our mother-sun, Burn away all but divinity."

She heard a door open and close behind her, but did not turn around. Oh Baba, she prayed silently, I've been so busy that I've forgotten you. And the task, the task! I've never even tried to find out what you wanted. Behind her closed eyes, she saw a circle of golden light, and Baba's smiling face appeared. *You may forget, but I do not. The task is at hand. You have begun well.*

Opening her eyes, Radha saw that Kamal had turned white, and sweat was dripping from his forehead. He had had a similar experience once before, when a missile attack was about to start. She feared that he was again seeing trouble before it happened. "What's the matter, Kamal?"

"I felt strange," he said, leaning against the wall for a moment. "A darkness came over me. Please, go on."

Kief's strong baritone was just singing out the words, "The only religion is the religion of love," when the front door burst open and six armed men pushed their way into the room, led by Radha's cleaning woman.

"You see," the woman shrieked. "They are worshipping strange gods. I heard them and you can see for yourselves they are heathens, defiling this place."

Radha jumped to her feet, trembling as she struggled to reach the basket where the baby slept. With each step, she seemed to be wading through deep water. Her heart pounded as Kamal tried to bar the door with his body. They could kill him, but he would still try to save his family. Again Radha had the strange feeling that Kamal held his own physical body lightly because his real life was on another plane. Perhaps that was where he had foreseen that the attack was about to take place. They had never discussed his clairvoyance, because she was afraid to know its source.

The tallest man pushed Kamal aside, and two others stopped Kief in his tracks, pinioning his arms behind his back. Baby Ibrahim started to scream, and Kori snatched him up, her pale lips moving in a silent Om Sai Ram.

The man who had pushed Kamal stood before the little altar, his club raised to smash it. Then he stopped. "Strange," he said, reaching out a tentative finger to touch the photograph. For a moment he froze, then dropped the club and prostrated himself on the floor, his head toward the altar.

Muttering to himself, another man took up the club and swung it back as if he would knock everything off the altar. But he, too, stopped in midswing, stepping around to look at the back of the picture. "Come closer, brothers, and look at this," he gasped. His mouth dropped open as the club fell to the floor.

Shifting so she could see around the men crowding in front of the altar, Radha caught a glimpse of gray ash pouring from the picture. A sudden wind shook the building, and a gust swirled through the room from the slightly open window. Though the petals of the rose shivered, the candle flame continued burning straight up as amber liquid ran down from Baba's eyes, pooling on the table.

"It is sacred here," the tall man cried, rising to his knees. "This is the Holy One promised by God." He reached out and touched his fingertip first to the amber liquid and then to his lips. "Taste and see."

"It is a sign from God," said another, after taking a sip of the sweet fluid.

"Amrit," Kori said, in her cool, teacher voice. "It means God is present here in physical form." She went to the altar and took a fingertip of amrit, placing it on the squalling baby's tongue. Ibrahim opened his eyes wide and stopped crying.

"I beg your pardon," said the cleaning woman, clinging to Radha's sleeve. "Forgive, please."

"Let us worship with you," the tall man begged. "We will come whenever you pray, if you will allow us."

"Yes, yes, I forgive you." Radha's eyes were staring at the picture, and she hardly heard her own words. "He is our Lord, and he has done a great thing."

Kori moved among the kneeling people, the candlelight haloing her soft gold and silver hair, as she touched each one's forehead with ash. "Whatever the name you use for God," she said, "let this remind you that God is everywhere and that God is love. *Loka samastha sukhino bhavantu,*" she whispered in Sanskrit. "Let all the beings in all the worlds be happy."

☙❧

Over time, the little group of worshippers grew until they had to meet in the large hall at the center of the commons. The picture was now under glass to protect it from the many hands trying to touch it. But still the vibhuti continued to fall, and people came from all over Jerusalem to take it away in little packets. Amrit flowed from the picture only on holy days of the great religions. So people of all faiths gathered in the hall to celebrate each other's festivals before Baba's altar.

Some worshippers, who came to see the miracles, brought symbols of their own religions for the altar. Within a few years, Baba's little picture was surrounded by a Burmese statue of the Buddha, a crucifix carved in Italy, a menorah from the home of a visiting rabbi. These and other objects stood on a brilliantly colored cloth woven by the wife of a Bedouin chief, whose quadriplegic son had stood and walked when the amrit touched his lips.

After coming home from his job as a grade-school art teacher, Kamal would sit before the family altar for hours. Ibrahim loved watching his father's face, which seemed to light up from within. But Radha was often annoyed at the lengthy prayers and would begin rattling the plates loudly at dinner time. Then Kamal would quietly wash his hands and come silently to the table, as if he were still in a state of prayer.

Ibrahim enjoyed placing the religious articles on the altar each Thursday night, but he often grew restless during prayers. One Thursday night, after celebrating his fifth birthday with the bhajan singers, Ibrahim overheard his parents when they thought he was asleep. Radha's voice was raised sharply, and he could hear every word.

"How am I supposed to know you love me when you never say so? When you pray all night instead of coming to bed with me? This is not a monastery, Kamal. And I won't be just the cook and cleaning woman around here."

Kamal's voice was so soft, Ibrahim could barely hear it. "I don't love you less for loving God. How can I explain it to you?"

"Words aren't enough," Radha stormed. "God has no body, but I do. Does that make sense to you?"

"Something holds us apart," Kamal said. "But I can't talk about it."

"Something I've done? Just tell me what." She was sobbing now, her voice muffled. "I can't stand the way things are between us."

"I should have known my guilt would cause this," Kamal murmured. "It is my fault, not yours."

"Guilt? You mean because you left your people for me? Give me a break, Kamal. They would have turned you into a criminal. You've hinted as much."

"I was a criminal," he said. "You do not know what I did, and I cannot tell you."

When they came out into the kitchen, Ibrahim heard the clattering of cups and then the splash of tea pouring through the drink synthesizer. He tiptoed over to the partly opened bedroom door and peeked through the crack. It served them right that he was eavesdropping, he told himself. He was too old to be put to bed at eight o'clock.

"Well, let's try talking about how you and God get along very nicely as a cozy twosome. How patriarchal and exclusive." Radha dragged her metal stool noisily across the white tile floor and plopped herself down. "It's so easy that way, and you don't have to spend any energy on me. After all, I'm just a temporary grabbag of blood and skin and bones, not pure spirit. Not perfect. So it's easy to avoid mistaking me for God."

Kamal stood behind her, his face haggard and pale. "I should have been a monk, not a husband," he said. "God has given me a faithful wife, and I have made her unhappy. What should I do to please you, Radha? I am stupid about these things."

She pulled his hand to her cheek. "Just touch me sometimes. I feel so alone now that Ibrahim is in school. Even Baba doesn't speak to me anymore. What do I want from you?" Wrapping her arms around him, she laid her face against his chest. "I want a holy marriage. I want to be your companion as you go to God. I don't want you to leave me puttering in the kitchen and watching the telecon by myself."

Unlike most families, they had chosen not to have one of the virtual reality systems that drew billions of people into imaginary three-dimensional worlds. Kamal said that he himself was already too removed from this world, and he also preferred that Ibrahim not lose touch with reality before he had experienced it. Instead, they had selected a simpler system that served as a computer, television, telephone viewer and message center. Radha enjoyed tripping, as everyone called it, and often went next door to her neighbor's apartment to travel into impossible worlds at the touch of a finger. After an experience of VR, the ordinary world seemed drab and dull. Perhaps, she thought, that's the way Kamal feels when he leaves his spiritual heights for our bedroom.

"I have been so selfish," Kamal said, stroking her hair. "All this time, I was trying to become a saint." Suddenly he straightened up, clutching his chest as he staggered toward the sink.

Radha was terrified. "I'll call the emergency number!"

"No, no," Kamal gasped, his voice faint and thick. "It isn't that. Something terrible has happened. I saw the sky ripped open and darkness spilling in on us. Quick, turn on the telecon. We must know what has happened."

Radha helped Kamal to a chair in front of the screen. Sitting on the floor, she leaned her head against his knees and passed her hand over the photo-electric selector. Within a few minutes, a report came through from what had once been Tibet.

"We interrupt the scheduled programming with a news flash just in from Lhasa via Chinese satellite," the voice said. "A private jet carrying the world-revered Indian spiritual leader, Sri Sathya Sai Baba, disappeared from radar at 3:33 this afternoon as it crossed the Nepal-Ladakh border. He was traveling to visit a Himalayan ashram when the plane disappeared from radar screens near the border. Due to the extreme weather conditions, authorities in Ladakh say there could be no survivors. Rescue teams cannot be dispatched because of a severe blizzard.

Satellite photos from the crash scene are expected shortly. Stay tuned to your round-the-clock news channel for further developments."

The anchorman continued reading from what was obviously a bio-sheet, "In recent years, Sathya Sai Baba has assumed world prominence as a spokesman for the unity of all religious faiths and as a builder of free schools and hospitals throughout Asia. He was known as the 'Man of Miracles,' and his followers are estimated to number more than two billion. Sai Baba named no successor, but has stated that he himself will be reborn in order to continue his worldwide activities. His reincarnation is expected near Mysore in South India, sometime during the next ten years. Tune in tomorrow at 6:00 P.M. for a documentary about this remarkable individual and his influence throughout the world. This station will now observe Sai Baba's passing with a moment of silence."

Radha waved her hand across the selector, turning the picture into the usual moving light show of interweaving shapes and colors that was the main wall decoration in their small living room. Her voice shook. "Light the altar candle."

They sat in front of the altar where Sai Baba's picture was kept when not being used for services in the big hall. "Don't be sad." Kamal's face was peaceful and his eyes were full of light. "Baba said he would leave when he was ninety-five, and he has."

"I'll never have a chance to go to India now," Ibrahim said, trying not to cry. "I'll never get to see the Holy One." For once his father was wrong, Ibrahim thought. There was a lot to cry about.

Radha looked at Baba's picture through her tears, then reached out to touch the glass. Her fingers came away without the usual gray smudge. "No more vibhuti," she whispered. "He's gone. I won't hear his voice ever again."

Suddenly a familiar burst of light appeared behind her closed eyes, and Radha heard the voice. *Do you think leaving the physical body is the end? I will never abandon those who love me. Never. But I am with you in a different way now. Only wait a little while and trust. I will soon call you to the task.*

10

Perhaps it was knowing that Ibrahim was to enter a kibbutz the day after his thirteenth birthday that made Radha feel so sad and drained. Although never psychic like Kamal, she had felt all day that something terrible was about to happen. She wished she could be as happy about Ibrahim's decision as he was. But the violent fighting over international borders and religious differences was so widespread that the impoverished UN forces were no longer able to provide protection in the Middle East. When the next war came, as it surely would, no one would be safe, not even in the open city of Jerusalem. Perhaps the imminent event that was chilling her to the bone was the beginning of another war.

Too nervous to stay alone at home, Radha put on a plastic poncho over her handknit white shawl, a gift from her mother many birthdays ago. She started out for the Kotel where her grandmother's people had always gone to mourn. The Wailing Wall, some called it, and Kamal said that he often saw tears running down the wall, as if the very stones wept. Well, they would be weeping today, she thought, because of the driving winter rain.

Radha walked fast, clutching the poncho hood under her chin to keep out the rain. It was falling so hard that the drops bounced into the air, and the cobblestone gutters gushed with muddy water that overflowed onto the slippery walk.

Only delivery vans were allowed in the narrow streets of the Jewish Quarter. Israelis were such reckless drivers that there would be accidents at every corner if the streets were open to passenger cars. She stopped to buy a falafel roll for lunch at a little stand near the Ha-Kotel Yeshiva school, which had refused to admit Ibrahim as a student. The school followed the old religious laws, under which he could not be considered a Jew because his mother was technically not Jewish. It didn't matter that Radha's grandmother had died a martyr, protecting Jewish school-children from a lunatic Arab assassin. She shook her head, wishing that her countrymen could hear Baba's message of reconciliation. Perhaps when Prema Sai arrived, the religion of love would become everyone's religion. Prophets and seers all over the world said that day was coming, but to Radha, it seemed distant and unreal.

After lifting her poncho to show the armed guards that she wasn't carrying a weapon, Radha walked carefully down the worn steps to the ancient square. Despite the rain, many black-hatted men were davening near the left side of the wall while women pressed their heads against the right side, as if being comforted by the shoulder of a loved one.

Little sprigs of vegetation grew in the crumbling wall, giving it the texture of a living thing. Three thousand years before, at a time when the Jews longed for a great kingdom, these stones had formed the outer rim of Solomon's temple. Now, this decaying relic of innumerable attacks reminded them how brief were the glories of the world, how permanent the condition of mortality.

Radha pushed a tiny, rolled up piece of paper into a chink in the wall. On it was written a prayer for Ibrahim's safety and another for honesty and truth in her marriage. She touched her face against the cold, wet, uneven stones. Kamal loved her, she was sure, but he was immersed in his own private world, unable or unwilling to tell her why he could not bring her into it. Radha had given up asking why and was trying to love him without making demands, as she felt Baba wanted her to. Her face damp with tears and rain, she turned away from the wall. Perhaps if she became a better wife, Baba would reach out and speak to her again.

On the way back, within sight of the King David Commons, Radha was passing under the high, time-blackened arch of the Jaffa Gate when she heard the rapid, metallic sound of automatic weapon fire. Suddenly she thought of Kamal, and a wave of nausea weakened her. "He'd be coming home from school now. Dear God, don't let it be him." She ran across the wide expanse of Mamillah Street, dodging the honking cars. On reaching the other side, she rounded the curve of the market stalls and entered the narrow stone lane that led to their condo complex.

A crowd was gathered around a man who had fallen. Blood and water flowed across the stones. Using her old t'ai chi skills, Radha forced her way through, sticking a knee here and an arm there to carve out a pathway. With a final jab, she broke through the circle that had formed around the man's body. Even before turning him over, she knew who it was.

"Get back, get back," Radha screamed, pushing so hard against the onlookers that some of them fell backward. "It's my husband. Call an ambulance." Her heart ached at the curious stares that intruded on her grief and Kamal's agony. "Leave us alone," she whispered, not looking up. Did they think they were watching a newscast or a film, that pain should have no privacy? Pulling off the poncho, she made a little tent to crouch under while she cradled her husband in her arms.

"It's good that you have come, my darling," he whispered, holding his hands tightly to his chest as if to stop the flow of blood. "I have things I must tell you before I die. You must hear them in order to free my soul. When you know what I am, you will not grieve over me. I knew Nazim's people would someday punish me for leaving his service. At least I told you that much."

"Never mind, never mind." Radha rocked him gently. "I wish I could stop the pain. I wish it was me instead of you."

"It does not hurt much. I am in shock, I think." His face was gray-white and his breath labored. "Listen to me. I cannot say this in the careful way I had hoped. Your grandmother . . ." He stopped as Radha wiped pink foam from the corner of his mouth. "It was I who killed her. I have begged God for forgiveness every day of my life since then, but until today I have not felt free of this crime. Now I am suffering the same fate, and it is right. This is why . . ." His voice started to fail again, but his eyes were clear and focused on her face. "This is why you must not grieve, but be glad I have paid my debt."

Radha sat rocking him mechanically, her heart cold and dead as stone. She opened her mouth to cry out, but no sound came. Is he making this up to keep me from mourning him, she wondered. No, Kamal would not lie. Staring at him with cold eyes, she could find no words of comfort. The grandmother she had never known had been murdered by this man. Perhaps Gina would have understood her as Kori had not. Why shouldn't she leave him right in the street, to die alone as her grandmother had?

Though blurred by a film of tears, Kamal's eyes were still open. He looked like a man awaiting a sentence, not one on whom a sentence had already been carried out. "I hope God will forgive me, since you cannot. Believe me, Radha, my love for you was never a lie. I was too weak to tell you the truth, too afraid of losing you."

A rush of memories flooded her mind—holding Kamal's hand when the labor with Ibrahim had gone on so long that she was screaming for a cesarean, his patience with the small boy who pulled books off the shelves and threw food on the floor, his arms holding her gently after they made love. Radha began to cry loudly, like a baby.

"I don't know if I forgive you. But I love you, Kamal. I hope that's enough."

Kamal smiled and closed his eyes. "It is enough."

Radha felt a dam burst within her, and a surge of light passed through her whole body. It was like the night when vibhuti first fell from Baba's picture. *You see how love does away with karma,* Baba's voice came from far off. *Dear little friend, you have just broken the chain of violence that has bound your two souls for a thousand years. Now it is finished. You must go back to your home, to your parents. Leave Ibrahim here so you can do the work you were meant to do.*

But I can't leave my son, she cried out to the voice as it faded from her mind. He is all I have left. *No,* the voice was strong again. *I am all you have left. He will be safer without you. Your task goes on and is to be fulfilled elsewhere, far from here. Prema Sai was born today. You must be ready to serve him.* A flash of joy shot through her, and Radha momentarily forgot where she was and who she held in her arms. Bowing her head, Radha formed the word "yes" on her lips as she bent to kiss her husband good-bye.

Ibrahim returned that afternoon to a dark, empty home. When the neighbors brought the news about his father's death, he did not go to the hospital, for he wished to say good-bye alone, in this place they had shared for thirteen years. Ibrahim lit the candle by Sai Baba's picture and sat cross-legged before the altar. He had just begun his prayer when he saw that the picture had clouded over. Leaning forward, Ibrahim touched the glass, and his finger came away powdered with gray ash. Then he watched as amrit began to flow again from Baba's eyes.

Radha took few belongings when she left Israel. Even her gold ring with the face of Sai Baba had been enlarged to fit Ibrahim's third finger and was now his. She hoped it would remind him to ask for God's protection. Except for her clothes and a few favorite books, everything was left for Ibrahim, including the condo. Its rental would provide for his education. Arranging a passport had taken some time, since Radha had entered Israel using Ayesha's. In order to verify her identity, the Israeli authorities had contacted their counterparts in Santa Barbara, now the capital of the new province of Mexical. Radha felt uncomfortable giving her family's name and address to the authorities, but she had no other choice, if she wanted to leave Israel for home.

The San Francisco waterfront, where her boat docked, was now lined with canals. As with most coastal cities, it had begun to sink beneath the waters of the melting icecaps. The Golden Gate Bridge had dropped at one end, its remaining tower trailing cables like a bedraggled queen. A causeway on floating barges carried passengers and cargo from ships to the port building, a sprawling, cement-block structure set among blackened, burnt-out buildings.

Radha nervously gripped her bag, wishing dusk had not already fallen. She didn't like waiting for Philo in this seedy, almost deserted terminal, which looked like an empty warehouse. Sea gulls were flying around under the shadowy, fifty-foot-high ceiling, where a few lights flickered behind dented, discolored, plastic screens. Small groups of young punks stood around eyeing the passengers.

Most of the others on her boat had also come down from Washington-Columbia and had quickly scattered into waiting electric taxis as soon as they got past the slow, indifferent customs officials. Not seeing Philo anywhere, Radha decided to wait in the women's room. Approaching the door, she heard a muffled scream and fumbled in her purse for the chemical canister Ibrahim had given her. He had told her to aim for the eyes, and that the caustic purple liquid would spray for ten feet, straight as a laser beam. Shifting the bag to her left hand, she kicked the door open.

Three howlers in black plastic jackets and tight pink fluorescent pants were wrestling on the floor with a black-haired girl wearing what at first looked like a rainbow. Her dark eyes wide and terrified, the girl was clutching the edges of her multicolored sari.

Radha swung her bag, heavy with books, into the ribs of one howler who stood up when she came in. He fell back against the wall clutching his chest. Aiming carefully, she sprayed the eyes of another man, who had jumped off the Indian girl. He screamed and his face turned bright purple. Radha avoided him as he stumbled around cursing and retching, his arms flailing as he tried to reach her.

She called out to the third howler, who still hung onto the Indian girl, preventing further use of the canister, "Let her go, or you'll get yourself a face to match your friend's. Move it."

The man rose to his feet and retreated warily. Suddenly he pointed at Radha and called to the others, "Hey, look. It's her, the one we're supposed to bring in."

Radha pulled the Indian girl out the door. "Come on," she said. "We've got to find a cop." She longed for Israel, where there were armed guards everywhere.

Radha's stomach tightened in fear when two of the howlers burst out of the bathroom behind her, knocking the canister out of her hand. They were joined by two others, and she was surrounded. Having lost most of her martial arts skills and without the advantage of surprise, Radha was helpless. Jason, she thought. Who else would be able to check passport records?

"Go," she said to the Indian girl. "They want me, not you. Run back to customs. Get someone to help."

"But I cannot leave you to such men," the girl said in hesitant English.

"You can't help. Get out of here." Radha kicked the knees of one man as he circled her, but another grabbed both arms pinning them behind her.

The Indian girl stood with her eyes closed. "Om Sai Ram," she said in a clear voice.

At the other end of the building the door swung open, and Radha could see three men come in. The dimness made it hard to tell who they were. As they came closer, she saw that one wore a monk's robe and carried a long wooden stave.

"Father Gregory!" Radha screamed, digging her nails into the wrists of the man holding her. "Philo! Over here."

The howlers took off, pulling their staggering, purple-faced companion along. A slender figure in black pursued them to the door, his hand slanted at a familiar angle, ready for action. Eddie. He had come for her.

Philo reached out, and Radha threw her arms around his neck. His face was thinner than she remembered, and under one high cheekbone there was a white scar that stood out against his tanned face. "You look great, Radha," he said, twirling her around. "Not much different than when you left."

"So do you." She kissed him on the cheek. "The blessings of Melody. Hope you know where I can get some in this hellhole. Don't Mexicalis pay their taxes, or what?"

"Who's got cash anymore?" Philo shrugged. "And this girl?"

Radha had been so busy with Philo she had forgotten the Indian girl, who stood silently outside their little circle. It took Radha a moment to remember. "Consuelo," she cried. "She looks just like Consuelo!"

"She does." With folded hands, Philo politely greeted her. "Namasté. It's not safe for you to be here. Can we help you find your people? Were you expecting someone to meet you?"

"My name is Shanti Patel. I was told only to come." She had large, shining eyes and thick, waist-long black hair that was neatly braided. She smiled and her face suddenly seemed like a child's, soft and rounded.

"Who told you to come here? Your parents?" Philo stared at Shanti with a puzzled look.

"That would be hard to explain," she said. "I must get my bags from customs."

"I'll go with you." Philo left with Shanti and returned carrying two canvas bags stamped with the Om Sai Ram symbol. "She has come from Puttaparthi to be a missionary," Philo said. "I hadn't realized that to the Indians we're a developing country."

"You're surprised?" Radha looked around the crumbling building. "Not exactly world-class architecture around here, is it? I hope the next missionary we get is a contractor."

"Or a hydro-engineer," said Father Gregory. "With the rising oceans, we can't build dikes fast enough."

"I am not really a missionary." Though soft, Shanti's voice had a firm edge. "I have just come to help, however I can."

"Right now, Shanti, I think we should help you." Philo's eyes held hers as if the two were alone. "We, too, follow Sai Baba. Maybe you were supposed to find us. We can take you back to my parents' farm. You'll be safe there."

"Not if we don't get out of here fast," Radha said. "Those men knew me. Jason sent them to pick me up."

"Jason? He's so faithful a lover after all these years?" Eddie Szu stood close to Radha, looking at her fondly. "Such good taste."

"Not love, Eddie," she said, handing him her bag. "Lust to own. Anything he once had his hands on, Jason thinks, is his forever. Let's go. We might not have much lead time, unless his communication system is as trashed as everything else around here."

Philo loaded the passengers and bags into a dented electric van. "Solar powered," he told Radha proudly, as she got in behind him. "We have about six hours before the battery dies. That should be enough to get us home. Shanti, sit up front with me. You can see better from here."

The Indian girl obediently climbed in and sat quietly, looking straight ahead, hands folded in her lap. Radha sighed as she settled back next to Eddie. It seemed as though girls like Consuelo and Shanti were always served first. Their gentle voices made people want to do things for them, Radha reflected, wishing her firm, husky voice could do the same. Women had to be soft to be loved, she reminded herself, tears burning her eyes. Would any man ever love her again, once he knew how hard she could be?

Eddie reached over and touched the corner of her eye with a fingertip, then laid it against his lips. "I'm glad you've come home, Radha," he said, protecting her shoulders with his outstretched arm as the van bumped along the potholed street. "I've been waiting a long time."

Rolling her head back, Radha gazed into Eddie's face, her breath catching in her throat. So he had not forgotten how much she had loved him. If he loved her, too, nothing would stand between them now. She was a grown woman, and he need not be afraid to touch her.

"I've waited, too, Eddie," she whispered in his ear. "You almost broke my heart when you shut me out."

"You were still a child." Eddie stroked her cheek, his touch light and tentative. "I had no right even thinking about you. But at night, you mingled with God in my dreams. I hope God was not as embarrassed as I was."

"The God who created such a world as this," Radha pointed out the window at the wrecked cars and windowless houses by the roadside, "is beyond embarrassment."

As they drove south to Santa Cruz, Radha hardly recognized the country she had left seventeen years before. Philo explained that many roads were now unsafe, with roving gangs carjacking and assaulting travelers. It was slower but wiser to take the side roads, through country villages. Some towns were now abandoned or taken over by squatters, often "cokies," the violent, brain-damaged children born of crack-addicted mothers.

According to Father Gregory, the new AIDS epidemic had claimed three-quarters of the population in Mexical. Many of the survivors had become celibate or had fled to monasteries like the one on her parents' farm, more often from fear than holiness. Muslims, Protestants, Buddhists. Every group had monasteries now, which, of course, paid no taxes. Bankrupted by the AIDS epidemic and the disappearing tax base, the health care system had collapsed along with most other government services. Earthquakes, fires and mismanagement had reduced Mexical to poverty. Since much of the population now lived by barter, little income was left to tax.

"You say everybody has guns." Radha looked at Eddie as they bumped up the overgrown road from the village. "Why don't they revolt?"

"Who is there to revolt against? Some rich landlord in Beijing?" Eddie shook his head. "No. The time for revolt has passed. Now we just try to defend ourselves against our neighbors."

The van moved more slowly as the road grew steeper, and the battery gauge began flickering off and on. Radha looked out the window at the lush winter vegetation. White wild flowers shone in the moonlight, and oleander bushes swayed as the wind from the Pacific sent fingers of fog into the hollows between the mountain ridges. Her heart beat faster when at last she saw lights from the farmhouse and the monastery half a mile above them. Eddie's faithful generators were still at work, fed by the pure water that streamed down the mountain, spreading life throughout the farm.

"We still have power, as you see." Eddie waved his arm. "Now that the oil's run out, everybody's scrambling for alternative energy."

"Too bad American oil interests kept us in the twentieth century for so long," Philo said bitterly. "The rest of the world moved on to other power sources years ago, while we still tried to squeeze out the last barrel of oil. How is it in India?"

"Not as bad," Shanti replied shyly, obviously not wanting to make unflattering comparisons between their two countries. "Twenty-five years ago, Sai Baba invited the American inventor of the Starburst Generator to settle in Andhra Pradesh and set up manufacturing there. Fusion energy was too far in the future for us then, and too expensive. Now India manufactures Starburst technology for all of Asia."

Eddie snapped his fingers. "De Sola's self-sustaining energy device." When Radha raised a questioning eyebrow, he explained, "Instead of converting energy from one form to another, De Sola generated it from an absolute vacuum. No pollution, no fuel costs. The Eurocom Corporation is making billions off its upscale version of the Starburst."

"I'm surprised you haven't figured out how to make one yourself," Radha smiled up at him.

"Can't get the parts. The last of the good tool and die men in this area retired ten years ago," Eddie sighed. "Making machine parts is a lost art, like chamber music and poetry."

As the red eye on the dashboard finally blinked off, the van groaned and lurched to a stop. Philo got out and opened the doors. "Guess we'll need your tractor to pull her into the solar hangar," he said to Father Gregory. "Lucky we got this far."

Radha, who had watched Shanti's soft, round mouth silently forming an infinite number of Om Sai Rams, wasn't so sure luck had anything to do with it. The Indian girl had prayed all the way home, keeping the protective mantle of divinity wrapped around them. It was the sort of single-minded devotion Radha wished her madcap, fickle mind were capable of.

Looking into Shanti's warm brown eyes, Radha felt the sudden joy of the familiar. She had seen this face, felt this presence before, but not in this lifetime. A memory flickered, and she saw a woman pushing a boy in his wheelchair through a crowded courtyard. And then the memory went out, like a candle flame in the wind.

She took Shanti's hand. "Come on. It's only a little walk from here. I want you to meet my mother. You'll like each other. Did Baba say what you were to do here?" Radha squeezed Shanti's hand as they walked. "You can tell me. I've been told I have a task, too."

"I know only that I was to come here and that I will serve Prema Sai," Shanti said as they walked together. "He was recently born near the city of Mysore, but no one knows yet who he is. It is hard to understand how I can serve him in India while I am here. Still, I know better than to disobey God's voice when I hear it."

"So do I." Radha gave the Indian girl a quick kiss on the cheek, then turned to her brother. "Philo, take Shanti in. I'm going to run ahead. I see Mother and Dad at the door, and for once, I want them all to myself."

❧

Brom Strassbourg looked down at the panorama of Paris that stretched below the towering glass windows of the Eurocom office complex. From here, a large portion of worldwide government and industry were controlled. It was Brom Strassbourg who controlled them. Only forty years old, he had risen to the top over countless bodies, Brom reflected, admiring his powerful biceps under the shimmering polysilk bodysuit. A few of his older executives still wore the dull-colored, two-piece suits of the twentieth century, but most worked out for two hours a day and chose clothes that showed off their efforts.

As he had worked to acquire his trim, rippling physique, so he had worked to achieve his position of power. At twenty, Brom had designed a new Starburst mainframe, based on De Sola's project in India. Brom's invention linked and augmented all the generators throughout Europe. By the time he was thirty, his corporation was manufacturing the only generators compatible with his mainframe. As a result, he controlled Eurocom, the old European Community, from the British Isles to the Urals. Now, he was attempting to pull Asia into his sophisticated network. He needed only the agreement of the UN to move from its temporary headquarters in Tokyo to the new fiber and glass structure already under construction adjacent to the Eurocom Towers in Paris.

The office monitor toned, and Brom nodded his head to turn on the transceiver. "Secretary-General Narayana Tewati is here," his assistant's cheerful tenor rang out. "Of the United Nations," he added unnecessarily.

Brom opened the door himself, not wanting the Secretary-General, a gentle, exquisitely polite old man from Madras, to think he took himself as seriously as he actually did. After being seated, Tewati looked Brom over, raising one thin white eyebrow. "I have been sent by the United Nations to inform you that the headquarters will be moved here next year, as you have . . ." He paused, considering the right word to use . . . "suggested."

As Brom rubbed his hands together and paced around the room, energy crackled from his tall, muscular body. "Excellent, excellent. You will not regret the move."

Tewati raised his hand slightly. "The Japanese insist on keeping an Asian sub-headquarters on their island of Oahu," he said. "It is a matter of national pride, you understand."

"As long as they know that the orders will come from Paris." Brom sat on the desk, stretching his feet out toward the Secretary-General. He knew that the gesture was insulting to an Indian, but did not let that stop him. "We'll hammer out the local jurisdictional details later. Japan must acknowledge that we will base the currency here."

"They and others object to your decision that each person who wants to conduct business must be fitted with the holographic trademark." Tewati placed his hands in his lap, palms up, and Brom could see he did not have the tiny blue chip imbedded at the base of his left thumb. "Perhaps I am a tiresome old man, but I see no purpose in this mutilation."

"It will prevent theft and fraud," Brom said, his voice cool. "Anyone who has the money to buy and sell can afford the operation. As for the others, it does not matter. Let them barter, let them starve. The new world order will advance faster without them."

"I will be among them," Tewati sighed. Twisting the heavy gold ring on his middle finger, he focused on the enameled image of a dark man with Afro-style hair. "Tonight I am submitting my letter of resignation to the General Assembly."

Brom's gray eyes turned frosty. "I would prefer that you stay, at least until the trademark is implemented worldwide," he said. "I would strongly prefer that." When he said twice that he would prefer something, everyone around Brom Strassbourg knew that he meant to have his way.

Tewati knew little of Brom's administrative quirks and cared less. "Regardless," he said, rising to leave, "I prefer to step down. It is reported that an incarnation of God has been born in my country. I mean to find him and to end my days serving him. Serving the United Nations, I fear, has become a matter of serving Eurocom and the interests of the rich."

Using his nine-inch advantage in height over the older man, Brom blocked the doorway. "You are the third person in a week who has told me of this birth," he smiled. When Brom Strassbourg smiled, showing his perfectly capped white teeth, he looked innocently beautiful. "I would like to know where I can find the child. Can you tell me?"

"He was born this year near Mysore," the old man said. "More than that, you will have to learn for yourself. Now, if you will excuse me."

When Tewati had gone, Brom rubbed his hands together and began to plan. A holy child born in India might become a religious symbol for the new order, even eclipsing the growing influence of Sai Baba. The Chinese, Brom remembered, had recognized the need for a malleable spiritual leader when they assassinated the Dalai Lama and installed their own lama in his place.

Brom knew that most followers of Sai Baba, known as Babans, had kept their own faiths, while adopting Sai Baba's ideals of selfless service and inner divinity. Millions served in the free Baban schools and hospitals that were springing up in every country. Brom intended to bring these people back into his commercial structure, in which money was the only reward for work. Only then could he have complete control. They would resist his plan for the trademark unless a world-recognized spiritual leader backed him up.

It should be easy enough to capture this child and mold him. He would tell his agents in South India to follow Tewati once the old man reached Mysore. Sitting at his desk, Brom activated the memoscreen. As he waited for the machine to come online, his fingers ran over the new trademark that would soon be imbedded in the hand of every person doing business in the world. He had designed it himself, to represent the three groups of six nations each that comprised Eurocom. The symbol was simple and universal in its appeal—three unified sixes forming a sunlike wheel, with three curved tails and a circle in the middle. It was sleekly attractive, even spiritual, some might say.

11

Radha was not surprised at how easily Kori absorbed Shanti into her life. Since the age of seven, the Indian girl had studied Sanskrit with teachers in Sai Baba's Puttaparthi ashram. Every night after questioning her, Kori corrected her own notes according to Shanti's answers. Showing a sudden desire to improve his own rusty knowledge of Sanskrit, Philo attended the sessions, too, reminding Radha of similar efforts he had once made to impress Consuelo.

Radha refused to study what she called a dead language, but accepted Shanti's offer of lessons in Telugu, the language Sathya Sai Baba had spoken. After dinner, they would sit at the kitchen table while Shanti drilled them in the South Indian dialect. She said that learning to read Telugu was not necessary, but seemed strangely insistent on teaching them to speak it. Radha wondered if perhaps Shanti wanted Philo to speak her own tongue in order to feel closer to him. Whenever his eyes strayed to Shanti's face, she would look down shyly and smile.

One day, while gathering eggs, Radha bluntly asked, "Does it bother you that Philo can speak only baby Telugu?"

Shanti placed her basket on a bench and fastidiously wiped her fingers on her apron. She would not eat eggs for fear of eating live embryos, but the rest of the family wasn't so fussy. Protein was hard to come by these days, especially since Kori forbade eating red meat. "I would like to be closer to him, yes," Shanti stared into the distance, toward the blue edge of ocean. "But it is not for that reason I teach you both Telugu."

"Why, then?" Radha asked. Having forgotten to bring a basket, she carried her eggs carefully in her apron.

Shanti began to walk toward the house. "I will tell you," she said, keeping her eyes straight ahead. "But we should all be together to discuss what I have to say. A decision must be made." She shrugged helplessly and shook her head. "It is embarrassing for me, asking others to make decisions."

That evening, the family gathered around the kitchen table. Eddie Szu sat next to Radha, his back straight, ready for action. After all these years, Eddie's hair had only a peppering of gray, and his face, strong and still as if carved from ivory, showed only a few lines above the heavy brows. He looked down at his long, slender hands.

Radha wondered why he so often studied his hands. It was as if he gathered strength from them. When attending services at the monastery, which she did more to be with Eddie than to pray, Radha would watch his strong hands folded over the pew. Eddie in prayer was like Kamal, absorbed in a world of light. She realized that she was drawn to such men because they balanced her sensuality and earthiness, reminding her, as Baba had, that she was more than just her body.

When they took holy communion from Father Gregory, Radha could see Eddie's eyes shining. Sometimes she felt guilty staring at him during such private moments, but watching Eddie was for her a kind of communion in itself. His goodness reminded her of God and kept her thoughts from wandering to how Eddie's hands might feel on her body.

Radha was glad that in the four months since coming home she and Eddie had trained for two hours every day, restoring her old t'ai chi skills. By focusing the physical tension between them on something other than sex, they easily fell back into their old bantering intimacy. Unlike Kamal, Radha felt Eddie was a man who could take her with him to God, instead of going alone. But she would not tell him she loved him, as she had told Kamal. This time she would wait, possessing her soul in patience, as Eddie did.

Before the others came, Radha told Eddie that he had been in her dream the night before, and his face had suddenly changed to Baba's. Astonished at seeing one face become the other, she hadn't heard what he was saying.

Eddie nodded. "It's Baba's way of reminding us to treat each other as divine incarnations. Namasté, Radha," he said, raising her hand to his lips and kissing the inside of her wrist. "I salute the divinity within you."

Kori smiled at them from the doorway. "I also had a dream about you two last night. Perhaps later I will tell you what it was."

Father Gregory and Brother Elijah came in and sat beside Eddie, followed by Shanti and Philo, who sat near Kief at the other end of the table. His voice musical and light, Philo took one of Shanti's trembling hands. "Shanti has told me what she wants to say to us all. She has asked me to help her say it." Radha had always been annoyed by the certainty and faintly amused detachment in Philo's voice. He was so in control of his world, she thought, untouched by passion, except for the transient kind that was easily satisfied and not subject to longing or regret.

After glancing around the table, Philo looked at Shanti. "Stop me if I say it wrong. She has had a vision in which Prema Sai asked her to help him."

"He was a baby, but had a man's voice," Shanti said softly. "He said I should bring my friends to Mysore to help him. He said four names, but I remember only Philo and Radha."

"After my dream last night, I am not surprised." Kori rubbed one hand with the other to ease her arthritis, which had flared up during the winter. The light over the table brightened her cap of silver hair. "We have heard rumors that some factions within the Sai Baba movement are trying to find the child. I suppose it is only natural that men seek power. Possession of the holy child would mean supreme power."

"Of course, Sai Baba's followers will not be the only ones looking for

Prema Sai," Kief said, shaking his shaggy gray head. He poured himself a glass of water and stared into it. "I'd guess there are politicos all over who would like to control him, including the international cartels."

"Yes, power is the reason some will seek the child. It has happened before," mused Father Gregory, shuffling his long legs into a comfortable position around the table leg. "Another incarnation in another place. Herod wanted to find the Christ child, to worship him, the king said, but . . ."

"God, when will they learn?" Kief rubbed his eyes casually, as if he was merely tired, but Radha knew there were tears in his eyes, as there were in her own.

"We've been directed to locate and protect the child." Philo's hand closed tightly around Shanti's. "You'll go with us, Radha?" he asked, looking out through the window, not at her. That was Philo's way, to look into the distance with his piercing, deep-set blue eyes, as though gazing into mysterious sources of wisdom that only he was evolved enough to penetrate.

Radha was silent a moment, waiting for the inner voice she had learned to trust. Two words flew into her mind, then faded as fast as they had come, *The task.*

"I'll go," she said. "But I've just come home. It's hard to leave so soon." Radha turned to Eddie, eyes pleading, her mouth closed tightly so her lips wouldn't tremble.

"I don't know if I'm intended to go." Eddie sat still, his back straight. "All I'm sure of is that I don't want to be separated from Radha again."

Elijah put his hand on Eddie's shoulder. "But you are one of us. We always thought you would become a monk." When Eddie took Radha's hand in answer, Elijah sighed, "Well, you are needed. I can see that."

"The holy child may need a doctor," Father Gregory said. "I am an old man, but still strong. I'll go with you."

"And I, too?" Brother Elijah's eyes brightened, his voice hopeful. Then he looked at Kori, whose face had clouded at his question. "Maybe not," he finished hastily, looking down.

"I want you to take my place, Elijah," Father Gregory said. "The monks will vote yes to that. What do you say, Kief? Have you enough help to run the place if three men leave?"

Kief looked up at the light. "It's been on my mind ever since Radha came back," he said, his voice low and grave. "Jason knows where she is, so we're already on borrowed time. He came for her before and he will come again. He is the military authority in this area, such authority as there still is, and we're at his mercy. I think you should go. Eddie and Father Gregory will be needed to help Philo protect the women and the child."

Radha's lips opened to protest, but her father held up his hand. "Yes, I know you're a warrior, but allow us to play our roles as men. We will protect you whether you like it or not."

"They must go very soon," Kori said. "In my dream, they were married, Philo and Shanti, Radha and Eddie. Just after they drove away, a storm swept in and destroyed the farm. I'm afraid we have very little time."

"Married to Radha?" Eddie's voice trembled. "I've dreamed of that too. But I can hardly expect . . ."

"Forget the past, Eddie." Kief put his arm around his friend's shoulders. "In this house you are loved. Believe it."

"It's settled, then. You will leave tomorrow morning," Kori said, her voice strong and impersonal, as if she were somewhere else. "You can reach the Ukiah monastery by vespers tomorrow evening and be out of Jason's jurisdiction."

Radha looked uncertainly at her mother, but Kori was staring into the distance, her eyes wide open as if trying to absorb more than human sight could hold.

"I'll rig the van with that long-life solar battery I've been working on since the old one died." Eddie smiled at Radha, his eyes crinkling at the corners. "Will you have this odd old Chinaman who loves you?"

"Old! For a man, fifty-four isn't old." Radha threw her arms around

him. "I'm not exactly fresh from the baker myself. Come on, Shanti.
We've got packing to do."

"Wait. Prayers first." Kori turned to the altar, where her icon of the
virgin and child was still side by side with Sai Baba's picture. On the wall
above the altar was a five-foot-long, roughly worked iron cross Brother
Elijah had cast as a gift for her. "We need your blessing on this task,
Father Gregory," Kori paused, "and on those of us who will be left."

A sudden pain knifed into the pit of Radha's stomach, and she ran to
her mother. "It didn't hit me until this minute that you will be staying
on the farm, you and Dad. Just when I've realized how much I love you,
I'll be losing you again. All my life has been about losing and letting go.
It's not fair," she cried, holding Eddie's hand with all her strength, as if
to warn God that she had better not lose him, too.

Looking across the table at her husband, Kori waited for his nod.
"We're old enough to hold our lives lightly," she said. "You must leave,
but I will not hide from what is coming." She lit the candle. "Now, we
will say the prayers and go to bed. Tomorrow will be a great day, and we
must be ready."

Just before dawn, as she often did, Radha dreamed of Kamal, who was
floating in a receding circle of light, his hand raised either in blessing or
farewell, she could not be sure which. Then he shrank into a single
bright point and disappeared. When he left this time, she sensed he
would not return. Tactful and self-effacing as always, she said to herself
upon awakening. As she did every morning, Radha prayed that Kamal
would be forgiven, but suddenly she realized that there was no longer
anything to forgive.

After showering, she ran her hands through her damp hair, hoping it
would dry in the sun. Since Radha didn't have a suitable dress to be married in, Shanti offered the rainbow sari. She herself would wear the traditional wedding attire, a flaming red sari, filigreed with gold, that her
mother had insisted she bring to America, although Shanti had no wish
ever to marry.

"My mother says that in the coming age not only gurus and avatars, but ordinary people like us will be spiritual teachers," Shanti told Radha, as she brushed the long black hair that fell below her waist. "Perhaps it has always been so." She began braiding a long golden ribbon into her hair. "Much work is done quietly by those who keep the message of love alive, spreading the word of God throughout the world. This is what we will do."

⮂

Standing before the monastery altar that evening with Eddie, Radha felt like a new creature, as she had once long ago when Father Gregory had baptized her. She thought about Shanti's words, as she and Eddie fed each other the communion bread. "Namasté," he whispered, placing the bread of life on her tongue.

"Namasté to you, dear one," she whispered back, bowing to her husband. They were consecrated as the hands of God in the world and would be one flesh, one instrument. The thought frightened her. Did this marriage mean she could never turn back, never again be free to go her own way? Then she looked into Eddie's eyes and saw her own face reflected in their dark depths, knowing that he was seeing himself in hers.

The sun broke through the dark clouds just as they left the chapel, and Radha held out her hands, as if to capture the earth and air of the farm one last time. She wanted to carry the feel of it with her wherever she went. Kori stepped into her daughter's open arms, making a small sign of the cross on her forehead with vibhuti. "The Lord Jesus Christ and his Blessed Mother go with you," she prayed, eyes closed as she lifted her face to the gray sky. "Sai Baba will guide and protect you always, my darling."

"We'll never see each other again, will we?" Radha gripped her mother's hands, wanting to stay, to rescue her, to die by her side, anything rather than to leave her.

"Not in this life, I think," Kori said, tenderly stroking Radha's damp hair.

Staring into her mother's eyes, which were full of light, Radha whispered, "You are one of those who's never coming back. You are already with God."

"As are we all," Kori said, her worn face brightening in a smile. "Now, we must speak of practical things." She walked briskly, guiding Radha to the room where Shanti was already packing. "The Prema ring I have already given to Philo, as Sai Baba told me to do," she said, hanging a leather pouch on a thong around her daughter's neck. "Your grandmother's jewels are in this bag. She gave them to me before leaving for Israel. You will find some diamond earrings, an emerald bracelet and a string of pearls. Use the pearls one by one as you travel. The rest will take care of you in India."

Radha's hand closed over the pouch as she gazed into her mother's eyes. Kori was giving her responsibility. Trusting her, not Philo. She swallowed hard, unable to speak.

"You are the one who has traveled and lived abroad," Kori said. "The others have less experience in the outside world. I trust you to watch over them." Looking toward the sun, which was again covered by dark gray clouds, Kori frowned. "Go quickly. There is not much time. I feel the storm coming."

Radha stowed her bag in the back of the van, leaving room for Father Gregory to lie on his mattress next to the back seat so he could stretch out his long legs. There was barely room for him after Kief loaded the box of supplies.

The priest said goodbye to his monks, lingering a moment with each one. He took Brother Elijah's hands last, giving him the kiss of peace on either cheek. "When trouble comes," he said, "you must hide in the hill cave, where we keep the winter food. Kief agrees that the monks are not to fight. Your job is to keep the monastery going, Father Elijah. There is no bishop here to make you a priest, but by my authority as abbot, that is what I declare you to be."

"Not stay to protect Kori?" The blood drained from Elijah's face, and he suddenly looked old. "How can I not stay?"

"You are still under obedience," Father Gregory said sternly. "I want your promise. You are to keep our monastery alive until the coming of the Lord."

What was left of the little community stood in a half circle watching the van drive away. They took the northern mountain road, avoiding the more traveled road up from the village. If Jason was approaching, he would take the easy, southern route.

When at last the van disappeared from sight, Kori handed Elijah the icon from her altar and her picture of Sai Baba. "Keep these safe for me."

Father Elijah nodded and looked into her eyes for a long moment before turning away. The monks followed him, carrying their belongings and the equipment they would need to set up a temporary monastery.

Tough as the scrubby mountain pines, Juan and Candelaria came forward, followed by the half dozen younger men and women who had settled on the farm over the years. "What do you want us to do?" Candelaria asked, her gnarled brown hands clutching Kief's carefully polished Winchester. "We are not soldiers, but we have fought off bears and wolves, and can fight off wolfish men."

After a glance at Kori, Kief said, "We want you to leave with the monks. They will need your help to start again. Take all the food from the kitchen and the blankets. Go. Hurry." Candelaria just looked at them without moving.

"We must remain here." Kori's voice was steady. "If we stay behind, the attackers may believe there are no others. But if the place is empty, they would track all of us down."

Knowing better than to protest, Candelaria took Kori's face in both hands and kissed her on the lips. The others grimly filed by, shaking hands but saying nothing.

Kori and Kief stood alone on the knoll and held each other. They didn't watch as their people followed the monks up the mountain, the last one taking great pains to straighten the trampled grass and hide their escape route.

Holding Kief's rough hand, Kori remembered the years of labor they had both put into this loved place. Her voice was light and tranquil as she looked into his eyes. "I think we will not see another day together, my love. Let us use the time well."

"You aren't afraid?" Kief put his hands on her shoulders. "I am, for you."

"You forget," Kori smiled, "I come from the people who invented the Götterdämmerung, the fall of the world into chaos. Smile, my dear. We are in the hands of God."

Cold, heavy drops of rain had started falling from the lowering clouds when they heard voices and the sound of trucks coming up the road. "I want to be in my house," Kori said with a low laugh. "It is not fitting to welcome guests out here in the rain."

"How can you be sure who's coming?" Kief followed her into the house, stooping to avoid the low lintel, as he had done ever since the house had been built. "You really do know, don't you?"

"In the old stories of my people," Kori said, taking the long metal cross down from the wall, "the Norsemen knew when their doom was upon them." Smiling, she held the hilt of the cross to her lips and went to the door. "Perhaps this is something I remember how to do from the old days of my people."

Kief stood beside her in the wide doorway, watching a gang of armed men, dressed in black, swarm over the ridge like a cloud of locusts. A harsh voice split the heavy, damp air as a thin, light-haired man took the lead. "I want the one named Radha taken alive," he shouted over his shoulder. "The rest of 'em you can trash."

"I can't do it," Kief cried out, his voice breaking. "I can't stand here and watch them kill you." Shouting and waving his arms wildly, he ran toward the intruders.

The assailants had obviously been told to save their precious ammunition. As she saw Kief brought down by the swinging rifle butts, a tide of blood rose behind Kori's eyes, and rage filled her until her soul was swamped. She drew herself up to her full height, not much less than the six feet of her youth. When the first man reached her, she swung the iron cross like a two-handed sword, knocking him to the ground. After hitting the next man squarely on the head, she howled an animal sound that shook her whole body. "Now, I am not pure enough to join God. I will return to serve the Lord Prema, when he comes in *Gloria Dei Patris.*"

Standing just out of reach of the swinging cross, Jason calmly shot the old woman point-blank in the stomach. Braced by the cross held close to her heart, Kori fell to her knees. "Om Sai Ram," she whispered with a smile. "You will not find my daughter, poor man. She returns the ring to its source." As her body closed down, the blood thundered in Kori's head and she heard a sound like a great house falling.

Before he set fire to the homestead, Jason looked down at the peaceful face of the woman he had killed. His face twisted with fury as the butt of his rifle pounded again and again into her bleeding body. Consuelo would not hanker to go home, he told himself, now that the old woman was gone. He looked forward to telling this most aloof and unmanageable of his wives that the woman she loved as a mother was dead.

Many hours later, after the invaders had left, the monks slipped down out of the hills. Finding the entire ranch and the monastery a smoking ruin, they searched through the ashes until they found what was left of Kori. She was clutching the iron cross, which was still hot to the touch.

Elijah prayed over her body, one thin, blue-veined hand resting on Kori's remains. "We will bury her under this cross, up on the hill, where she can feel the sea wind," he said. "The new monastery will be built over the altar of her bones." Kneeling in the ashes, he began to sing the Mass for the Dead, *"Requies aeterna . . ."*

The last of the winter rains turned the ground to mud, making it ready for seed.

On her wedding night, Radha stood in the dim little chapel of the Ukiah Monastery, as enameled figures of gold-edged icons seemed to look through her with dark, staring eyes. The deep roar of monks' voices curled into her ears as if she were listening to the sea through a conch shell. How her mother would have loved this place, Radha thought. She blinked back tears and sniffed, making up a story in her mind that her parents would hide in the caves where they would be safe if Jason's men attacked. It was something she had done as a child, making up stories about how she wanted the real world to be. A story was at least better than the surge of fear, the flood of swirling thoughts that threatened to drown her if she couldn't hold events at arm's length and manage them.

Radha sighed shakily and wiped her face with the rough sleeve of her sweater. Eddie held her other hand against his heart, watching her face instead of the monk who was swinging a gold incense holder, sending out a dark thread of smoke that spiraled up into the dome above them.

"Let my hands rise to thee like the evening sacrifice." Eddie sang the words of the liturgy, his eyes so warm and intense that Radha had to look away. He was inviting her into a communion so total that it could drown her, and she did not know how to answer. For such a man, she would need to be sure of her divinity and his, to put aside her ego with its games and small passions. Eddie was asking her to consecrate herself to a marriage that was much more than the joining of bodies.

Shanti had explained that in the tradition of her people, when a marriage is consummated, the man becomes a god and the woman a goddess. Like hub and spokes of a wheel, together they roll a fiery chariot into bliss. No trace of separateness remains. Radha shuddered at this idea, for deep inside her was the desire to keep a little bit of self hidden away as security. Suppose God planned, of course with her best spiritual interests at heart, to strip her of every earthly pleasure and security? She dropped Eddie's hand and gripped the pouch of jewels hanging around her neck. I could not bear to be helpless, to be vulnerable to whatever comes, she prayed silently. I'm not strong enough.

Recognizing that fear was the real reason for her reluctance to let go, her cheeks reddened with shame. "Wash me with hyssop and I shall be purer than snow," she sang, her husky alto merging with Eddie's baritone. As the priest sprinkled them with holy water from a little pine branch, a pang of nostalgia swept over her for the canopied Jewish wedding she had never had.

In their little room after the vespers, they pushed the two narrow beds together. Radha sat beside Eddie, trying to explain how she felt, wanting to be clear of past ghosts and present desires that drove her like a leaf in the wind. But she couldn't complete the prayer of surrender, Mary's prayer: "Be it done unto me according to thy will. Whatever it takes to unite me with thee, that I ask, O God." As the "whatever" stuck in her throat, she looked at Eddie with bleak, defiant eyes. "My will be done," were the words that came to her, but she was too ashamed to utter them.

"Maybe you can begin with another kind of surrender." He gently ran his hands through her hair and down her shoulders.

"You mean to you?" Radha drew back, unsure about Eddie's idea of surrender, but afraid he might have some odd Oriental notions like expecting his wife to kiss his feet.

"To us," he said, kissing her gently on the lips. "To what we can become together." Then he pulled her down against his body. "The bridegroom gives his life to his bride as Christ gave his for the church," Eddie whispered. "I will give mine to you, Radha, in the same way."

As they made love, she had a sense of being a wide, fertile field, swarming with bees and flowers. Her husband was a great cloud raining down on her. Faceless and wild, they were ecstatic as birds hurling themselves into flight. Radha felt like an awkward virgin on this unfamiliar ground, where bodies and souls were indistinguishably merged.

Later, when she was falling asleep in his arms, he was just Eddie again, with a mole on his shoulder and a thin, slightly wrinkled neck. But she loved him no less for being his small, human self. As they burrowed close together under their single blanket, the warmth of his body protected her from the cold wind that came whistling through cracks in the plaster walls.

⚬⚬⚬

The next morning they left the monastery, traveling up the old Interstate Five to Washington-Columbia. Radha did not join in their conversation about what the third Baba, Prema Sai, might do to change the world. She sat back, quietly watching the distant mountains become clearer and more rugged as they drove north.

Driving as fast as the frequent potholes allowed, Philo gestured with his free hand. "Why do people forget what Shirdi Baba did?" he asked, glancing fondly at Shanti. "Just because he had fewer followers doesn't mean he had a smaller role in all that has happened. He taught duty to God and tolerance of all religions. Those have to come first, before we're ready for the more popular stuff."

Shanti curled her small brown fingers around Philo's waving hand. "You talk as if you had been with Shirdi Baba, as if you knew him in the flesh, the way I knew Sathya Sai, when I was a child."

"Yes. I feel as if I do know him." Philo nodded his head vigorously. "Just last week I had a dream where he frowned at me and shook his finger, saying that I must not forget there are others in my world besides me."

Radha wanted to interrupt and say that Shirdi Baba was right. Her brother had always gone his own way, not considering the feelings of others. He thought everyone should be like him, strong, needing no one. At least he seemed to need Shanti, if only as a backboard to bounce his opinions off. Since Shanti seldom seemed to have any opinions of her own, Philo was able to maintain the illusion that she agreed with him, whether she did or not.

Leaning over the back seat, Father Gregory scratched his silver-thatched head until his thick hair stood on end. "If Shirdi Sai spoke for duty, then Sathya Sai taught us to see the divinity in every person and love that divinity, just as Jesus did. My question is, what is left for Prema Sai to teach?" Father Gregory had a deep fear that he had misplaced the meaning of his life when he chose to abandon everything for God. He clung to the hope that God would offer a sign that his course had been the right one. Patiently, the priest had waited for the sign which did not come.

Nobody answered until Shanti cleared her throat and said, "Prema Sai will give humankind the understanding that not only does God live in everyone, but that everyone is God, with a human face. Only then will we learn to love each other as God loves us."

"As I am in the Father, so you are in me and I in you," Eddie murmured. "Jesus said the same thing, but people couldn't hear it."

"So we can't truly love," Radha said, "unless we see the other person as divine." She stared at Eddie, wondering if she could possibly love him as if he were God. It would take more than willpower, maybe some kind of transformation of the entire human race, to make people see themselves and each other as divine. Prema Sai has his work cut out for him, Radha thought, looking through the mud-spattered windows at the fortified houses they passed. In each fortress, an armed man was king, ready to do battle with his brother.

"We'll stop at the Seattle airport," Philo said, veering back onto the main highway. "I've heard they have three planes a day leaving for India."

"We should save money if we can." Radha squeezed her leather pouch, thinking how insignificant the contents seemed. "We don't know how much things will cost in India."

"Shanti?" Philo turned off the highway at the rusty green and white airport sign. "Is India more expensive than here?"

"I grew up near the ashram, and nothing was expensive there," she said, shaking her head. "Sathya Sai Baba had insisted on that. I don't know what things cost anywhere else. My ticket was given to me, so I don't even know how much it was."

Radha didn't say what she was thinking, that they were walking into the unknown, and that Philo would learn the hard way to value his sister's experience. She folded her hands over the pouch, as if to remind everyone who was in charge of the money.

A light spring rain was falling when the taxi dropped them at the airport. At Philo's insistence, they had sold the van for Washington-Columbian cash, hoping the money would be enough for five one-way tickets to India. As they stood in the ticket line, Radha brushed her palms over her wet hair and shook off the rain.

When it was time for Philo and Radha to step forward, the clerk impatiently snapped his fingers. "You." He jerked his chin at Philo. "Show me your trademark."

The others anxiously waited behind the yellow line, gripping the handles of their bags. Having no idea what a trademark was, Philo looked at Radha, then back at the clerk, shrugging his shoulders. "Do you want to see our passports?"

"What are you people, hicks?" The clerk pulled Philo's hand over to the light on the desk. "Nope. No trademark, no tickets."

"How about this?" Radha held out the cash, shaking it under his nose. "You know what money is?"

"So tell us," Philo said coolly, stepping in front of her. "What's a trademark?"

"The order came through three months ago," the clerk said. "You gotta have the holochip in your hand, otherwise nobody will sell you nothing." He raised his voice. "Now, move on or I'll call the cops."

The group left the ticket desk and conferred in the corner of the airport. Clearly resigning any responsibility, Shanti sat on her bag, a little behind the others. Radha glared at her, wondering why it was that other women found it so easy to enter a dream world and not come out until the men had decided what to do. She gripped her brother's arm. "Nice work, Philo. No plane tickets, and the van is history. Any other great ideas?"

"If memory serves," Philo said, "you were the one afraid to leave from San Francisco, so we had to drive north. It wasn't my choice."

"The fact remains," Radha said, overriding any reminders of her own responsibility, "you insisted we sell the van before you knew whether or not we could get tickets."

Eddie put his arm around her. "We've got to remember what our whole trip is about. Some good will come of this, if we look for it."

Glancing around, Philo spoke in a sharp voice, "Where is Shanti? And Father Gregory?" He found them just around the corner in the lounge area, sitting on either side of a small man with tousled white hair and thin white eyebrows that rose to a point over his nose.

Shanti introduced the man as Narayana, a retired businessman on his way home to India. "Look!" she exclaimed, her eyes bright. "He is wearing a ring Sai Baba made for him forty years ago."

Radha pulled up her bag and sat at the old man's feet. "Your name sounds familiar," she said. "What kind of business were you in?"

"My name is a common one," he said, "and what I did, alas, was unimportant. Come, tell me why you are scolding each other." He looked inquiringly from Radha to Philo.

Embarrassed, Radha looked down, wishing her voice were not so loud, that she had not blamed Philo for something they had all agreed upon. Her cheeks flushed, and she realized that blaming Philo was what she always did, before he could blame her. They were still caught in the web that had trapped them since childhood, and now this stranger was taking Kori's role, making peace between them. Radha wondered if she would always need someone else to make peace for her, and within her.

"We're in trouble," she said to the old Indian, finding comfort in his soft brown eyes that crinkled when he smiled. "We need to get to India. But we don't have a trademark, whatever that is."

"Nor do I," Narayana said. "I am traveling the only way I can, by private transport. Without the trademark, no one can travel any other way."

"Who decided everybody needs a trademark?" Father Gregory's fingers were running over his rosary at a furious rate, as they often did when he was trying to figure something out.

"Brom Strassbourg, the head of Eurocom, has decreed that no one can buy or sell without the mark. His way of keeping track of everyone. It will prove very inconvenient to us ordinary people, I fear." The old Indian shook his head, reflectively twisting the ring with Sai Baba's face on it.

Father Gregory sighed, "It sounds to me like the prophecy is being fulfilled." His big hand closed over the cross of his rosary. "The Beast is demanding that everyone wear his mark. It is beginning."

"What beast?" Radha asked, her heart beating hard. "What is beginning?"

"The time of persecution," Eddie said. "What Christian scriptures call the Last Days before Jesus comes again to save his people."

"Earthquakes, floods, famine," Father Gregory added. "We have them all now, plus immorality, pestilence and a scorching sun." He rolled his rosary into a ball. "Maybe we should have just stayed home to wait for the second coming."

"We've always had natural disasters," Radha argued. "Is it really any worse now than it was before?"

"I think perhaps it is," Narayana said, rubbing his chin as he stared into the distance. "In my work, I was often exposed to the ills of the world. So many of the young are dying of the new AIDS virus and so many others from poverty and violence. There seems no pity left, no simple kindness."

Shanti leaned close, as if she wanted to put her arms around him. "Don't give up hope," she whispered. "Our savior, Prema Sai, has been born. God is once more on the earth."

"You know of Prema Sai?" The old man stopped twisting his ring and stared at her.

"We are going to him," Shanti nodded, "to serve him, if we can."

"I, too, am going to see him," Narayana said, looking around at the circle of faces. "I may be too old to serve him, but I can serve you. A friend is coming to drive me to the Bellingham port, and another is sending a yacht to take me to Madras. You are welcome to join me."

"Jai!" Shanti cried, clapping her hands. Radha had never seen her so excited. "Thank you, Sri Narayana. Sai Ram!" She bowed to him, hands pointed under her chin.

"You may all call me Narayan," said the old man, rising so slowly that Eddie put a hand under his elbow. "For too long I have been burdened with heavy titles. I am too old for anything but simplicity. Come, my friends. The man who will drive us is waiting at the door."

Sitting on a jump seat in the limousine, Radha wondered who Narayan really was. No one but the very wealthy and powerful had access to luxury like this. Then she remembered seeing his face on the telecon just before leaving Jerusalem. The UN had sent its top official to persuade the Arabs not to invade Israel's vulnerable midsection. Arab troops had been surging toward the Israeli border through the new Palestinian state. This man, Narayan Tewati, had offered the Arabs a UN-sponsored loan that would help industrialize the western half of Jordan and Arab towns on the West Bank. Of course, the Arabs were not told that the Israelis would pay for most of it. Having struck a temporary peace between two mortal enemies, Secretary-General Narayan Tewati left while he was ahead.

That meant grim days to come for Israel, Radha sighed, remembering that her son's kibbutz was only thirty miles from the border. Whatever the risk, perhaps she should have insisted that the family return to America when Ibrahim was a baby. But even had he survived the threat from Jason, he would have missed the benefit of his Israeli education. Kori had often complained that in California her children had slipped into barbaric ignorance, playing with coarse, unkempt children who used poor English and spat. Well, Radha thought, her mother could not have complained of Ibrahim, for the boy was skilled in Arabic, Hebrew and English. Though only fourteen, he was planning to study ancient languages at Hebrew University. Her parents had passed on their academic genes, though they would probably never know it.

The evening mist hovered over the blue ridge of mountains to the east as they drove into Anacortes, the harbor town south of Bellingham. Fingers of water from Puget Sound jutted inland between irregular rolling hills, covered with azaleas, clumpy rhododendron bushes and the ragged red-barked madrona trees. Mount Baker rose in the distance like a white fist over the ridge of foothills. Beyond were the Cascades, a line of snowy mountain peaks that rippled like a high, white-topped wave.

Before carrying her bag down to the waiting yacht, Radha paused to look back at the lush greenery and flowers dripping with dew. She wanted to tell everyone that she would stay here, for this was paradise. The mission she had believed in since first hearing the voice in her head now seemed preposterous, as though she had confused a movie with real life. In order to find some mysterious child, she was leaving one of the few places on the planet where they could live unhampered by the whims of gods or men. Since she was always tangling with Philo, Radha thought, maybe it would be best if she and Eddie used some of the diamonds to buy a little farm in this magical place. Her brother and the others could continue on with the rest of the jewels. Then Philo would be supreme high commander of everybody in sight, just the way he wanted.

"My dear child." Narayan's voice, reminded her that the others were all waiting on the boat. "Once having put your hand to the plow, do not look back," he smiled. "Or a stone will fly up and hit you in the head. Remember always, dear Radha, the high purpose for which you have come into the world. The service that you do for others is the service you do for yourself."

Embarrassed that Narayan seemed to know her selfish thoughts, Radha reluctantly lifted her bag and followed him onto the gleaming, stream-lined yacht. She had not expected to hear the voice of God from the mouth of this little Indian man, who had wealthy friends in high places.

As the ship moved out of the harbor, Radha stood beside Eddie at the rail, watching the small, loaf-shaped islands slide by. Like my life, she thought, like everything else in my life I have had to leave behind. She tried to cheer herself up by thinking of Prema Sai and how he would love her. But all she could see in her mind's eye was the face of her son, shrinking to a dot and disappearing, like the last island before the open sea.

12

Holding his head in his hands, Nazim let Consuelo's letter drop to the floor. As he sat on the pile of cushions Yasmin had arranged for him in the corner of their tent, the cold wind surging down from the hills chilled him to the bone. Without being asked, Yasmin brought hot tea she had heated on their primitive gas burner and sat next to him. He absently patted her shoulder so she would feel appreciated. Yasmin yearned for approval and constantly broke into his periods of silence to ask what he might want. His wife wanted attention, Nazim supposed, as much as he wanted silence. She was trying to do what she thought Fatima would have done, and it was not Yasmin's fault that she did not have Fatima's instinct for self-effacing service.

It must be hard on poor Yasmin, he thought, glancing at the few conveniences in this, their temporary home on the newly drawn border with Israel. He had, of course, offered to set her up in the house they had left in Amman years before, but she had insisted on accompanying him. She must have thought him a foolish old man, wanting to die among his people, sharing their poverty, since he could not relieve it. The great schemes of his past had resettled most of the Arab refugees, but somehow they remained as poor as always, still living in tents, still tending their scrawny flocks and tiny vegetable gardens.

He glanced at the letter again, pulling the edges of a worn wool blanket around his thin shoulders. Was this what things had come to since he and Homer Healey had schemed to replace the American government years before? Murdering an old couple and burning down their farmhouse, all to find this woman who so obsessed Jason? He did not so much desire Radha, Nazim reflected, as he desired revenge. She had insulted Jason by rejecting him, so he had ended by killing her parents. A foolish son of a foolish mother.

Nazim closed his eyes and stared into the darkness. He should not have placed his hopes on Jason. His foster son was a barbarian who had never understood the scriptures. Nazim winced, remembering how the boy had squirmed through the lessons which he and the imam had tried to teach. He also realized he had guessed wrong in his choice of America. He would have done better going to Paris, now capital of the Unified European Community, in order to influence its rising star, Brom Strassbourg.

"The building without a firm base," he thought aloud. "Do not build it high. Or if you do, be afraid."

"Surely you are not afraid." Yasmin poured more tea, though he did not want it. "You have never been afraid of anything."

"You do not know," he murmured, "how much I fear that I have ill-served Allah. So many are dead because of me, so few better off."

"You are thinking of Kamal, perhaps?" Yasmin ventured, rubbing his cold feet as she often did, since his circulation had begun to fail.

"It would be a great comfort if Kamal were here now. The men who shot him hoped to please me but took from me one of the few pleasures I might have had in my final days." Not wanting to hurt her feelings, he glanced down. "Except for you, of course, my dear. Now, bring my writing table. I must answer Consuelo."

Nazim had much to say to the woman who ran Jason's household and had more influence on him than anyone else. She should be made aware of certain world events that were forming a disturbing pattern. "The small national and tribal governments of the West," he wrote, "are gradually falling under the economic influence of the European Community and its corporate network. It is only a matter of time before the non-industrialized Muslim world will also be threatened.

"Europe's central Starburst mainframe, which controls all the generators from Britain to Siberia, has nearly eliminated the need for oil. With this mainframe, Brom Strassbourg now dominates the European community and clearly means to dominate the world. The more primitive Asian Starburst can be operated independently, but is not powerful enough to run the subtle, interlinked technology of the West. For that, Brom Strassbourg's mainframe is needed. Of course, now that neither East nor West is dependent on fossil fuels, the Arabs have little left to bargain with but threats of violence.

"It would be wise for Jason to link up with the Muslim countries of Asia," Nazim continued. "They will have access to the new generator being developed by India, without paying European prices for connecting to Strassbourg's mainframe in Paris. You would also do well to turn Jason's eyes toward the Pacific and invite representatives from Malaysia, Indonesia and Vietnam to invest in Mexical, before the region collapses in poverty, disease and violence. I am concerned about the drought, now that the Healies in the north have closed off the water supply before it can reach San Francisco."

Nazim ended the letter with a polite wish that Jason be well. It is bad enough to have no water, he sighed to himself, thinking of the boy he had raised. Worse, to have no character. Telling Yasmin to mail the letter, he lay back and watched the camelhide ceiling swaying above him as the tent poles bent in the wind. Some men had bad dreams, but Nazim saw worse visions when he was awake. If a man's sleep is better than his waking, he said to himself, it is time to die.

Consuelo seemed to sense his need for spiritual comfort, just as Fatima had. She studied the scriptures of several faiths and often wrote to him of what she had learned. This time, her letter included a picture of Prema Sai Baba, the great prophet who had recently been born in

India. The picture, as Nazim held it close to his dim eyes, looked like pictures he had seen of Jesus, with the long dark hair and short beard. He did not understand how anyone could tell what the infant would look like as an adult. Still, Nazim propped the picture beside him and studied the face, which had a curious appeal.

Perhaps this was the prophet coming to announce the last days before the Judgment. He remembered the Koran's words that the earth would be rocked in a final convulsion and men would be burned by a scorching fire. Surely that day was at hand. Earthquakes were occurring everywhere, and the sun's rays scorched the earth without mercy, now that the ozone layer had dwindled almost to nothing. If only the Arabs' billions had been spent on saving the rain forests and the Palestinian refugees, instead of on gambling and fine cars.

His heart fluttered erratically like a door flap shaking in the wind, and Nazim wondered if perhaps the only Judgment is the moment each man must face as he dies, the moment when God fills up his senses like the noon sun. Surely this prophet of India, this Prema Sai, would remind the dying to seek refuge from the scorching fire of the unjust. "O, let me be deemed to have been fair," Nazim prayed, tears stinging his eyes. "Stand witness for me before God, O prophet with the gentle face, that above all things, I sought justice and truth."

As he gazed into the deep, shadowy eyes of Prema Sai, the words of the Koran hummed in his ears like bees' wings. *My son, God will bring all things to light, be they hidden inside a rock. He is ever disposed to mercy.* Yusef Nazim smiled as he fell asleep, hoping that Yasmin would not be too disturbed when she could not wake him.

Consuelo was still wearing the black caftan she had put on weeks before, when Jason told her that Kori was dead. When he had objected, Consuelo cut her long hair to shoulder length and warned that if he complained again, she would shave her head completely. He knew her well enough to believe it. She could never forgive him, Consuelo said to herself, as she stared out the window into the garden. She had stayed in her room for more than a month, refusing to speak to him. He could hardly object, since Ayesha was there to take over the household. But Ayesha had a limited culinary repertoire and could not handle his correspondence.

Consuelo leaned over to smell the jasmine, which was just opening its small white trumpets to herald the arrival of spring. It was time to stop mourning, she decided, running her sturdy fingers through her tangled black hair. Kori would not have approved of this withdrawal from duty, nor would Nazim, whom she had grown to love in the year before he had left. Many times they had sat together on the white stone bench under this very window, talking about the nature of God. He had allowed her to order Sanskrit books, then asked her to read to him about Brahman, the unknowable, the formless one, whom he was sure was the same Allah he worshipped under another name.

A rustle across the room caused Consuelo to turn. Someone, probably Jason, had slipped a letter under the door. As usual, he was trying to win her back without losing face. Since he had forced her to marry him nearly twenty years before, their roles had subtly shifted. She had known at the time that she was only a stand-in for Radha. But after so many years and the birth of his two sons, Jason seemed to have convinced himself that she was the one he had wanted in the first place. However, Radha had once been his, and it galled him to have lost her. Consuelo carefully destroyed the few letters and pictures that her friend had discreetly sent via travelers coming to America from the Middle East. Since Radha was a lazy correspondent, most of Consuelo's foreign mail came from Nazim.

She sat down to read Nazim's letter, which Jason had obviously opened first. It was true that they should link up with the Muslim countries in Asia. She had often told him so, but he was too stubborn to listen. Jason wanted no help; he would rule alone as Premier of Mexical. His parents, Annie and David, had learned long ago not to contradict him. Besides, Annie had grown immensely fat and lay around all day watching music videos and action game shows on the telecon. David, who had Alzheimer's, couldn't remember where the bathroom was, let alone the location or significance of Asia. So it was up to her, Consuelo reflected, to insure that her eighteen-year-old son Rumi would inherit more than an empty title and a home under siege by starving barbarians. Ali, their fifteen-year-old, should inherit something too, but because he so strongly resembled Jason, Consuelo did not trust him.

There was a tentative knock at the door. "All right, Jason." Consuelo remained in her chair, studying the letter. "You can come in. The door's not locked."

"I thought you might be over your snit by now." Jason stood awkwardly in front of her, since the only other chair was well across the room. His thin, graying hair had receded from his forehead, leaving a large, bony expanse that made him look more intelligent than he was. His jaw was set at a grim angle, in an expression learned from Nazim. Jason used it whenever he expected her to disagree with him. He pointed at the letter. "After all these years, Nazim still writes to you, not me."

"I suppose he knows you will read the letter anyway," Consuelo replied, not looking up.

"You gonna let your hair grow nice and long again or keep it in a mess, just to put me off?" He waved his arms in the air, as he did during pep talks to his men. "Where are the sweet little women anymore? Where do I have to go to find a wife that will show me respect?"

"Have you tried Bangladesh?" Consuelo leaned back in her chair and stared at the ceiling.

"Aw, honey, y'know I don't want nobody but you." Jason reached out to touch her, but she pulled away, holding the letter between them.

"We need to talk about this," she said. "Kuala Lumpur and Singapore each want to set up Starburst plants here, a dozen manufacturing centers up and down the coast. We could get out from under the oilmen once and for all."

"I ain't under nobody, y'hear?" Jason clasped his hands behind his back and walked around the room, staring fiercely at the Mexican tile floor.

"Of course you're not." Consuelo rolled her eyes, praying for patience. "You have valuable territory that everybody wants, and you can get a high price for it. Insist that they pay you for protection and providing trained workers. That way you get something for nothing."

"I guess they'd know I'm smarter than them if they have to pay for my advice," Jason mumbled. "I'll think about it. But it's me that decides, Consuelo. Remember that."

"Something else for you to think about," she said, going over to the vanity table to brush her thick, coarse hair. "Nazim warns against Eurocom. But why not meet this Brom Strassbourg and get Eurocom investing here, too? Nazim would be astonished, and it's not easy to astonish Nazim."

"Hey, that's true." Jason snapped his fingers. "He'd see that I'm a better operator even than him. If this Strassbourg guy would come out here, we could pick his brains, get this place going again. I remember how it used to be, and I'm sick of the pigpen it is now." He was smiling, obviously glad to be pleasing both himself and her at the same time.

"So you're ready for me to write those letters?" Consuelo hoped he would stay with business, since she did not want the same hands that killed Kori to touch her, not ever again.

Jason pulled at the buttons of her black robe. "In a while, honey. I been waitin' a long time for you to come around."

Consuelo sent her spirit far away, thinking of the task she had accepted and of the Sanskrit words that danced in her mind like tongues of fire, *You are the master of your senses. Where there is purity, there is divinity.* Jason never guessed that she was not really in his arms.

❧

Radha was surprised at the speed of the bullet train that took them from the new seaport to the inland city of Mysore on the Karnataka plateau. Even though the AIDS epidemic and the coastal floods had taken a third of the population, those who were left seemed healthy and prosperous. They were well paid for their work and had neat, solidly built homes. The rich, black soil of Karnataka produced more than enough to feed them, and many were growing wealthy selling excess food to Africa. Tewati said that the epidemic had hit even harder there and that the desertification would take another generation to turn around. India's Starburst machinery was already at work in East Africa and the southern Sahara, powering huge irrigation systems and desalinization plants, like the ones between Madras and Mysore.

Shanti explained that Karnataka, which had been settled for more than ten thousand years, had always been a garden place. Even the metamorphic rocks were rich in both iron and gold, she said. As in all earthly things, the ordinary and the sublime were inextricably tangled in Karnataka.

As they passed over the gentle rise of the Eastern Ghats, worn down by water and wind to a shadow of their former height, the sun reflected off the quartz in the gray-green rocks. When the train reached the southern upland of Karnataka, the country became more rugged—a series of plateaus between jagged, rocky hills. These ghats, Radha learned, were natural steps up the western side of the mountains facing the Arabian Sea. She could understand why the maharajahs had chosen to live here above the green rice paddies and slow, brown rivers, more than a thousand feet over the steaming plains.

Their little group would rest for a few days and consult Tewati's friend at the main Sai Baba center, now the spiritual heart of the city. After the dirt and noise of coastal cities, the trees and wide streets of downtown Mysore were a welcome relief. Still, the heat was oppressive and the air heavy with unshed rain.

Tewati's friend had reserved rooms for them at the Hotel Siddhartha, a government guest house. From her balcony, Radha looked across the lush gardens at the Maharajah's white marble palace. Rising like a giant

wedding cake against the skyline, this sprawling, intricately carved structure was a monument to the marriage of Hindu and Muslim architecture. How many civilizations had risen and fallen here, she reflected,
blending into one another through mixed marriages like her own and
Philo's. It seemed as if the course of nature would blend humanity into
one family, despite the racists who struggled to keep their people pure of
alien blood. Though Sai Baba's ideal of harmony among all religions had
gained billions of adherents around the world, many hearts were still
closed where the marriages of their children were concerned.

At the Sai Baba Center on Mirza Street, just a short, shady walk from
their hotel, they met Jagdish, Tewati's friend who had sent him word of
Prema Sai's birth in the nearby village of Gunaparthi. As Radha sat on a
plastic chair between Eddie and Father Gregory, she wondered if her
long silk skirt would stick to her legs when she stood up. Shanti had
warned her to dress respectfully, in keeping with the Sai organization's
rigorous code. Religious Indians were as firm about modest clothing as
were Orthodox Jews. Radha felt they had reason to be strict, since the
very air of Mysore was sensuous, permeated by the odor of incense. Her
head swam, dizzy with the sweet scent of jasmine laced with the pungent
aroma of sandalwood.

Jagdish, the head of the Sai Center, was a stiff-backed, middle-aged
man who had a heavy streak of vibhuti across his forehead. He lit a long
sliver of blue-tipped sandalwood, gratuitously adding to the aroma
already hanging in the warm, moist air. "You are not the only ones who
have come looking for the child, Sri Narayan," he said, his crisp British
accent clipping the fast rolling music of his Indian English. "I have
recently been contacted by representatives of Eurocom and also an
American religious group. Hellies, I believe they call themselves, rather
ominously, I might say."

"Healies," Radha corrected him, ignoring Shanti's slight shake of the
head. "Christian fundamentalists. I'm sure they'd like to get hold
of the child. Prema will welcome everybody into his Parousia, but

fundamentalists think they're the only ones who'll be invited."

Jagdish cleared his throat and nodded curtly in her direction. She could see that being corrected by anyone, let alone a woman, did not sit well with him. "We here at the center are prepared for any threats to the child's safety. He has already been moved from his birthplace at Gunaparthi to secret quarters here in Mysore."

"The group Brom Strassbourg sent," Tewati's voice was low and serious. "I am perhaps to blame for that."

"We directed them to some inaccessible villages up in the Western Ghats," Jagdish said. "If the heat doesn't finish their search, the monsoons will. You understand, Sri Narayan, that the Sai Centers are totally opposed to Western influences on the child."

Radha opened her mouth to argue the point, then closed it firmly, rolling her eyes to the ceiling, which was elaborately painted with a blue-faced Krishna and his female retinue. This man, who Tewati said was a great scholar of the Vedas, clearly had no use for any point of view but his own.

"I have longed to see this child since Sai Baba's prophecy of his birth forty years ago." Tewati's gnarled hands twisted together in his lap. "Can you arrange a darshan for us?"

Jagdish moved the chair back from his desk, as if to distance himself. "No Westerners are allowed," he said. "And even you, Sri Narayan, will have to be taken in a car with blackened windows to where we have hidden Prema Sai."

"You've got him living like a prisoner?" Radha burst out. "Don't his parents find that just a little highhanded?"

Jagdish frowned, vibhuti from his forehead sifting down as his thick, dark brows came together. "They bow to the necessity of protecting the holy child and understand that he must be in the care of his devotees. We cannot allow any influence from strangers who come in the name of other gods." He stared balefully at Radha, as if she represented some heathen conspiracy.

"Other gods," Radha muttered, folding her arms as she looked at the floor. "Unless you're still in the last yuga, there's only one God. I thought word had gotten around."

"I would like to go with Sri Narayan," Shanti interrupted before Jagdish could escalate his battle with Radha. "Since I am not a Westerner, would I be allowed?"

"You come here representing another Sai Center?" Jagdish straightened the papers on his desk. "Not every center has the same plans for the child Prema as we do."

"I come from Prasanthi Nilayam," Shanti said, her voice stronger than before. "And the politics of the centers have never concerned me."

Pushing aside the pile of papers on his polished teak desktop, Jagdish rose from his chair. "Very well. I will take the two of you this afternoon. Sri Narayan, will you join me now for tea? The rest of you will excuse us, please."

When they were outside in the gated courtyard, Philo turned to Shanti. "Good thinking. Maybe you can help us follow the car."

"And how is she supposed to do that?" Radha held the damp coil of hair off the back of her neck, praying for a breeze. "They probably won't even let her open a window."

"I think Philo's expecting she'll wear a sensor," Eddie said. "We should be able to buy cellular equipment somewhere around here. I'll tinker something together so we can track the car."

By the time they were ready to leave that afternoon, Eddie had pinned a tiny round transmitter to Shanti's choli, the short-sleeved blouse she wore with her silver and olive-green sari. When the dark blue sedan with blackened rear windows turned off Harishchandra Road into a jumble of smaller streets, the taxi carrying Radha, Philo, Eddie and Father Gregory followed at a discreet distance. To avoid being pursued, the driver of the sedan twisted and turned through residential back streets. If not for the steady beep of Shanti's transmitter, the trail would have disappeared.

After their circuitous route, the sedan stopped at a small apartment house on Dhanvantri Road, close to the railroad station. Almost hidden among the large hotels, this building was surrounded by a pointed iron fence. The taxi waited half a block away, until Tewati and Shanti had entered with Jagdish.

"Strange," Father Gregory said, "we're visiting the Nazareth of our time." He looked out at the graceful figures of sari-clad women and dark men with white cloths twisted around their bodies. "I don't suppose the people looked much different back then."

"Those do." Radha sat up straight, pointing at three fair-skinned men in shorts and open-necked shirts, who were heading for the apartment house gate. One carried what appeared to be a large camera bag, so heavy it pulled his shoulder down.

"Wait for us," Philo said to the driver. "My guess is that these guys belong to Brom Strassbourg."

"Eddie, you and Father Gregory go for the one with the bag," Radha said, running to keep up with Philo's long strides. "Philo and I'll take the other two."

"Hold it," Eddie stopped outside the open door to the apartment house. "Hang back just a little. We can't be sure they're not tourists. Not yet."

Entering the cool, high-ceilinged hallway, they could hear the fast, firm steps of the three men on the tile floor. "They're just around the corner," Radha whispered, her hand on Philo's arm. "Sounds like they've stopped."

"I say we get them before they're through the door," Philo said. "We don't want to endanger the child or Shanti."

When they heard a muffled explosion, all four ran, following the sound. "They blew the lock," Eddie said. "We've got to hit that guy with the bag before they get their torps out." Eddie had told Radha about the new weapons that found their targets automatically through heat sensors.

"Okay, go!" whispered Philo, as he ran through the door and tackled one blond man who was reaching for his torp. Radha cried out a warning when a second man pointed his weapon at a dark, slender woman holding a baby. The woman's mouth was open in a silent cry. Radha's heart pounded painfully when she realized that Brom's men had been ordered to kill the parents when they seized the child.

Moving lightly despite his age and size, Father Gregory darted in front of the mother and child just as a flash of light shot from the torp. After Radha and Eddie knocked the gunman against the wall, Philo snatched the weapon as it slid across the waxed floor.

"Father Gregory," Shanti cried, running to the priest, who had fallen forward when the missile hit his chest. "We'll get help." She bent over, cradling his head in her lap.

The three men saw their chance and took off, shoving Radha aside as she tried to stop them. Framed by the doorway, Philo stood in the hall and leveled the torp, then paused and lowered it. He came back into the room and shut the door, his eyes closed as his lips moved silently.

"Find a blanket, somebody. He's going into shock." Radha had a cold, heavy feeling in her heart as if she had taken the missile herself. A bitter taste rose in her mouth when she remembered Kamal shivering in the rain, blood foaming from his mouth.

A tall, white-haired Indian man who had been standing beside the woman and child took a blanket off the couch and laid it over Father Gregory. "I am afraid he is dying," the man said. "Jagdish, will you call for an ambulance? The telecon is in the bedroom."

Father Gregory opened his eyes wide. "Let me see the child," he whispered, his voice rasping in his throat.

The slender woman knelt beside him and silently held out the baby, a lively year-old boy with thick, black curls and large, brilliant eyes. "This is Amar," she said. With one plump hand, the holy child reached out to Father Gregory. As the tips of their fingers touched, little Amar smiled.

"Now let me depart in peace, O Lord," the old priest murmured, "for I have seen your face."

Radha gently closed his eyes and rested her forehead against his. She remembered the dream he had of coming face to face with Jesus, how he had thrown open his arms, crying out, "I would die for love." And so he had, reminding them all that death is a small thing, especially when traded for new life. Gazing up at the mother and child, she studied the woman's gentle face. Probably in her mid-thirties, Radha thought, not the young girl they had expected. As she looked into the woman's eyes, her heart stopped pounding and her mind became quiet.

Radha jumped up. "Narayan, you stay with Father Gregory's body until the ambulance comes. We'll meet you later at the hotel. We're taking Amar and his parents with us."

Jagdish stepped between Radha and the little family. "He belongs to us. Do not dare to interfere with what we have planned for him." His full lips smacked together harshly, as if he liked the taste of his words. "I will not allow it."

"And a fine job you did of taking care of him." Radha's grief at losing Father Gregory was spewing into hatred of this rigid, controlling little man. The thought flashed through her mind that what she hated in him was exactly what she hated in herself, but she went on talking anyway. "It was our priest who died for this child."

She turned to the baby's mother and held up Philo's hand, pointing to his ring. "We were sent to help you. This is the only proof we have." Her voice was shaking. "Will you go with us?" Suddenly the whole enterprise seemed preposterous, and she felt as she often had in nightmares, that she was wading hip-deep in mud and sinking with every step.

The woman wrapped the end of her pale blue sari tightly around the child and looked into each of their faces. Then she nodded. "My mother told me to wait for strangers who possessed such a ring." She turned to the tall, white-haired man next to her. "Husband, you must say it. Shall we go or not?"

"I will pack our things, Devi," the tall man nodded without hesitation. "It will take some time, sir." He bowed slightly to Philo. "My wife and child will go with you now. Please to pick me up in one hour behind the Agarwal Hotel. It is not far from here. Your driver will know it."

"You do a great wrong, Giridhar," Jagdish hissed, shaking a finger in the older man's face. "You are devotees, you and your wife. Yet you entrust the life of God to these strangers? Westerners who will try to bend the child to their own purposes?" Jagdish's face turned dark copper and his whole body trembled.

"I was told what to do," Devi said quietly. "I must go where I am sent. Do not grieve, Jagdish. You will see us again." Without a backward look, she followed Radha out the door.

"We must take them to a different place." Radha walked beside Devi and the child, turning to talk over her shoulder to Philo. "Jagdish knows our hotel, and those three men might know, too."

"Maybe they were told to kill the child if they couldn't take him alive," Philo said slowly.

"Like Herod killing all the male babies in Nazareth just to be sure Jesus was dead," Eddie said, folding his hands in front of him. "The Hindus could be right about history moving in a spiral, not a straight line."

When Radha shyly tickled Amar's hand, he buried his face in his mother's shoulder, then peeked at her. As she made a motorboat noise with her lips, the baby laughed out loud and clapped his hands.

"Why did you name him Amar?" she asked.

"That was my father's name," Devi answered.

"Why not Prema?" Radha was suddenly uneasy.

Devi shook her head. "To me, he is just Amar. Prasadamara Krishnan is his full name."

Radha pushed the bangs off her forehead and wiped the sweat from her eyes. Did they have the wrong child? But the woman had dreamed about them. They would have to be content with that.

"My name is Devichamundi," the dark woman said. "You may call me Devi."

"Devi, meaning goddess," Philo murmured. "Appropriate. Chamundi was the Mysore goddess who killed a demon to save her people." He had Kori's memory and never forgot her stories, while Radha couldn't remember them moments after they were told.

"Durga. By another name, the mother Kali. She swallows her children when they die." Shanti spoke in a far-off voice, as if walking in a daze.

"Kali is the mother of us all." Devi said, moving the restless baby to her other shoulder. "He will need to nurse soon."

Walking back to the taxi, they passed under olive trees as the hot sun spattered through the leaves. Radha reflected that India had always been a country of mother-worship. Kori once told her that Shakti or feminine power is the active strength that creates the world from the passive, earth-bound masculine power. It was said that Prema Sai would embody this great feminine force in order to divert the world's headlong rush toward chaos and set many human feet on the path of love. No wonder strong, unyielding men wanted to control him or even kill him. She suddenly longed to be alone where she could weep for Father Gregory and her parents.

Radha stopped in front of a modest home with a sign on the gate. "Let's stay in this rooming house for the night," she said, hoping that a decision, any decision, would end the chattering of her thoughts. "They'll be checking the hotels."

"Good idea. Shanti and I will guard Devi and the baby here," Philo said. "You two take the taxi back to the hotel and get our things, then pick up Giridhar." Giving Radha no chance to argue, he looked over her head as he spoke to the others.

Eddie answered before she could, heading off any disagreement, as if he and Philo had a silent pact to stop her decision-making in its tracks. "We'll ditch the taxi and walk after we meet Giri, so no one will follow us here."

Radha stared coldly at Philo, wanting to show that she remembered details he had overlooked. "Since you're staying with Devi and the baby, you'd better keep the torp." Eddie handed over the weapon and stood for a moment watching little Amar, whose small round mouth was making sucking noises, even though his eyes were closed. "A shame that such sweetness must be defended by force," he said.

"We are defended by more than force." Devi's smile lightened her worn face. "Thank you, my friends, for being the hands of divinity, shielding my family." She bowed and followed Philo into the house.

Before going to pick up Giridhar, Eddie and Radha directed their taxi, now loaded with luggage, to drive through Mysore's back streets in order to lose any car trying to follow them. Just after sunset, they pulled up at the rear of the Agarwal Hotel. In the gathering shadows, at first they could see no one among the trash cans and parked vans. Then Radha spotted a dark figure slumped over a pile of boxes. A long-necked tambura lay on the ground next to him, strings face down.

"It's Giridhar," she whispered. "I remember his brown shirt." She knew before they turned him over that he was dead. His delicately lined face was covered with bruises, and his mouth was smashed. "They tortured him before they killed him." Radha's voice caught in a sob. "Probably trying to find out where the mother and child are. He wouldn't have told them even if he'd known."

"We'll have to leave him. I'll call the hospital from a public telecon and tell them where his body is." Eddie picked up two of the boxes. "Bring the other box and the instrument. Hurry."

～∽⌒∾

Upon hearing the fate of her husband, Devi said nothing, but as she bent over the baby sleeping in her arms, her tears fell onto his cheeks. Amar woke up and was reaching to touch his mother's cheek when a fine sifting of vibhuti began to fall from his palm. The strings of the tambura, which was standing alone against the wall, mysteriously began to twang, resonating like the sound of glass chimes in the wind.

No one moved except Shanti, who sat at Devi's feet and bowed her head low before touching the vibhuti to her tongue and forehead. "He is the holy one," she said softly. "Now there is no doubt."

"We must decide what to do next," Radha said, pacing the room as she glanced at the baby, from whose hand the gray dust continued to fall. "Amar must be protected from Strassbourg's men, or whoever it was that killed Giridhar."

"I'm sure it was Brom's men who killed him." Philo absently streaked vibhuti across his forehead. "Jagdish may be a fanatic, but he's no killer."

"Brom Strassbourg knows that the child is in Mysore," Radha said. "So we've got to get out of here. Maybe drive somewhere tonight." The voice came softly into the back of her mind, then drifted to the forefront. *Bangalore. Bring Tewati with you. In Bangalore you will be safe for six years,* the voice said. *Then you must go to Puttaparthi. Six years. Do not forget.*

Radha leaned over and held the baby's hand, wondering if it was his voice she had heard. "Bangalore, then," she said, her voice so deep and calm that Philo stared at her. "Tonight we'll drive to Bangalore. Eddie, go find Narayan."

"Shouldn't we just leave?" Philo said, running a hand through his thick brown hair. "He may tell Jagdish about our plans."

"We must take Narayan," Shanti said. "A man must help to raise the child as a Hindu, now that his father is dead."

Devi gave a long, trembling sigh as Amar gently touched her face, leaving an imprint of gray powder on her cheek.

⁓⧓⁓

Eddie found Tewati sitting on the floor of his room between two packed bags, as if he somehow knew of the plan without being told. To avoid being followed, they went down the back stairs to meet with the others. Radha was afraid Strassbourg's men would trace them if they hired a taxi, so she traded a handful of pearls for a used electric van. Avoiding the checkpoint where officials inspected cars for illegal immigrants and drugs, Tewati guided them out of Mysore by the back road through Shrirangapatnam. With Strassbourg's power growing wherever international trade flourished, the risk of being stopped by his men was greater on established routes like the main road to Bangalore.

"Bangalore is a good choice," the old man said to Radha as he leaned his head back against the seat top. "It is high, cool and has many parks. The child will flourish there."

"It was not a choice," Radha said. "I received the instruction in my head. Sometimes I'm spoken to in this way," she finished uncomfortably, staring out the window at the crush of tiny houses with tin roofs that lined the narrow road. Despite the economic boom, Indians in the countryside lived as they always had and kept their old beliefs, which probably did not include personal messages from God. She wondered if Tewati, saintly though he was, might think she was a dangerous lunatic, hardly one who should be caring for the holy child.

Instead, Tewati opened his eyes wide and looked at her intently. Then he began to describe the tradition in which he had been raised, how yogis learned to still their thoughts, assuming postures that allowed prana, the divine spirit, to pour through them, teaching them what to do. The teachings had come earlier, three or four thousand years before Christ, when Krishna was born among the great yogic rishis of Mohenjo-Daru and Harappa, the ancient cities of the high Indus civilization. Western scholars liked to believe it was their own people, rough Aryan nomads from the mountains, who brought the Sanskrit words of the Vedas and Upanishads to India a thousand years before Christ. But the seals of the ancient Indus people bore images of men seated in yogic postures and inscriptions written in an early form of Sanskrit. Hearing that these ancient rishis had come from the Himalayas more than ten thousand years ago, Radha wondered if their breathing practices had kept them warm in the relentless cold of the mountains.

"The ancients," Tewati said, "did not worship the violent Vedic gods, but Savitri, the power behind the sun, and Atman, the source of life, the divine spirit within all beings. All that we call real was dreamed by

Brahman, the formless, invisible spirit that humankind calls God. Thus," he explained, "myth is only the surface of the sphere known as the Hindu religion. The practice of union with the divine Spirit forms the inner core of Hinduism." Tewati turned an invisible ball between his hands and studied it with a bemused expression, as if he were a god studying the spinning world for signs of life and the smoke of worship.

Radha leaned forward, watching Amar's sleeping face as he lay sprawled on his mother's lap. For a moment, he looked like pictures she had seen of the young Vishnu, lying on an infinite ocean, the lotus of creation rising from his belly. Then the moment passed, and Amar was only a tawny-skinned Indian boy, whose plump cheeks worked in his sleep as he dreamed of taking his mother's milk. Wondering if she had been dreaming, Radha looked at Tewati and saw that he, too, was staring at Amar, as a smile widened his wrinkled cheeks.

"One expects such miracles from avatars," he said softly to Radha. "But still, it is always a surprise."

"My child will grow up with this holy one as a big brother." Shanti placed her hand on her belly and looked at Amar. This was the first she had told anyone about being pregnant. "Eddie, you must take my supply of Melody. I will not use it now."

Radha was glad the Indian girl had offered this gift. Eddie would not refuse the anti-aging compound if it came from Shanti, who had a way of winning agreement with whatever she wanted, perhaps because she so seldom asked. Or perhaps because the others, especially Radha, sensed that Shanti was in a cosmic flow where she did not speak only for herself, but on behalf of some oceanic being, in which she swam easily, while Radha kicked and struggled to stay afloat. In any case, Radha reflected, she would now have what she wanted most—Eddie at her side, in his full strength and vigor. Perhaps she would not lose him, as she had lost so many others.

After they settled into a modest, gated house near the Kempegowda Circle and the city market, it was Tewati who spent the most time with Amar. The old man would sit cross-legged on the ground for hours, holding his japamala beads between thin brown fingers, his eyes focused on Amar as if he was seeing visions. If he was, he told no one, but only looked with the same wondering expression that Radha had observed when the two of them saw Amar as the baby Krishna.

Amar took his first steps in the walled backyard, which was lined with oleander bushes. At two, he would stand over the basket watching little Murali, Shanti's new baby. Singing to her in lisping Telugu, he repeated the holy bhajans his mother had sung to him.

Since it was considered too dangerous for him to be seen by the neighbors, Amar's only playmate was little Murali. Most people on the block didn't suspect there were children in the whitewashed, two-story cement house until one Friday afternoon when Murali's colicky screams alerted them. As Murali screamed in her mother's arms, Amar came padding in on bare feet, followed by Radha. His big brown eyes were full of tears. "The baby hurts," he said to Shanti. "Can't you help her?"

"No, Amar," Shanti said patiently, laying her soft hand on the little boy's curly head. "The pain is in her tummy. My milk is not good for her, I think."

Amar kissed the baby's hard, distended little belly. When he lifted his head, there was a yellow stream of amrit snaking across Murali's skin.

"Drink this, Shanti," Amar said. "Your milk will be good now." Smiling as the baby fell asleep, Amar hitched up his short blue pants and left the room, with Radha close behind. She wanted to stay near the child, and would have hugged him if she dared. Sometimes he hugged her, as he did the others, but already Amar had a solitary dignity that made everyone but his mother and Murali hesitate to touch him uninvited.

Amar went directly to his mother, who was setting the table in preparation for dinner. He sat down at the table and propped his round chin in his hands, while Devi brought out two tall, carved brass candlesticks with white candles. Radha watched from the doorway as Devi covered her head with the end of her sari, lit the candles, and held her hands over her eyes, praying silently.

When Devi had finished, Radha entered the room. "Why do you do that?" she asked. "It's the same ritual my father's people did every Friday night."

Devi raised her delicate black eyebrows. "I don't know why, but the women of my family have always lit the candles on Friday. My grandmother brought these candlesticks with her when the family left Cochin many years ago and moved to a place north of Bangalore. My husband," her voice faded as she looked sadly at the flickering candles. "My husband was born near Mysore, not I."

Bending down to examine the candlesticks closely, Radha wondered if she might see a Star of David among the twisting gold vines. Although the candlesticks bore no sign of Jewish origin, she knew she had just watched an ancient, familiar ritual. "Your mother was Jewish," she said, staring at Devi. "Or at least some woman in your family, somewhere, sometime, must have celebrated Shabbat." Tossing his head back, Amar laughed and hugged Radha around the hips.

"I have no knowledge of that," Devi replied, shrugging. "We are Hindus now, whatever my ancestors might have been long ago."

Radha went into the kitchen and began stirring the curried vegetable stew. Sitting on the floor, she stared at the vegetables simmering in the golden brown sauce. As much a Christian as she was a Jew, Radha saw Christianity as the universal form of the older religion. But for Jews like those she had known in Israel, the Messiah would have to carry another name than Jesus and must, of course, have a Jewish mother. They had suffered too much at the hands of those outside their faith to believe in a messiah who was not a Jew.

She leaned over the rising steam and smelled the pungent curry, so much like what her mother used to make. Radha remembered Kori's

Christian icon sitting next to the picture of Sai Baba and shook her head, wondering why people had such a hard time calling God by more than one name. It was as if they thought the human stomach could accept only white rice, or that the sun shone only on one chosen people, while the rest lived in darkness. People needed to feel special, just as she had always wanted Kori to think she was special. But Philo was always the favored one. And now? Even as a grown woman, she still wanted Philo to admire her and show it by giving in to her. He was all the family she had left, and she still saw Kori in his precise, elegantly angled face.

While stirring the stew, Radha daydreamed that little Murali might grow up to love her aunt even more than her own parents. Then, if Eddie died first, Murali would be there for her and she would not be alone. In many ways the thin, long-limbed baby reminded her of Kori. Except when crying with colic, Murali was calm and observant. Rather than waving her hands about randomly like most babies, she moved purposefully and had quickly learned how to seize an object she wanted to examine.

Yet, despite the resemblances, Radha was sure that Kori was too holy to have returned to this world. Pouring the curry into a serving bowl, she sighed softly. It would be a long time before Radha could accept the fact that she would not see her mother again.

13

Ibrahim Al-Essa was about to finish his undergraduate work in Oriental languages at Hebrew University. A full year ahead of schedule, he was deep into his dissertation about the structural similarities between Hebrew and Sanskrit.

Three years earlier, in a freshman political science class, Ibrahim had sat beside Sarah Ordman, a black-haired beauty from an orthodox Jewish family. From that first day he was determined to make Sarah his wife, but her family would not allow her to marry outside their faith. At least she was not being forced to marry someone else and had promised she never would. They often met outside the walls of the Old City, in the little park near the Russian Church, where no one in her family was likely to see them.

"You could become Jewish," she said, flipping a lock of her long, glossy black hair over her shoulder as she leaned forward on the park bench. "It's only the religious difference that bothers my family, you know. They like it that you're a Hebrew scholar."

"Not their kind of Hebrew scholar, I'm afraid." Ibrahim scratched at the still unfamiliar beard he had grown to please Sarah. "When I told your father I was also studying sacred texts in Sanskrit and Arabic, a curtain fell between us, like the one between the men and women at your synagogue."

Sarah examined her short, business-like nails. "I know you don't like anything that divides people," she said. "But isn't it a fact that everyone is part of a tribe, whether they call it that or not? They love their own and hate the others. Isn't that how it's always been?"

"Maybe. But not how it will always be. Sai Baba says to follow your own religion, but don't knock anyone else's. Realize that everyone is following his own path to God. To Godhood." Ibrahim added the last words with some trepidation, since Sarah was resistant enough to a universal religion without his adding the divinity of man.

"Godhood?" Sarah's dark eyes flashed, and she tied her red muffler so tight around her neck that she almost choked. "You think men are gods, Ibrahim? Take a good look at history. Just because Sai Baba has billions of followers doesn't make him right. We Jews are used to being in the minority. No man can be God. It makes me sick that you think so."

"Can I tell you about Baba?" Ibrahim ventured, his hands curled tightly around his knees. He knew that if only he could hold Sarah, kiss her soft, red lips, run his hands through her hair, she wouldn't fight him so. And he wouldn't feel the constant ache that he carried with him to bed, to his studies and even to his prayers. "He came to teach us to love and serve each other, as I want to love and serve you, Sarah." He took her hand and caressed it with a wild fervor that was meant for all of her.

She pulled her hand away. "It's no good, Ibrahim. I'll have to get over you. Not see you anymore. There's no way I could live with a husband who believes that Ha-Shem, pure spirit, would take a human form. Or that mere human beings are gods. We've got more than a curtain between us. It's a stone wall." She stood up and began to walk away, shoving her hands into the pockets of her ankle-length gray coat.

"Sarah, wait!" Ibrahim ran after her, his eyes on the black curls bouncing and rippling down her back. "I won't give you up." He swung her around firmly, holding her by the shoulders when she tried to break away. "If becoming a Jew is what I must do to have you, I'll do it. Look." He tugged at the scraggly brown fringe around his jaw and smiled. "I've even got a bit of a start."

"You'd give up your own belief for mine?" Sarah's face softened and she swayed closer to him.

"What I believe," he said, "is another matter. I will go on praying five times a day as a Muslim. I will go on believing that Allah wants all men to love each other as he loves us. But yes, I will accept the laws of your faith, if you will have me no other way."

Sarah took his face between her hands and kissed him lingeringly on the lips. Then she let him hold her body against his, as he had never been allowed to do in the three years they had known each other. Sarah knew exactly how to punish or reward him, Ibrahim thought, hoping that marriage would end their power struggle.

"We will speak to my father about this," she said. "Being a rabbi, he will know what to do. But you mustn't tell him your weird ideas. Or me either. I don't want to know." She held his hand tightly all the way back to her parents' apartment in the Jewish Quarter, as if afraid he would change his mind and run away.

Rabbi Ordman was in his study when they arrived. Though no taller than his daughter, he was an imposing figure. His thick neck and broad shoulders looked dangerously top-heavy on his otherwise frail body. No one knew what the rabbi did in this tiny book-lined room for eight hours a day. He couldn't be reading; his eyes had given out ten years before from studying the small, dancing letters of his Torah. Now he peered at the world through glasses so thick the weight of them reddened and blistered the high bridge of his nose.

When Ibrahim entered with Sarah, her father did not shake hands, but merely waved at the two worn leather chairs opposite his desk. He stared at them, as if trying to see through them to the wall of books at their backs. Sarah had always said her father was more comfortable with books than with people. This quality, she felt, was all he had in common with Ibrahim, except that both of them were kind, the two kindest men in the world.

Sarah waited, but her father said nothing. Finally she cleared her throat and gestured at Ibrahim. "Father, he will become a Jew. He has agreed to it."

"My Sarah is a beautiful girl," the rabbi said, stroking the hairs of his unruly beard, which sprang up again as soon as his hand had passed over them. "But she is not so beautiful that a man should sell his soul for her. We must discuss your beliefs. You are a Muslim, I understand, so you obey our dietary laws."

"That is true." Ibrahim nodded. "My father insisted on what you would call a kosher household."

"And you are able to read our scriptures?"

"I study them every day." Ibrahim felt his tight shoulders relaxing. This interview was no worse than the usual grilling in his upper-division classes and about as impersonal.

Rabbi Ordman rose, shoving his chair into a precariously balanced pile of books that trembled but did not fall. Suddenly turning toward Ibrahim, he leaned over the desk on two balled fists. "What do you know of your family, young man?"

"Does that matter now, Father?" Sarah was nervously curling the ends of her scarf and loosening them again. "His great-grandmother lived as a Jew and was protecting Jewish schoolchildren when she was shot by an Arab gunman. She was a martyr. Everyone knows the story."

"Not everyone knows, however, who the gunman was," the rabbi said, fixing his small bright, brown eyes on Ibrahim. "I have made it my business to find out. It was your father."

Ibrahim jumped to his feet, his throat tightening so that his words came out thick and harsh. "You mean, mean old man. My father was a saint. The men who gunned him down were the terrorists."

Sarah clung to his arm, shaking it. "Wait, wait. He has proof. I've known about it but didn't want to tell you, Ibrahim. It doesn't matter to me."

"It does to me." Taking off his glasses, the rabbi sat down and pressed the heels of his hands into his eyes. "Sarah is my only child, and her children will be my only grandchildren. They should maybe also be the grandchildren of a murderer? Understand me, our family has never had such shame as this."

"I will see your proof," Ibrahim said, his voice cold and distant. "Show me." He went through the handful of documents as Sarah and the rabbi watched silently. At last he laid them on the desk, his hands trembling, and looked directly at the rabbi. "It appears that I have a second reason to abandon my family for yours. As of now, I am without a family and a past. Will you have me as I am?"

"Father, you can't say no!" Sarah cried, kneeling at the rabbi's feet and holding his hands tightly. "I won't marry anyone else. Not till Solomon's Temple is rebuilt on the Mount. I swear it."

"I seem to have no choice," Rabbi Ordman sighed. "My Sarah's strong will has always worn me down in the end. You have known each other for three years, and to keep you apart any longer would be inviting you to sin. When Ibrahim has become a Jew, Sarah, you may become his wife."

"Excuse me, but I need to know where the washroom is," Ibrahim said, ignoring Sarah, who was reaching out to him. When he was alone, Ibrahim held his hand tightly over his mouth so no one could hear, leaned his head against the mirror, and wept.

Sitting under the banyan tree, whose thick roots snaked under the high arched gate leading to the alley, Radha shelled peas as she watched the children playing in their sandbox. They were like her own grandchildren, she reflected. Since her grandson, Solly, was so far away in Jerusalem, Amar and Murali seemed much more real to her than he did. He was only a name and a handful of pictures, while they were a whole childhood full of hugs, scraped knees and stories being read over and over again while they curled up on either side of her.

Now nearly seven, Amar had picked up reading on his own and often read to Murali. Tewati was teaching the boy Sanskrit, and Amar studied alone a few hours each day, occasionally asking help from Shanti or the old man. Radha wondered if perhaps Amar was not so much in need of help but enjoyed seeing their faces light up as they read the ancient wisdom of the Vedas with him.

Radha often found herself observing the boy's face as he played, absorbed in building precisely engineered block towers inside walls of sand, then steering trucks and cars through the tunnels underneath. Murali tried to build as he did, but her towers would fall whenever she didn't leave enough clearance under the blocks.

Today, when her tower fell as she tried to push a small truck through the tunnel, Murali stood up and kicked the blocks, shrieking. "I want to do it right, like you, Amar. Why can't I do it right?" She sat down and put her face in her hands, sobbing. When she couldn't be perfect, Murali invariably lost her temper.

His eyes wide and bright, Amar looked up from the other end of the sandbox that Eddie had built for them. As tall as Murali, he was wiry and extremely quick with his hands. "Don't cry, Murali," he said tenderly. "I'll fix it."

Sitting back on his haunches, he raised his hand, palm down toward the jumble of blocks. In a shimmering blur, the blocks reassembled into a tower, as Murali clapped her hands with pleasure.

"This time, try a little car," Amar said, tossing her one of his. "That truck is way too big to go under the tower."

Radha stared at him, wondering if she should tell Devi what she had seen, but decided to keep it to herself for a little while. She laid aside her pot of shelled peas, folded her hands in her lap, and rocked back and forth. It was well past the normal time for Amar to go to school, she thought, but if he used his powers like this, he would certainly be noticed. Once he entered school in Bangalore, Amar could not be protected from curious questioners, and those who were more than curious, wanting to control him for their own purposes. She had been told to take the child to Puttaparthi when he was seven, and that time had clearly come.

Hearing muffled sounds, like a backfiring car, Radha jumped up, knocking over the pot. As the peas bounced down the steps into the yard, both children came running to gather them.

Shanti burst out the back door, followed by Devi. "Hurry," she gasped. "Eddie and Philo are holding off some men who tried to break in the front. Go to the van."

"Shanti, run and get the jewels from my desk," Radha shouted, "or we'll be begging in the streets for our dinner."

Devi gathered Amar up under one arm and dashed for the gate, where Radha was already fumbling with the rusty key. She could hear shouts and the sound of furniture being overturned as she used both hands, trying to turn the key. "Amar," she cried in despair, "I can't turn it. Do something."

When the child reached out, amrit gushed from his fingertips, pouring over the key, the lock and onto the ground. The thick, honey-like liquid seemed to lubricate the metal, allowing Radha to easily turn the key in the lock. They rushed toward the van, which always sat fully charged with a key hidden under the front seat. "What about our men?" Shanti cried, throwing herself into the back beside Murali. Devi was already in the front with Amar.

"We've talked about what to do." Radha turned the ignition, praying that Eddie's new, briefcase-sized Starburst engine would work. "The men will follow us to Puttaparthi."

As the van roared down the alley, Shanti leaned over the front seat and laid the pouch of jewels in Radha's lap. "Just this morning I restocked the van with food and clothes, as you said must be done every week."

"A good thing, too." Radha glanced in the rearview mirror, wishing she could see Eddie and Philo. They could hold off three or four men, she told herself, unless the men had torps. If Eddie didn't have time to grab theirs, he and Philo could be dead. Tewati would be useless, probably napping upstairs right through the attack. Radha's lips began to move silently. Strange how she prayed whole-heartedly only when she was afraid or had completely lost control of a situation. If she turned to God only when she was suffering, then suffering was what she could expect.

The van turned down Hosur Road, toward the main boulevard, and they heard the shriek of wheels on concrete. "They're following us," Shanti cried, holding Murali close, so the child wouldn't try to look out the window. "At least they've left Philo and Eddie alone," Radha said, gripping the wheel tightly with both hands.

Escaping her mother's arms, Murali stood to look out. "They have shooters," she wailed. "One is leaning out the window." She flung herself into Shanti's lap and held still, afraid to move.

"How about it, Devi?" Radha steered around a pothole and pushed harder on the accelerator. With humpbacked cows and street vendors wandering into her path without warning, she was afraid to take her eyes off the road to check the mirror. "Are they going to shoot?"

"I think so." Devi's eyes were closed. "You cannot go faster?"

Bouncing up and down on the seat in excitement, Amar called out, "Warp speed, Auntie!"

As Radha swerved to avoid a motorbike, one torp missile tore through the plastic window on Devi's side. "We aren't going to make it," Radha whispered, her breath coming in short gasps, as it did when she was about to cry. "There's no way. Amar? Can you help?" She glanced at the child, who was calmly looking straight ahead.

"I thought you'd never ask. Turn now, *bangaroo*," he said, speaking suddenly very much like an adult. "To the left, then to the right."

Radha could not help smiling that Amar called her "darling," as his mother called him. She pulled the wheel sharply as he directed, and the car sped into a maze of narrow alleys.

"Now, you see? Go in there." The child pointed to a small warehouse with an open door. "Mother, jump out and close the door behind us."

Trembling in the dark, they heard a car approach, then pass by.

"Couldn't you just make their shooters disappear, Amar?" Murali finally asked. "Couldn't you make those men die?"

"No need to kill anyone. Just get out of their way." Amar hugged his mother. "May we have some sweets while we wait?" he asked. "I have some in my pocket."

"Amar can make sweets come out of his hand," Murali said, clapping with delight. "But he won't let me have them unless Mama says yes."

When the boy leaned his head against her shoulder, Radha felt a warm thrill. Caressing his smooth cheek, she looked at the other women and said, "It's time we were at the ashram. We can't hide him much longer."

Since Radha stayed on back roads all the way to Puttaparthi, the trip took a long time. Philo and the other men had taken the new bullet train from Bangalore and, as prearranged, were waiting in the lobby of the Prasanthi Arms, one of the many luxury hotels that lined the broad streets near Sai Baba's ashram, Prasanthi Nilayam. The great hotels had been built to house the affluent who found it difficult to adjust to the simple accommodations at the ashram. Beyond the high, turreted walls of the old city, residential and commercial areas spread out into the foothills. By the end of Sai Baba's life, the ashram had been fortified to prevent mobs from surging in, crowds so desperate to see the avatar that they might resort to violence. Radha hoped the new torp turrets and security checks would provide Amar with the measure of safety that his handful of protectors could not.

Philo reported that Brom's henchmen had sped off as soon as they realized Amar was gone. "Do you think they followed you north?" He kept one arm around Shanti and the other around Murali, who had fallen asleep in his lap.

"No. Amar saw to that." Radha glanced at the boy, who smiled and took his mother's hand.

"It was time," he said. "We had to leave that place." Hearing Amar's voice, Murali woke up and insisted on sitting beside him.

"Puttaparthi should be safer than anywhere else." Philo kept his voice low, since hotel guests were milling around the lobby. "But if word spreads that Prema is here, Strassbourg's men wouldn't let a mere gate stop them."

"Then you think we should go on keeping him hidden?" Radha asked. Elbows on her knees, she leaned forward and looked thoughtfully at the children. "Murali will be going to school soon, and he would be alone."

Tewati turned to Amar, who was reading a story to Murali and pointing out words so she could learn to read. "Children, excuse us," the old man said gently, covering the page with his hand. "We must ask you something, Amar. If we send you to school with Murali, could you refrain from doing anything," he cleared his throat and paused before adding, "unusual?"

"I will go to school," Amar said firmly. "And I promise not to make sweets." Reading the disappointment on the little girl's face, he smiled at her. "No, not even sometimes, Murali. I will be like everyone else."

"Can you keep such a promise, Amar?" Devi leaned close to her son and took his face between her hands. "Or do these things happen before you have time to think about them?"

"Be sure I will do no harm," the boy said, "to myself or you. I will be discreet, Mother. And now, I'm sure everyone is tired. Shall we find our rooms?"

More and more often, Radha noticed Amar acting like an adult. Then, he would quickly return to building block houses with Murali or tossing stones into puddles. Radha wondered if he was adult enough to avoid bringing dangerous attention to himself and to them all.

Tewati had invited them to live with him in the three-story house that Sai Baba allowed him to build at the edge of the ashram. Puttaparthi itself, like Bangalore, seemed too full of indifferent strangers, coming and going, doing God only knew what holy or unholy business. Still, without even having seen the inside of the ashram, Radha felt peace settling over her like sleep when she thought of the little mandir her grandmother and parents had prayed in and the great one built later next to the stadium fields.

Passing through the entrance gate to the ashram, they saw the stained, worn statue of Lord Ganesh, the remover of obstacles. Radha felt an impulse to dip her fingers in the coconut milk that rolled down the steps in front of the elephant god. Evidently a sacrifice of coconuts had just been made, and she felt that here at Prasanthi Nilayam, the Abode of Highest Peace, sacrifices might not be quite so hard.

14

Jason was unable to persuade Brom Strassbourg to meet in Mexical, though his region had become an important base for both Eurocom and its related Asian corporations. But at least he had agreed to meet in Paris, which Consuelo had always longed to see. She and Rumi, a tall man and darkly handsome like his mother, were in no hurry to meet Strassbourg. They had spent the morning in the Cluny Museum, examining medieval Christian artifacts. Monastic art was one of Rumi's passions. A skilled painter, he found it hard to obey the Muslim prohibition against representing the human body. Sometimes he would break the rule, creating landscapes that showed men and women at work or worship. These would be hidden away in his large folios, to be seen only by his mother.

Rumi and Consuelo often kept secrets from Jason. The year before, when Jason was away from Santa Barbara on business for several months, they had driven north to Santa Cruz and searched out the old farm, which was now a monastery. Consuelo's parents had died in a typhoid epidemic, as had so many other people she had loved. But when Father Elijah embraced her, it was as if she had seen him just the day before.

The old monk showed them around the grounds, stopping to pray near the wooden altar over Kori's grave. Carved niches framed her icon, a picture of Sai Baba, and a photo of Kori as a young woman. Rumi

275

lingered over Kori's picture, his fingers aching to sketch the delicate planes of her face and her large, clear eyes.

"You, too, find her beautiful," Father Elijah's voice quavered. "I knew her soul, in so far as one human being can know another's, and it was even more beautiful than her face. See that hint of a shadow at the corners of her mouth?" The old man pointed. "When I look long enough at that shadow, I sense her presence as she was in life."

"I would like to stay a while." Rumi sat in front of the picture and took out his sketch pad.

Elijah stood watching as the young man drew Kori's portrait. "We have too little art here," he said, when Rumi had finished. "Perhaps you would do us the favor of painting holy scenes on these bare walls while you're visiting."

So Rumi spent a month painting the chapel walls with scenes from Elijah's holy books, transmuting them as his imagination moved him. While painting, he felt Kori's eyes following him from her portrait, and living images flowed from his brush with an ease they never had before.

Walking around the chapel with Father Elijah, Rumi was happy at the priest's pleasure in his work. As their stay was ending, he told Elijah that he would like to return someday to live at the monastery. "Do you think I could become a monk?" he asked. "Is that possible for a Muslim?" He held his breath, waiting for the answer.

"Of course it is possible. Here every man is free to find God any way he can." Father Elijah ran his fingers meditatively over his long white beard. "But tell me, my son, have you no experience with women? Do you not feel such a need?"

"No. I feel that in another life loving a woman caused me great suffering," Rumi answered, vigorously cleaning his brushes. "Now, my only desire is for God."

"It is a serious thing," the priest said in his light, gentle voice, "to cut yourself off from the love of women, for we need such love to soften the heart." The old man sighed, "I remember how it was for me to love a woman I could not have, and I will always grieve her loss. Yet because of her, I learned to look beyond myself and am grateful."

"You see how that kind of love brings pain?" Rumi rolled up his clean brushes in a canvas holder. "I find it easier not to seek love outside myself. It is wiser to love only God, who does not change or die."

"Nevertheless," the old priest murmured as he followed Rumi out of the chapel, "Can the heart that has not felt the pain of human love know how the heart of God hurts for us?"

It was not until Rumi was on the way home with his mother that he realized Father Elijah had been speaking of his own love for Kori, a love that had led him more deeply into God than he could have gone alone. Not wanting to think about how Kori's wise, bright eyes and warm smile had pierced his own soul, Rumi held the wheel tightly and focused on the potholed road.

❧

Rumi had begun to draw when he was sixteen. It had been an unexpected gift, one that came in the midst of a heavy depression. Rumi had always kept his fears to himself, and in his early teens often thought of suicide. What he most feared was becoming a man like his father. He saw the revulsion on his mother's face whenever Jason came into the room and wondered if she would someday look at him in the same way. One afternoon he had wandered on the beach, imagining how it would feel to go so far into the ocean that the waves would carry him off. As he walked toward the water, staring out at the horizon, he heard a voice in his head, a pleasant, tentative male voice.

"You don't know me, but I have been watching you for some time. My name is Kamal. If you are frightened, I will go away and not disturb you further."

Rumi stood still, curling his toes in the sand, afraid to move. "What do you want from me? Are you trying to keep me from killing myself? Are you an angel?"

"No. I'm not an angel. Just a man who lived not so long ago. I wish to perform a task in your world, a task that will pay for something I once did. Will you help me?"

"I can't even help myself," Rumi said, twisting his hands together. "I just want to be out of here. How could I possibly help you?"

"Since I need a living body to accomplish what I must do, and you don't want yours anymore, we could work together. Divinity is coming to the world and we could be part of the new Golden Age."

"Where would I go if you took over my body?" The boy was shaking and he clenched his teeth to avoid throwing up.

"In your society I would be called a walk-in," Kamal said. "You could, if you choose, pass on to other realms, or we could become one person, with separate memories of the past. I would bring you all I have. My art and love of literature. My love of God."

Rumi felt a warmth flood his being, as if he were in the arms of a gentle woman. "You are an artist?"

"When I put my hand on God's creation, it comes alive in art," the voice said. "This gift I will bring to you, with the help of God."

"Then come." Rumi stood facing the horizon, arms spread out, his heart open. "I welcome you. Use me as you will, to do good in the world."

From that day on, Rumi had been a new person. He had not told even his mother of the soul who shared his life, but she was aware that something had shifted within him. When she looked at his drawings, she would stare at him, wondering how he had learned to draw things he had never seen. Rumi knew his drawings of forbidden human forms were safe with her.

∽)(∾

They met Brom Strassbourg in his luxurious suite overlooking L'Étoile, with its frenzy of traffic around the carved stone arch. Rumi had no desire to meet the tall, bronzed man, but his father insisted, pushing him forward. With a slightly contemptuous twist of his narrow lips, the Director of Eurocom glanced down at Rumi's extended hand, but did not take it.

"Your son, I suppose, will govern after you?" Strassbourg sized up the young man, wondering if he was as stupid as his father, or to be reckoned with, as his informants said the mother was.

"I 'spect so." Jason leaned back on his heels, trying to appear at ease. He had told his wife and son that he didn't much like Europe, with its sissy men wearing silk bodysuits and talking all the time about the vintages of their fancy wines. "One of these days, he'll run things just as smooth as I do," said Jason, standing in front of Consuelo, obviously wanting to keep her in the background.

Ignoring his frown, Consuelo stepped around her husband. In the studied way of a man who knew he looked important, Strassbourg folded his arms across his wide chest. "I've heard of you," he said, trying to stare down the small, dark woman. But she held her ground and resolutely stared back, no expression on her round face with its high Indian cheekbones.

Strassbourg tried again to elicit a response. "My investigators tell me you were raised with the woman who now controls Prema Sai, the child some say is the Messiah." He said the final word, Rumi thought, with a light amusement, as if it were a joke between them.

"We don't know nothin' about that," Jason interrupted, his voice rising with a fretful twang. "The reason we're here is we want Eurocom to—"

"Not so fast, Jason," Consuelo said, taking Strassbourg's arm and leading him to the couch under the broad window. "Director Strassbourg must first have tea, then tell us about his concerns."

Rumi sat alertly poised at the edge of his curve-legged antique chair. He could see that his mother was going to find out what Strassbourg knew before telling him anything about her childhood friend.

"You understand," Strassbourg said, now speaking only to Consuelo, as if he knew she was the power in the family, not Jason, "that this old friend of yours is a fanatic? That she belongs to a group that intends to control the world?"

"And turn it holy," Consuelo added noncommittally.

"Not exactly what I have in mind," Strassbourg went on, taking her few words for assent. "I'm building a unified, corporate world order with no place for religious fanatics, especially fanatics who are planning a revolution."

Rumi's thoughts wandered to the peaceful monastery where Elijah harvested vegetables with his monks and prayed at sunset, lifting hands and incense as offerings to God. Such men needed nothing, wanted nothing, and were thus a danger to Brom Strassbourg and his world order, in which men lived to buy and sell, not to pray and love. Father Elijah had said he knew the Messiah had returned to earth, for he felt it in his old bones. Rumi would live to see the day of the Lord, Elijah said, and everyone would rejoice when he came in his full glory. Everyone but Strassbourg, Rumi thought. Pulling a little pad from the inside pocket of his jacket, he began to sketch the director's features, glancing up from time to time as Strassbourg talked. The man had a bull-like cast to him, and Rumi could not help sketching in horns and a nose-ring, once the face was finished.

"Your friend is somewhere in India. We know this much." Strassbourg leaned one arm along the back of the couch behind Consuelo's shoulders, ignoring Jason's frown. "Can you tell us where?"

"I'm sorry." Consuelo shook her head, pushing back a long strand of black hair that had escaped from her braid. "I've heard nothing from her in all these years, except when her son was born and again when he married."

"So, she has a son." Strassbourg began pacing before the window. "Useful to know. If we take him into custody, she will have to come forward with the Indian boy. What woman would sacrifice her own son to protect someone else's?" He was at the door before Consuelo could answer.

"She'll give you nothing," Consuelo cried out, her hand over her heart. "Nor will her son."

"That we will learn as soon as we find him." He waved away Jason's attempt to stop him. "Tomorrow, Monsieur, there will be time to talk about investments, but not now." Strassbourg opened the door and was gone before Jason could utter a word.

"We must send word to Radha's son," Consuelo whispered to Rumi. "I will call his university tonight."

When he looked at his mother's stricken face, Rumi knew what she would want him to do. By that evening he intended to have a ticket to Bombay, from where he would begin to search for his mother's friend and the child who was in her care. Rumi's heart leapt at the thought of India. He wanted to dance in the street as if he had just been released from prison. He had no idea why, but the very name of India resonated within him, as did Jerusalem and Mecca. Above the triumphal Roman arch outside the building, Rumi watched a flock of white gulls flying toward the sea and felt no less free than they.

෨෬෭

Ali had been playing checkers all morning with Ayesha, his second mother, and was glad for the diversion of Rumi's farewell letter. He ripped it open and read aloud to Ayesha, who was nibbling a piece of Annie's fudge as she watched an old Homer Healey tape on the telecon. Ayesha did not want to become as fat as her mother-in-law, so she tried to limit herself to one piece a day. To make the fudge last longer, she slowly ran the grainy, sweet taste over her tongue. Jason paid little attention to her as it was, and Ayesha feared that if she gained more weight, he would never visit her again. He said as much the last time he had come, looking distastefully at her spreading waistline and graying hair. Jason cared only for appearances, not like Homer, whose tender words and gentle smile made her feel loved.

Although the minister was long dead, for Ayesha he was still alive. As she watched his old tapes played by the Christian telecon net, subtly, hardly realizing it, she was becoming a born-again Christian. The pure, impersonal Allah, whom she had been raised to worship, seemed not to care about women, only men. But Jesus loved women and loved gently, as women do. He loved even her, plump and ignorant as Jason said she was. Jesus knew her heart was pure, and she adored him for knowing. When the minister called for people in the video audience to come forward and give their hearts to Jesus, she wept and prostrated herself on the floor. Ayesha burned with love and gratitude for the one who gave her salvation, lifted her out of a loveless life and took her in his warm, accepting arms. Sometimes she could not be sure whose face she saw behind her closed eyes, Homer's or Christ's. But she knew she felt loved and was strengthened in her ability to love even Jason, though he mocked and abused her.

She had invited Ali to watch the tapes, and he, too, had given his heart to Jesus. Now Ali visited her every day for the telecast, not minding if he saw the same ones over and over. After each show, they would shed tears and hold each other's hands tightly. Ali welcomed Christ's love, for he felt that his mother and father cared much more for Rumi than for him. Strangely, he did not hate his brother, as Ayesha had hated Consuelo before Jesus came into her heart. Ali adored Rumi and wished he was wise and holy like his brother.

Until finding Jesus, Ali had always felt weak and small. He was in fact quite small, a head shorter than Rumi, with thin, blond hair that hung over his high forehead. When Ali looked in the mirror, he felt that only Jesus could love his scrawny body and washed-out, bony face. But Ayesha would hug the boy and assure him that he would grow into a fine-looking man. She said that Jesus didn't care what either of them looked like or how stupid others might think they were. Their faith had saved them, and Jesus loved them as a mother hen loves her chicks. The blood of the lamb covered them, as Homer Healey said, and they were whiter than the whitest snow. Ali, who thought himself too white already, told Ayesha he wasn't much reassured by this message, but his faith in the promises was otherwise strong.

"Rumi says he's going to search all over India to find this holy child." Ali folded the letter and slipped it back in the envelope. "I'm afraid he's going to lose his soul."

"The Antichrist," Ayesha nodded her head wisely. "Rumi thinks this Antichrist is God. We must pray for him. But not now. It's time for Homer's Hour." She turned on the telecon and folded her hands reverently.

Homer Healey's message was preceded by a news flash from the head of the Healie movement, Waynel Masters, a blond, velvet-voiced man with the face of an angel. Gripping Ali's shoulder, Ayesha straightened up. "He's going to tell us about the end of the world," she breathed heavily. "Last night the announcer said that at three this afternoon, Waynel will make a prophecy."

Though most of the time he imitated Homer Healey's warm smile and gentle tone, today Waynel was obviously churned up. His hands twisted earnestly together as he stared solemnly at them from the telecon screen. Ayesha waited anxiously, licking her fingers, which were still sticky from Annie's fudge.

"Brothers and sisters," Waynel drawled, his southern Rs fading into silence. "I have news that will shake even the most faithful." The woman seated next to him, whose gleaming platinum hair stuck out all around her face like a halo, sighed audibly and looked as though she was about to cry. Waynel held up a huge black Bible with both hands and laid his lips reverently against its cover. "It says in the Book that you will be shaken. But you will not be moved if you know the prophecies."

"Now he's going to tell us." Ayesha turned up the sound. "Aren't you crazy to know?"

Ali's eyes were frozen on the screen. "I gotta get us a Bible," he said. "This afternoon I'm gonna go buy one and sneak it in."

Waynel Masters had laid down the Bible but kept his long fingers curled around it. "The Antichrist has come, folks. It's that simple.

Thought you'd want to know." He paced in front of the bright-haired woman, who held a crumpled handkerchief, occasionally dabbing her eyes. "He's turned up in India, among the heathen who live in sin and believe in a thousand gods, their eyes darkened to the truth of the Gospel."

Waynel swallowed hard and shook his head. "He is called Prema Sai Baba, and he claims to be Christ come again." The minister thumped his fists together like cymbals. "We all know what that means, don't we, folks? The Beast of Revelations has come, and all over the world people will be forced to wear his mark. Earthquakes and famines are everywhere. The Muslims are about to destroy the Jews. The Second Coming, folks, is just around the corner. Like the wise virgins, you better be ready. Scrub your lamps and line up early at the church door, or the Bridegroom will look right through you like you aren't there."

The woman with the strange hair was now weeping loudly, her handkerchief over her mouth, eye makeup running down her cheeks. Waynel put his arms around her, and they rocked back and forth.

"I say unto you that the Antichrist will torment the believers, trying to scare them into renouncing Jesus. He will come like the snake in Eden and tell you that men are gods, not the poor, miserable sinners we are. He is the Devil, folks, and God will throw him down as he once threw Lucifer down from heaven, with a crash that will rattle all the windows of earth."

Ali put his hands over his eyes and sobbed in Ayesha's arms. He now knew his life mission. It was destined. That was why God had made sure Rumi's letter and Waynel's announcement came at the same time. God wanted him to have no doubts. Ali would someday track down the Antichrist and fulfill his purpose on earth. To save Rumi and others like him from hell and eternal damnation, this false Messiah must be destroyed. Until that day, he would pray and keep the faith, growing in grace until God touched his lips with the coal of fire. Ali could see himself making straight the way for the Son of God to come in glory on a cloud. When the Rapture began, the everlasting arms of the Almighty would take him up. And Prema Sai, the Antichrist, would be dead.

∽⦿⦿∽

Ever since Jason decided to continue living at their Paris hotel, Consuelo had been on edge. The only place in this glittering cosmopolitan city where she felt comfortable was in the deepest basement of the Cluny Museum. There she would sit for hours before a statue of the Black Madonna that stood in a niche not often visited by the public. Under the blackened, arched roof of what had been a monastery refectory a thousand years before, a series of holes, which seemed to lead nowhere, had been dug in the irregular stone. One excavation led down into another, with ladders between them. The archeological work seemed to have been abandoned long ago, for dust had sifted over the rough stone surfaces.

The eyes of the Madonna looked inward and her lips curved in a slight smile. Her dark face was turned toward the empty holes, as if she waited for the one who would discover what lay at the bottom. Perhaps this dark-faced goddess was Pra, worshipped by the ancestors of the human race, who wailed her name as they put their dead into the dark, devouring earth. Her face was kind, not like Mother Kali's terrifying face, with its wide-open mouth and vacant eyes. Each goddess, Consuelo thought, represented both birth and death and carried the whole world in her womb.

Studying the Great Mother's face, Consuelo felt herself catapulted back to a time when women were the spiritual guardians of the race, when men revered them for bringing food from the earth and children from their bodies. There had been a time, a Golden Age, when there was no word for war and men lived without weapons, when love was the highest form of worship.

Now, Consuelo thought, as she started the long climb back to the museum lobby, domination by Brom Strassbourg and his cohorts had turned the world into a well-oiled machine where only money and power were worshipped. Surrounded as she was by such men, Prema Sai and the new order seemed just a faint scent of sweetness in the wind. She knew of others, like her son Rumi, who did not wear Brom's holochip or compete feverishly to amass worldly goods only to sit on them, hissing like dragons guarding their hoards. The quiet multitudes, who farmed the earth or served as healers, teachers, artists and builders, were waiting for the day when God would return, as he had promised. They called him by many names, these patient, ordinary people, but they had faith he would come.

When she reached the hotel, Jason and Brom were waiting for her. Imitating Brom, her husband had begun wearing silk bodysuits, which sagged on his narrow shoulders and bulged over his pot belly. Thanks to the rich life of Paris, Jason had given up all his Muslim dietary laws and now ate and drank as he pleased. Consuelo was not happy to see him drinking wine with Brom, since afterward he became surly. She realized that Jason's Muslim faith had been all that stood between him and bestiality. Now he was no better than a jackal, and much less distractible. In fact, he had begun to look rather like a jackal, his big, irregular teeth snapping together in his long face whenever he spoke. He was snapping now, since he had assured Brom she would be home an hour ago.

Ignoring Jason's frown, Consuelo sat at the glass and metal table where they ate their deathfood, as she called his Parisian banquets. "What do you want, Brom? I suppose it's more information about Radha or Ibrahim. I didn't have any before, and I don't have any now." She was tired and slipped off her fashionable shoes, knowing, but not caring, that Jason would disapprove her lack of modesty.

"My investigators suspect that Ibrahim is in Jerusalem. Have you heard anything from your friend?"

"Would I tell you if I had?"

"It would be worth your while. Think about it. I'll find him sooner or later." Brom pulled out a chair and sat down so close to her that she could see her image distorted in his pale gray eyes. "I just want to know about this new religion. My employees are caught up in it."

Consuelo talked right into his face, since he was determined to lean into hers. "What exactly is it that you object to? For one thing, it's not a new religion, just living the way all great faiths have taught. A regime of love, selflessness, kindness. Subversive? I don't think so."

"Could be." Brom checked his smooth chin for stubble, then glanced into the mirror on the wall over the gilded ebony side table. "It's like some kind of drug. People are getting lax, won't enforce the rules. Whole companies within the system are letting workers make decisions and share my profits." He leaned forward, his face hard and blank as concrete. "I can be sure of no one. Respect for authority is down the pipe. Can you tell me what is happening?"

"You've got the power, Brom." Jason tried to edge between them. "All it takes is power and they'll do what you say. You can make 'em do anything."

Brom turned his wide shoulders and blocked Jason off. "I need to know, and you must tell me."

"There's nothing much to tell that you would understand." Consuelo pushed her chair back and folded her arms. "Prema Sai is raising the level of spiritual energy in the world. It's like pumping oxygen into a sick person's hospital tent. You either breathe it or you die."

Brom slammed his open palm down on the table so hard he cracked the glass. "That explains nothing. What about my workers and managers breaking rules? The tax collectors winking at barter? Soldiers quitting the army to dig sewage ditches in Africa?"

"Read this." Not wanting Brom to come any closer, Consuelo shoved a book into his hands. His looming body made her feel suffocated, as she felt when Jason pulled her into bed. "The author is a well-known scholar of comparative religion. If he can't explain it to you, no one can."

"*The Age of God*, by Abraham Hoffman." He held the book at arm's length. Despite his growing farsightedness, Brom refused to wear corrective lenses. "A Jew, I suppose."

"I suppose." Consuelo walked to the other side of the table. "It's a bestseller all over the world. I'm surprised you haven't seen it. In this book, you'll find everything that's known about Prema Sai and what he plans to do." She uttered a silent prayer that God would help this man of silk and steel to conquer his rampaging ego and accept the reign of love in the world. As likely, she guessed, as Brom searching out the Black Madonna to give her ancient lips the kiss of peace.

"Prophecies," Brom snorted, leafing through the pages. "The ravings of lunatics in loincloths and hair shirts." But he took the book with him when he left.

❧❧❧

Sarah Hoffman had refused to read her husband's book about Prema Sai, but at her father's request she brought him a copy. Tucked between its pages was a picture of Radha and Murali smiling, their arms around each other. Together, Sarah and Rabbi Ordman sat in the dim, book-lined study, while he pored over a few pages again and again. On his forehead the rabbi wore a light like a miner's lamp. Attached to his thick glasses was a surgeon's magnifying glass. Lips pressed firmly together, he shook his head sorrowfully from side to side.

"Father, your eyes are no good for reading. Let me read it to you," Sarah said, leaning over to pull the book away.

The rabbi slapped at her hand. "Such a yenta you are, Sarah, always into my business. Your husband's business too, I suspect. Always fighting with him, complaining to me. Why did you marry him if he makes you so angry?"

Folding her shapely arms over her plump stomach, Sarah sat back. The body that had once driven Abraham crazy was now matronly, but her full, pink face still resembled that of a renaissance Venus, with voluptuous lips that now pouted more often than they smiled. Fed up with her father and her husband, she was pouting now. She often cried out to Abraham that their little boy, Solly, was the only male she could trust, and sometimes she meant it.

"How did I know marriage would make me so angry?" Sarah demanded. "How does any woman know ahead of time what it's like to spend her days sorting bugs out from grains of rice and counting the days allowed for making love? By the time I finish picking and counting, making love is the last thing on my mind. It is so with all the young women I know. Our Orthodox men are out having a life, while we do nothing but breed and clean. If I am angry, it is because of the rules, Father." She glared at him.

"Child, do not blame me for the rules." Rabbi Ordman sighed and looked down at the open book. "They have kept our people alive and pure for thousands of years. You expect life to be easy. You always did. Now this husband of yours, whom you wanted so much, turns out to be a traitor to his own religion and to ours." He tapped one paragraph with his crooked, stubby finger.

"I will read to you. 'Unimpeachable sources in India report that Prema Sai's mother is descended from the House of David, as the Moshiach must be. It is well-documented that Jews have lived in Cochin, in South India, since the time of the Diaspora. Prema Sai's mother was descended from the Jewish families of Cochin.' So, Sarah, what do you think of your husband's Indian Moshiach?" Rabbi Ordman's voice quavered, as if tears were near the surface. "He is making up this information, yes?"

"I think this Prema Sai is a fraud, just as you do," Sarah burst out. "But no, Abraham is not making it up. I searched through his private papers. He keeps them in a locked metal box under the bed, but I found the key hidden in his desk. See, here is a letter telling about Prema Sai's Jewish mother, saying that the boy is living in a place called Prasanthi Nilayam. She is there also. My husband is not a liar."

"I will keep this letter," Rabbi Ordman said, holding it over his head when Sarah tried to pull it away. "Better in my hands than yours."

After Sarah flounced out, protesting that no one trusted her with anything of importance, Rabbi Ordman sat reading the tightly written pages over and over, his brow wrinkling and his eyes tearing from the bright light. Though the rabbi's heart was pounding, he could not pull himself away from the words until he knew them by heart. Finally he placed the papers in his desk drawer and put on his tefillin. "I must pray to keep myself pure of the evil one's words," he said aloud. "I must not be drawn away from Ha-Shem." Eyes closed, he bowed his head and rocked back and forth, trying to dispel the persistent image of a young boy with eyes like black diamonds, compelling belief.

❦

Abraham Hoffman, once Ibrahim Al-Essa, was cleaning out his desk at the university. He wasn't sorry he had been asked to leave. He had felt a sense of freedom the moment his chairman notified him of the board's decision. Poor old Ari always stammered a little when he had to enforce unpleasant orders. His voice cracked as he told Abraham that people more powerful than he had made the decision. Not even the great scholar Abraham Hoffman could be retained at the university after writing that an Indian boy was the Moshiach, despite the boy's having a Jewish mother.

Then there was the little matter, very little of course, that Abraham himself was not quite a Jew. He had often been seen praying in the mosque, and everyone knew the story of his terrorist father. Ari bit his full lips and looked as if he were about to cry, the way he always did at bar mitzvahs.

Abraham patted his mentor's shoulder, telling him not to go on, that he understood very well. Glancing over his shoulder at the solidly packed walls of books, he decided to send for his library later. Just his personal papers in this one packing box would be enough for now. Abraham left the room feeling curiously light and joyful.

Sarah was in tears when she greeted him at the door. He had called ahead with the news, hoping she might have gotten over her fury and grief by the time he arrived home. Assuming that his wife would probably be too angry to cook, he had stopped for a falafel snack at his favorite Arab restaurant near the Jaffa gate. Often he came here at difficult times, finding it a comfort to talk with Ahmed, the proprietor of the Petra Hotel, who would drink thick, sweet Turkish coffee with him while they discussed the untranslatable intricacies of the Koran.

"It's all over, then?" Sarah cried. "No more university? Just because of that crazy book?"

"That crazy book has made us half a million shekels already," Abraham said with a smile, "and will make millions more. You won't suffer from it, Sarah. I promise you."

"I was so proud of you being a professor," she said between hiccups, pounding her wet face against his chest. "I don't care about the money. I care about what people think."

"You mean your father." Abraham tossed his black jacket on the chair. He had never liked the traditional black suit and changed into light blue pants and a silvery-gray silk shirt. "It's your father you're worried about, I know. He hasn't spoken to me since the book came out."

"I have broken my father's heart by marrying a man with weird ideas. Look, have you got a dybbuk or what? How could the Moshiach be born in India, even if his mother might be Jewish? Which is a huge 'if,' let's admit." She stamped her foot so hard the candlesticks rattled on the buffet. "Such ideas you have. Solly is crying in his room because everybody at school says his father's gone totally meshugge."

"What do you want, Sarah?" Abraham fastened his shirt and put on a yarmulke, which rode uneasily on top of his thick, wavy hair. "The job is lost and the book is already being sold around the world. What do you want me to do?"

Tears running down her face, Sarah sobbed, "I want you to recant. Disown everything. Apologize."

"Apologize to whom?" Abraham shrugged. He was used to her outbursts and no more upset by them than he had been by his mother's.

"For what? I told the truth. And my religion is my own business."

"No, it's ours," she choked on her words. "It's everything we've built together. Our child, our Shabbat meals, the prayers we say before we make love. If you were still a Muslim, we'd just be two dogs mating, not husband and wife. Your soul would be somewhere else. With one of those houris in harem pants."

"You can't understand what it is to be a Muslim, Sarah," he said, opening the door. "And I won't try to explain it now. When you're calmer, I'll be back."

Since the elevator was slow, Abraham ran down the fire escape, his metal-tipped shoes resounding on the stairs. Just before reaching the street, he saw a limotank with dark-tinted windows and a torp turret parked at the end of the spacious, tree-lined alley where his father had been killed. As a sudden stirring of uneasiness twisted low in his body, Abraham backed up to the wall and slid along the rear of the building, then ran toward the front.

Another limotank with Eurocom insignia was parked in front of the apartment. One man sat inside, and two others were striding up the front steps. Abraham remembered the warning that had come five years ago from his mother's friend, Consuelo. So much time had gone by that he had almost forgotten Brom Strassbourg was hunting for him. Probably his change of name had put off the pursuers. Taking his great-grandmother's family name had made Abraham feel almost invisible, as if he were scarcely real, even to himself.

Both the university and the publisher had been given strict instructions not to reveal his address. The thought suddenly struck him that Sarah's father had a wide circle of friends, and not all of them wished Abraham Hoffman well. Whoever had betrayed him, it didn't matter now. After running to the kosher deli, he called the police, asking them to come and protect Sarah and Solly. Then he took a side road that cut into the Old City and backtracked to the police station just inside the Jaffa Gate.

Two officers had immediately been dispatched to his apartment house, and Abraham waited for them to call back. He felt sure that who-ever was pursuing him would hide only until the police were gone. Now that they knew where he lived, Abraham would be a constant danger to his family. Even after the call came, saying that Solly and Sarah were safe and the men were gone, he knew he could not go home.

After leaving by the side door into David Street, Abraham glanced nervously at everyone who passed by. He began to imagine that anyone who looked at him was one of Brom's henchmen. Long ago his mother had offered to teach him t'ai chi so that he could defend himself, and now he wished he had taken the opportunity to learn. But like his father, he wanted to be left alone, fearing nothing, wanting nothing but a life of love, prayer and study. Now Abraham had lost all three and was more alone than even he wanted to be.

Stuffing his yarmulke into his back pocket, Abraham ran all the way to the Arab market, a few streets from the enormous dome of the Holy Sepulcher Church. There he bought a gray-and-white striped caftan and a keffiyeh for his head. They would not be looking for an Arab. But just as the shopkeeper handed him the bag, two men in dark glasses and blue silk bodysuits stepped in the doorway.

Abraham brushed past the Arab shopkeeper and through a curtain into the back room, where a young girl at a sewing machine calmly ges-tured at the door behind her. Apparently she mistook him for a terrorist being pursued by the police. Once outside, he turned the corner, his plastic bag flapping behind as he ran. No time even for the disguise, he thought, gasping for breath. His heart skipped erratically as he heard footsteps and shouts behind him. Desperate for cover, he squatted behind a low rack of leather jackets, flinching at the sharp, acrid smell. Like his mother, Abraham had chosen not to eat meat or wear leather.

"You are interested in buying, Adoni?" The old salesman squatted next to him, as if he were used to customers who wanted to sniff the merchandise.

"Not now," Abraham hissed, peering through the garments at the approaching men in blue suits. "I'm hiding, for God's sake."

"Oh, gotcha," the salesman whispered, standing up. "And can I interest you gentlemen in a leather helmet?" he asked smoothly. "I have just the color. Blue-dyed ratskin." He hung onto one of the men, wheedling. "Only one thousand shekels. Too much? For you, then, it is seven hundred."

The two men pushed the old man aside and ran down the street, shoving their arms into racks of clothes and knocking curtains aside. When it seemed safe, Abraham came out and bought a wool muffler from the salesman, out of gratitude.

"Look out, they're back," the salesman cried, ducking for cover.

As the two men came around the block, one of them pulled out a torp from his hip-pack. Clutching the package to his chest, as if it could protect him, Abraham slipped past a falafel stand and down the slippery stone steps that led to the Holy Sepulcher Church. Crowds were milling around as he entered the round, high-ceilinged hall that seemed more like a crusader fortress than a church.

"Come, kiss the holy rock for only half a shekel," a toothless, brown-robed Franciscan monk called, gesturing toward a little tunnel under the huge altar.

Abraham briefly considered the tunnel as a place to hide, then decided it could be more a trap than a haven. Hearing a disturbance at the door, he knew it must be the gunmen. He vaguely remembered a stairway that led deep under the church. Hoping memory would serve, Abraham turned left and was relieved to see the stone steps. He hurried down, running awkwardly on his heels, so the metal taps on the toes of his shoes would not be heard.

The ancient underground sanctuary was low and rough-hewn, resembling a cave. It dated from early days, before the grandeur of Constantine, when Jewish believers had huddled together at their Lord's grave, saying prayers and breaking the bread that was his body. The

curving walls met overhead, and he could feel a throbbing energy, like a
heartbeat, emanating from the moist, black surfaces. Someone had
prayed here, Abraham thought, prayed with the kind of terrible intensity
that could ward off death. His hand over his heart, he stood uncertainly
in the middle of the room, feeling the urge to prostrate himself in prayer.

Then he heard a faint humming in his ears, and faraway words filled
his whole body like the beat of music. *Abraham, you must follow me a
long way now. Leave this place and find your wife at the Jaffa Gate. From
there you will go to the airport. Tickets will be waiting for you at the Air
India desk. Come, beloved. I have longed to see you.*

Abraham closed his eyes and swayed in ecstasy, even after the voice
was silent. Then he crouched behind the blackened altar and slipped on
his Arab headgear and caftan. Feeling more at ease, he climbed the long
stairway, ignoring the two men who jostled him on their way down.
Abraham's ears tingled and his eyes burned with tears. He had no doubt
who was calling him. And he was no longer afraid.

Her scarf pulled low over her forehead, Sarah was waiting for him in
front of the Jaffa Gate Coffee House, their favorite meeting place. When
she sprang into his arms, he could feel her body trembling.

"I ran all the way," she said, pulling him inside, where they sat down
on low stools with torn plastic covers. "I heard those men talking before
the police came. If they find you, they'll kill you, unless your mother tells
them where Prema Sai is. That's what they said."

"A long time ago I was told this might happen," Abraham said, holding her tightly. "But I didn't want to frighten you."

"We'll have to leave Jerusalem," Sarah sobbed, her face pressed against
his shoulder. "Where can we go that you'll be safe? Strassbourg owns
most of the world, and fundamentalists have what's left."

"Not all of it, my darling," he whispered, gently stroking her hair.
"But you must stay here. You have a family and a home. The book roy-
alties will provide money to live on. Strassbourg's men won't bother you
once I've disappeared."

"When will you come back? Soon?" Sarah shook him. "I just know Ha-Shem is taking you away from me because I was such a bad-tempered wife. Will you come back at all?"

"I don't know," he answered. "When it's safe. I don't even know exactly where I'm going."

"If you need money, call Ahmed," she said. "I could send it through him. Strassbourg's men will probably watch the house. I've put fifty thousand shekels in this bag with your passport and prayer book. Some food and clothes, too. You must remember to eat kosher wherever it is you're going."

"God be with you, my love, and with Solly," Abraham held her tightly against him. "Now, you had better leave through the back door. I'll go out the front. They're not looking for an Arab."

"Lehitra'ot." Sarah kissed him hard on the lips. "You are still a Jew. Say we will meet again, yechiri, beloved. Just say it and I'll wait as long as I have to."

"We will meet again," Abraham said as he gave her a little push out the door. "Wait for me here in Jerusalem."

He hailed one of the Arab taxis parked under the Tower of David, just a few steps from the restaurant. The early afternoon traffic was light, so they raced across Israel's heavily populated industrial midland toward Tel Aviv, veering off a few miles east of the city toward Ben-Gurion Airport. The promised tickets were waiting, and he saw with surprise that they were not to South India but to Mecca, then on to Nepal and Ladakh, in the Himalayas.

❧

Hugging Solly, Sarah sat in her father's study. "Abraham's gone," she wept. "Probably for good. I was a bad wife and have lost my husband. Father, you must tell me how to get him back. You have always known how to make miracles happen."

"My child, you depend too much on others," Rabbi Ordman

grumbled, keeping his rheumy eyes on her face. "That has always been your foolish way."

Solly wriggled out of his mother's arms and reached for the velvet bag, which held his grandfather's treasured tefillin. "No," the rabbi said, carefully placing the tefillin in a drawer. "They will be yours someday, little one, but not yet."

"Those men ransacked our apartment, Father. They broke my ceramic pot collection, every pot, looking for something."

"I take it they did not find what they were looking for?" Rabbi Ordman pulled open his desk drawer, checking to see if Radha's letter to Abraham was still there.

"How do I know what they were looking for?" Sarah gave the squirming Solly a smack to keep him still. "Whatever it was, they seemed not to find it. They left angry and said they would find Abraham wherever he went."

"But he is gone, you say? He did not tell you where?"

"I suppose he is joining this Prema Sai Baba in South India," Sarah said. "He didn't tell me. He tells me nothing important."

"Nor does he tell the place in this book." The rabbi laid his hand over the glossy cover of Abraham's bestseller. "Only in the letter."

They heard scuffling outside the door, and a cry from the housekeeper brought them to their feet. Sarah pushed Solly behind her as two men, dressed in blue polysilk bodysuits, burst into the tiny room. One trained a torp on the rabbi, and the other pulled Sarah up against him, his hands around her neck. "Where is your husband?"

"I don't know. I haven't seen him for the past two days." Sarah's voice was shaking.

"You must know where the child Prema can be found," he demanded. "Surely Abraham Hoffman's mother told him where."

The first man came closer to Rabbi Ordman. "We can tear this place apart," he said in a low, menacing voice, "or you can give us what we've come for."

"And what is that?" His voice calm, the rabbi stood up, looking taller than he really was. "I have nothing of yours."

"We found no letters in the Hoffman apartment," the man said. "We've already been to the university, and his personal things are gone. Come, there must be letters from Abraham Hoffman's mother. They must be somewhere. Tell us, or we will kill first your daughter, then the child." Sarah screamed as he placed the barrel of his torp against her neck.

"I see I have no choice." The rabbi reluctantly opened the drawer and handed over the letter. "Perhaps it is the will of God that this false Moshiach be caught before he harms the world. Here is what you seek. In it you will learn the place where the child can be found."

"And a picture," the gunman said, snatching the photo of Radha and Murali from the drawer. This could be useful."

"Father, no," Sarah choked. "I think Abraham has gone to defend the child. They will kill him, too."

Rabbi Ordman shrugged his shoulders and spread his hands as the men fled. "What I have done, I have done," he said. "*Gott vill helfen.*"

15

It was mid-August and the monsoons were late. The sky over Prasanthi Nilayam was sickly pale like the cracked land, and the vegetation had turned brown. The glaring sun made Radha dizzy. Sweat ran down her neck at the slightest movement, and a prickly rash spread wherever skin touched skin. The others had adjusted to the climate, even Philo with his fair complexion. But Radha went into a stupor from March through August, going out of the house only when necessary. Eddie had installed ceiling fans in the living room and bedrooms, but Radha said the fans did nothing except push the hot air around.

She preferred to sit on the verandah, from where she could see children playing in the Chitravathi River, while women washed clothes nearby. Despite the city's new laundromats, many Puttaparthi women still did their wash the old way. Watching them, Radha felt a little envious of the laughing and splashing that went on at the riverbank.

She also had a good view of the luxurious building Sai Baba had constructed to house visiting heads of state. There, Muslim and Hindu leaders had come together under his guidance, attempting to end the conflicts that had turned their country into a war zone for six hundred years.

At least they were moving toward peace, Radha thought, unlike the Middle East, where the Muslim-Jewish antagonism continually threatened the existence of Israel. Most Middle Eastern leaders had refused to meet with Sai Baba, unwilling to give up control over their suffering peoples. For them, she sighed, Shalom was still only a word. Leaning back in her cane rocking chair, Radha closed her eyes and prayed, as she did every day, for the peace of Jerusalem.

After his nap, Tewati came out to the verandah, and lowered himself slowly onto his floor cushion with a heavy sigh. He, too, often seemed to be in a stupor, though not from the heat. Only when Amar came for Sanskrit study or just to talk, did the old man come alive, and those times were less frequent now that Amar was twelve years old.

"Have you seen him today?" Tewati spoke so low Radha had to lean over to hear him.

"Not since he left for school." Even the effort of talking turned Radha's cheeks hot, and she hoped Tewati would go back into his usual reverie. "Eddie and I will meet him in a little while and bring him home."

"He tells me that we no longer need to meet him after school," Tewati said. "Did you know this?"

"Yes. Of course, he's right," Radha agreed, fanning herself briefly, then giving up, since the motion made her hotter than before. "Overprotecting would only call attention to him, so we walk at a distance to avoid being noticed."

"It is hard, is it not, to give him up? Surrender him to whatever will come?" The old man's thin hands lay peacefully in his lap, and it seemed that nothing was hard for him.

"For me, giving anything up is impossible," Radha sighed. "It has to be snatched out of my hands after a fight. That's always been my way."

Tewati smiled, carefully wiping a bit of dribble off his chin. "There was once a great English bishop who was asked how he stayed so calm when mind and matter were continually in an uproar. 'Never mind,' he told his questioners. 'Doesn't matter.'"

Sometimes Tewati sounded just like Amar, who often said that everything happens just as it should. "If that is so," Radha once asked Amar, "why did you bother coming into this world? The whole planet is in such pain," she said. "If I could change things as you can, I would do it." Then she told him all the things she thought should be changed—no more starving children, no more cruelty, no more wars.

Amar heard her out, his head cocked sympathetically. "Do you know what is real or unreal?" he asked. "Can you see how nothing is still, even for a moment, but always changing, dying and being reborn like clouds in the sky? Do you worry that such and such a cloud will not stay the same shape? No. You just watch it pass by and love the God in everyone and everything. Isn't that what you do, Auntie?"

Then he gave her a quick kiss and darted off to play with the crowd of friends, who never left him alone. Like everyone, they wanted all his attention. Radha was left to think about how she always forgot to love whenever she began to worry. Perhaps Amar was telling her that only love would free her from anxiety, would pull her out of her exhausted, cranky self. The coming of the monsoon rains would also help. "Narayan," she said, "will the rains never come?"

"Soon, perhaps." The old man squinted at the blazing sky. "But not a single cloud yet," he said, rearranging his cramped legs to restore the blood flow. Closing his eyes, he withdrew from the outside world to wait for Amar's return.

The screen door creaked open, and Eddie came out on the porch. Somehow he always looked cool and dry, perhaps because he walked with such economy of movement that he hardly seemed to move at all. Yet, despite the difference in their ages, he was always a step ahead of her, wasting no energy on complaints or worries. Being near Amar was enough for him.

"It's time to go for the boy," he said. "If you're too hot, I'll go alone today."

"No. I want to go." Feeling dizzy after pulling herself up, Radha leaned on Eddie's arm for a moment. To have a little time with Amar, even at a distance, she would endure the heat. Over the years, Radha had watched Eddie and Amar grow increasingly closer, and she tried not to let them be together without her. As she hurried to keep up with Eddie, a familiar, anxious lump swelled in her throat, and she felt like a child again, trying to come between Kori and Consuelo.

As Radha approached the sprawling white building Sai Baba had designed for the boys' middle school, she covered her mouth against the dust coming from the adjacent construction project. A tall crane was lifting blocks of concrete and placing them on top of the new school auditorium. Wavering bands of light from the relentless afternoon sun made her feel dizzy, as she shaded her eyes and looked toward the school, hoping to see Amar. Many of the younger boys were already scattering from the school entrance, hurrying home to escape the heat.

"I see him." Eddie pointed at Amar, looking grown-up in his immaculate white shirt and long white pants. "We'd better stay here and wait. He prefers it."

Many boys swarmed around him, gesturing and talking, jockeying for a place at Amar's side. He listened first to one, then another, focusing his warm, bright eyes on each one in turn. Several ran ahead to watch the huge crane, then ran back, urging Amar to come and look.

Radha watched Amar walking briskly in the center of the group. He seemed never to run out of energy, she thought, probably because he expected nothing and gave everything. It took so much effort to keep her own interests separate from other people's, planning how her needs would be served and worrying that they might not. In this intolerable heat, she hardly bothered to plan anything, and for a moment experienced the comforting lassitude she felt before sleep, when worries held at arm's length finally dissolve in the dark.

One boy, younger than the others, was standing directly in front of the half-built auditorium, pointing at the concrete block being lifted high above him. Hearing a sharp sound like a gunshot, Radha looked up and saw that the cable had snapped. She shouted a warning as the huge block plunged toward the boy.

Suddenly the gray mass of concrete began to shimmer, then dissolved in the sunlight. Radha looked at Amar, who was standing with his right hand raised, as a blurred gray cloud slowly collected in front of the trembling boy. After coalescing into a firmly defined mass, the cloud again became a block of concrete.

Radha was shivering and her mouth hung open, too dry to utter a word. Now he's done it, she thought. Everyone will know and nothing can be done to hide him. Here in India, rumors of miracles spread like typhus, and soon crowds would descend on them. Along with those who came to worship would come those who wished the child harm. As Amar stood there, vulnerable and gentle, her heart hurt with such love for him that for a moment she could hardly breathe.

One boy prostrated himself at Amar's feet. "You are Prema," he exclaimed. "I've always thought so, and now I know. You are Prema Sai."

One by one, the others knelt to kiss his feet, then sat back in silence, gazing at his face. In a split second, Radha saw Amar's whole countenance become luminous, changing from gold to faint blue, then to pure white, as if he had swallowed light. Amar suddenly seemed to tower over them all.

"Yes. It is time to tell you." His voice was full and strong, not the young voice they had heard every day. "I am Prema Sai." Then, once again his face became the one they knew, and his voice was his own. "Don't be afraid. Be happy. That's why I am here." He smiled his radiant smile and held out his hands to them all.

"Will you still play with us?" The little boy he had saved looked ready to cry.

Prema walked over and put his hands on the boy's shoulders. "Not anymore," he said softly. "For now, it would be better to tell no one what you have seen. Soon enough it will be known." Then he looked at Eddie and Radha. "I must be about my business."

That evening, when Radha pulled the window curtain aside, she saw that a crowd had gathered in front of the verandah. No one shouted or pushed. They just stood hand-in-hand, waiting patiently like the silent flock of bulbul birds in a nearby tamarind tree.

"You aren't going out there?" Radha's voice was trembling. "They could mob you, start a riot, anything."

"No they won't, Auntie," Prema's eyes were shining and peaceful, as if he were looking at something beyond her sight. "They will only love me." His eyes seemed to reflect the whole universe. Radha was almost afraid to look into them for fear she would see too much, something that would blast her away like the winds that had sprung up this past hour, bringing dark rain clouds.

Prema walked onto the porch and held his hands out to the people, like a mother reaching for her children. "What you have heard of me is true," he said. "But you need not worship or bow down. Once that was necessary, but now I tell you that you are the Atma, you are God. You are as I am. You are love, you are the breath of God, you are all that is. Once the sages told you to say '*Tat twam asi*, I am That.' But I tell you to say 'I am I.' There is no difference between you and All That Is."

He smiled in that warm, confiding way that always made Radha want to laugh and cry at once. "Truth to tell, there is no I, either. Bow down to each other, not to me, for it is each other you must recognize as God, each other you must worship with the devotion you would give me. Do you wish to please me, my beloved friends? Then love one another."

Prema waited for a few moments as people stood in little groups, arms reaching around shoulders, heads resting against heads, until the whole mass of people seemed to merge into a single, murmuring organism, and the bulbul birds began to sing their ecstatic, twittering song. When the rains started, the first heavy, cooling drops fell on Prema's open hand.

After coming back inside the house, he went directly to Devi. "Mother, I will need a few things to take with me," he said. "I would like you to put some clothes in my school backpack, and a bit of food. The kind that will keep."

"My son, my son," Devi stammered. "Where will you go?"

Radha exchanged glances with Eddie and Philo. Now that the boy had come into his full strength, their role was over. Though she knew that nothing had the power to harm him, how could she bear to let him go? Even now, when he so much as left the room, it seemed darker.

Prema smiled and took Radha's hand, smoothing it with his fingers, probing and pushing as if he were working out a splinter, until she relaxed. "Radha, do you think I will forget you? Not talk to you anymore?" His eyes lost their mystery and twinkled at her as they always had. "We have been friends forever, you and I. When you were unhappy, I was there, loving you. I have spent lifetimes winning your heart. And now that it is almost mine, I will never let you go."

She clung to his hand. "It is yours. My heart, I mean."

Returning her hand to her lap, Prema said lightly, "Not yet, *bangaroo*, not yet. But soon."

A knock at the door made Radha jump, for they were not used to callers. Philo stepped out on the verandah to talk with a group of visitors, but before the door closed, Radha caught a glimpse of several men in red and yellow robes.

"They are here," Prema cried out, joy in his voice. "I am so happy. Please bring them to me."

Philo opened the door, allowing one young Westerner and three monks in Tibetan robes to file in. They knelt down to touch Prema's feet with their foreheads, but he quickly helped them up, seeming impatient for the ritual to be over. "You must rest after so long a journey," he said, showing them to the low table in the dining area. "Rest and eat. I will serve you myself."

"No, my Lord, no," the leader protested, his cheeks crinkled from years of biting winds. "It is we who should serve you."

"Well then, we will serve each other, as it should be." Prema laid out bowls of dahl with rice, then poured white, creamy lassi into their cups.

When he sat down, Murali was close beside him, her delicate face turned to his like a flower to the sun.

Devi shrugged her shoulders helplessly and turned up her palms. "Son, who are these men? How do you know them?"

The oldest introduced himself as Dhattu, head of an ashram in Ladakh, deep in the Himalayas. He bowed to Devi, then to the rest. "We have come looking for our Lord," he said. "Signs led us to South India, and this young man has helped us find you." He nodded at the young Westerner, whose fine features looked as if they had been chiseled in golden brown marble by a master carver. Though this young man was much taller than Prema, the two could have been brothers, Radha thought.

"My name is Rumi," the young man said. His eyes were warm, and it seemed he could not stop looking at Radha. "And I believe you are Radha. You remember Consuelo? She showed me a picture you sent her."

He looked very much like Consuelo, Radha thought, though his jaw was more angular. His thick, shoulder-length black hair hung straight to his shoulders like folded crow's wings. She came close and looked into his eyes. "Philo," she exclaimed, "it's Consuelo's son!" Radha took Rumi's hand. "Why did you come?"

"My mother told me to warn you that Brom Strassbourg intends to take your son prisoner unless you give him Prema Sai. I saw this man, and he will do anything to have his way."

Radha's heart pounded, and she had to lean against Eddie's shoulder. "Does Ibrahim know?"

"It helped that you mentioned the university when you wrote of his wedding," said Rumi. "We left word for him there."

"Will he be able to hide?" Radha clasped Eddie's fingers tightly in her own. "Ibrahim no longer uses his father's last name, and he's changed his first name to Abraham. Let's hope they can't trace him." She swallowed repeatedly, trying to push down the fear that welled up like a hard bulb in her throat.

"Why do you think Amar is the boy you seek?" Tewati's hands trembled as he clutched a napkin, attempting to hold them still. "He is Hindu, not Buddhist."

"Our last lama told us to search for Issa, whom you know in the West as Jesus. After his resurrection, Issa returned to the Himalayas, where he had studied as a young man before beginning his mission in Israel. Our lama said that Issa had been reborn in South India as Prema Sai."

Eddie drew in his breath. "Jesus said he had visited other peoples who were not known to the Jews. Even many Christian scholars are convinced that Jesus traveled throughout the East before beginning his mission." He turned toward the monks. "And he stayed at your ashram?"

Dhattu swallowed his food slowly and deliberately before answering. "The story of Notovitch, the Russian explorer, is well known. At the turn of the twentieth century, he was carried to Hemis to be healed of a broken leg. While the monks nursed him back to health, he read their ancient accounts of Issa's stay in the Himalayas."

"And you believe our Prema is Issa?"

The monks nodded, and Dhattu said gravely, "We know it. And we have come to take him to our monastery so we may serve him."

"No," Murali cried out. "I need him. Leave him here a little longer. Next week I will be in a play, and he promised to watch me." She hid her face against Prema's shoulder. "You promised!"

"Murali, I will see you wherever I am. Don't cry," Prema stroked her soft, wispy brown hair. "And I will come back one day for you. You must be very good and strong while I am gone. Here, let me wipe your face."

"Can this be true?" Radha looked wildly from Prema to Devi. "Next people will tell us he's the Prophet Mohammed. He is Prema. Isn't that enough?"

"Radha, *bangaroo*," said Prema, his arm still around Murali, whose face had turned pale and frozen. "It is all the same. You think Jesus was only the Son of God, not God? He said he was the Son because the people could understand no more than that. But he was God as I am, as you are. We are all one great wave of life and love that rolls everywhere. Can you call this part Brahma, this Prema, this Issa, this Radha? Is your hand not you? Your heart? Every cell in your body? Just so, all of you are cells of my body, and I am inseparable from you."

"But why must you leave?" Radha cried, desperate not to lose him, to hold him by any means she could. "Haven't we taken good care of you, done everything you needed?"

Prema gently took Radha's arm, leading her into the kitchen where they could be alone. "I have a favor to ask, Auntie. You don't have to say yes."

"What is it?" she wiped her sleeve across her wet eyes. "You know I'll do anything you ask."

He held up his hand. "Wait. I want to take Eddie with me. It's for his good, to live with these monks, and for mine, to have him as my closest friend. He has earned this blessing over many lifetimes, as Arjuna, as John the beloved disciple. Others, too, whose names you would not know. You will be with us in this love, *bangaroo*. Will you say yes?"

"But he's the one who keeps me from falling apart," she burst out. "How can I let him go? Without him I'd be crazy. You know how I go into orbit over every little thing." She wanted to scream and throw herself at Prema's feet, or turn back the clock to when he was a baby in her arms.

Without Eddie she would be as lonely as a comet careening across the dark, empty sky. First she had lost her parents over and over again to Philo, and finally to death. Then she had lost Kamal. Now she would lose both Prema and Eddie. Maybe her son Ibrahim, too, if Strassbourg had his way. No one would be there for her, no one, and it would be like that forever. Radha cried out loud, clutching her throat, as though she were suffocating. For the rest of her life, she would feel this loss, from her getting up to her lying down. Why did she always love men who loved God more than they loved her? Men for whom she was not enough? Unable to catch her breath, she ran to the sink.

Retching and gasping, Radha bent over until Prema placed his hand flat against her back. All at once she was empty. Warmth and peace were flowing through her, from her middle outward to her limbs and head. This was how she had felt after Ibrahim was born, perfectly content. If she really loved Eddie, loved him as she loved herself, she would have to let him go. She had lost so much, Radha realized, because she had to learn not to need so much, and loss was the only way she would learn it.

"I will always be with you. Don't be afraid," Prema whispered, brushing his face so close to hers that she caught the faint scent of jasmine that always surrounded him. "Your son Abraham will also be with me where I am going."

"You will take care of him," Radha said, releasing her breath in a long sigh. "And you will take care of me. I understand." She held her hands together in a namasté of surrender. "Eddie can go. I'll be all right."

With his right hand, Prema made a swirling motion, then handed her a pendant on a thick gold chain. On one side was his face and on the other was Eddie's. "So you will never forget how much we love you," he said. "Now, he will need your help packing. Go, dear one. I must give some time to my mother and Narayan, for I am feeling their grief also."

Radha noticed that Philo did nothing to help with the preparations. He simply stood at the door, his deep-set eyes shadowy and blank, his narrow lips pressed so tightly together they were nearly invisible. Although Philo had begged to go along, Prema said he must stay to guard the women. As he stood mute, looking stooped and diminished, Radha felt sad for her brother, who was so unused to being left behind. Always, he had been the favored one, and now he was being emptied, as painfully as she had been over the years. When she took his hand, he seemed not to notice.

By midnight, Prema and Eddie were ready to leave. Under a sky black with rain clouds, everyone stood in a silent circle on the verandah. Prema said it was best to leave at once, so the ashram people would not see them. He was careful to say nothing precise about where they were going. After helping Eddie secure his backpack, Rumi shouldered his own. He asked Radha to send his mother word that he would return with Prema Sai, but not for many years. Eddie said nothing at all about returning, and she could not bring herself to ask.

Following Eddie into the yard, Radha was immediately drenched by the driving rain that had turned the air gray. She didn't kiss him good-bye, just laid her cheek against his. For once, she had nothing to say.

As she watched the men start down the muddy road, the hoods of their plastic ponchos pulled over their heads, Radha stood between the pillars of the verandah, her arm around Murali. Just as they disappeared from view, she heard a familiar voice in her mind, *I am with you now and always, as your sunshine and your shadow,* the voice said. *Look for me everywhere, for I am everywhere, holding up the world, turning the galaxies, spreading the universe to infinity. And don't forget to play marbles with Murali, so she won't be too sad.*

Radha looked at Murali, and her heart jumped when she saw Prema's features pass like a wave across the girl's tear-stained face. But Murali's own face returned instantly, and Radha kissed her on the forehead, reverently, as she would have kissed God. For had not Prema said there was no difference?

∽◦◗◦∾

Two days later, other men came to Puttaparthi seeking the child. Murali saw them first and ran into the house to tell her mother. Shanti, who was ironing a sari, straightened up with difficulty, holding one hand to her back. She was seven months pregnant and found it hard to stay on her feet for long. Three hours of ironing was too much, Radha had warned her, before leaving with Philo to buy the day's groceries.

"Hush, darling," Shanti said to Murali. "You will wake Narayan."

"Two men," Murali insisted, her arms around her mother. "They followed me into the ashram. I'm sure of it. I saw them pointing at me, asking someone who I was."

Tewati came into the room, rubbing his eyes. "Perhaps these are

Brom's men, searching for Prema Sai. Last night I had a dream that they would soon be here. Devi," he called into the back bedroom, "you must come. It is happening, as I warned you."

Devi's silver and black hair hung loosely down her back, and she was tucking in the end of her sari as she entered the room. "Murali, run out the back door and warn the ashram police. You must not be here when these men come." Taking a long, last look at her mother, Murali did as she was ordered, leaving the back door swinging behind her.

"Courage," said Shanti, taking Devi's hand. "We have always known this would happen."

"Even before I was born, I knew about this moment." Devi's voice was calm.

As the men burst in the front door, Tewati stood in front of the two woman, trying to shield them with his body. "What do you want?" he asked, his voice low and steady. "If you seek the child, you are too late. He has gone and we do not know where."

"Tell us," one of the men said, poking Tewati with the barrel of his torp. "Or we'll shoot the old man."

"We don't know," Devi cried, throwing her arm protectively around Shanti's shoulders. "Prema told us nothing."

"He told his mother nothing about where he was going?" The man sneered, his weapon trained on Tewati. Even before the silent shot landed in the old man's heart, the torp was leveled at Shanti.

"Surely you won't make me kill this pregnant woman?" He addressed Devi. "It's up to you. Tell me where your son has gone, or she dies and her child with her."

Shanti stood with her hands folded over her wide belly, whispering "Om Sai Ram," over and over.

"Even if I knew, I would not tell you," said Devi. "Shanti and I are prepared to die. Our lives belong to Prema."

A second hiss from the torp brought Shanti down, blood flowing from a hole in her forehead.

"Again, I ask you, where is your son?" The taller of the two gunmen prodded her with his weapon.

Devi was silent, though her lips formed the same prayer Shanti had said before she died. Suddenly they heard a siren in the distance. "The little girl must have gone for help." The shorter gunman stood at the back door, passing his torp from one hand to the other. "Let's get out of here."

"One more time." With his weapon jammed against Devi's heart, the tall man said, "Tell me."

Devi closed her eyes and shook her head. She was smiling when the torp flashed, killing her instantly.

"It's no use," the tall gunman muttered. "Even if the others know, they won't tell either. Let's get back to Paris and tell Strassbourg that we've lost the trail."

By the time the police arrived, the men had climbed over the garden wall and disappeared into the village. Radha and Philo ran through the front door, with Murali just behind. Crying aloud, Philo bent over Shanti's body and laid his ear against her heart. Blood from her forehead stained his face as he sat on the floor, gently rocking her. Murali patted her mother's swollen belly, whispering comfort to the baby dying inside, hoping he would hear.

"They wouldn't tell about the monks coming for Prema," Radha gasped, her hand tight against her throat. "That's why they're dead."

A slim man dressed in white rushed in carrying a white box marked with a red cross. "Stand back," he said. "Let me examine them." Kneeling down by Shanti, he put a scope to where the baby's heart would be.

Philo inhaled great gulps of air between the words that kept flowing from his mouth, regular as a heartbeat. "My God, my God," he said over and over again.

"I'm so sorry. No sign of life," the doctor said, moving on to the other two. "Death was probably instantaneous." He put his scope away, methodically clicking the box shut. "They are with God. We must take their bodies to the river."

Murali stood alone in the living room, forgotten as the others accompanied the dead. Philo carried Shanti in his arms, not allowing anyone to touch her. Murali was glad he had forgotten her, for she did not want to see her mother's funeral pyre. Arranging her dress around her long, thin legs, she sat before the altar, looking into the eyes of Prema, whose picture, framed by flowers, stared back at her.

"We are not our bodies," she whispered, remembering the words her mother had often said. "The body is like a shadow. Do I mind that my shadow is long or short or disappears? It was like that with Mother and the others. Only the shadows are gone." Tears coursed down her pale cheeks and she longed for Shanti's arms to be around her.

Suddenly, Murali's breath caught in her throat as she felt Prema's presence and heard his voice in her mind. *Don't grieve, bangaroo. They are with me in joy.* Light flashed behind her closed eyelids, and she gasped, her eyes burning. For an instant Murali could see her mother's radiant form before it dissolved in a fire brighter than the one that would burn her body on the shore of the Chitravathi.

❧

Abraham took the ticket to Mecca as a gift from Allah, allowing him to take the pilgrimage his faith required at least once in a lifetime. Once there, he spent many days praying before the black rock that embodied the unchanging strength and mystery of God. Then he went into retreat with a Sufi master and fasted for a month.

Abraham felt that he could join Prema only after peeling off the alien layers that hid the core of his being, even from himself. Only when the old Sufi said Abraham was ready to meet God, did he leave the Holy City, his heart an empty vessel, ready to receive what God would give him.

During the flight from Katmandu, Abraham reviewed what little he had been able to learn about the tiny Himalayan province of Ladakh. He recalled that the state was bordered by Kashmir and China and had the fewest people per square mile of anywhere in the world except Antarctica. As the throbbing, dented little plane lurched down toward Leh, the capital, Abraham clutched the backrest of the empty seat in front of him. Flying low, just under the dark, scudding clouds, the plane seemed about to be impaled on the four-mile-high mountain peaks below. He saw no sign of human life, only bare granite crags and rugged walls of ice glittering blue in the occasional shafts of moonlight between the clouds. A river cut deeply between two mountains, surging like a bobsled through the narrow, twisting valley. As the plane flew through the gorge just above the water, its wings seemed almost to touch rock on either side. As was his habit in bad moments, Abraham closed his eyes and prayed in all three sacred languages, hoping, as he had explained with mock solemnity to Solly, to catch the ear of whomever was free.

As Abraham left the plane, a dull ache started somewhere in the center of his head. His skin prickled in the cold, dry wind that tore at the thin wool jacket and swirled powdery dust into his eyes. It was all he had to protect him from the cold, since his luggage, according to the authorities, had disappeared. He was returning to God, Abraham said to himself, almost as naked as he had come into the world.

From the air, he had noticed few prominent buildings in Leh. Once outside the tiny air terminal, he had a closer look at the ancient ten-story palace, a relic from the days of the maharajas, perched on a spur of rock overlooking the town. Looming above the palace was a large monastery that was a thousand years old and looked it. Corn and wheat grew at its base, barely clinging to the unpromising soil. Six-foot-high prayer walls with carved stone Buddhas ran here and there throughout the block-long town. These monuments had obviously been constructed with more care than the open sewer running down the main street.

Gazing up at the monastery, Abraham wondered if that was where he should go. As he stood still, uncertain what to do next, a man with intense, wide-set eyes and shoulder-length black hair approached from behind. "You are Abraham," he said, "and I am Rumi. Prema Sai sent me to bring you home."

Abraham was too startled to speak. He was not sure whether to bow or shake hands with the young man, who wore a quilted jacket over his red and gold robe. He offered a tentative hand, which Rumi touched lightly, apparently just to be polite. No handshakes among these monks, Abraham thought, filing away the information.

As they stood in the little stone courtyard outside the terminal, Abraham thought his head would burst. His heart was beating rapidly, and he felt sick to his stomach. The pilot had said the city was 11,500 feet above sea level, and Abraham could tell that after a lifetime in low-lying Israel, the altitude would take some getting used to.

"If you're panting like this now, you'd never make it up to the monastery," Rumi said, hailing the driver of a bullock cart. "We need to rest for a few days at Lamayaru so your body can adjust. You should take oxygen before you sleep. Pulmonary edema can kill newcomers."

"Is that the monastery where we'll be living?" His hands laced under his head, Abraham stretched out in the cart, looking up at the few stunningly bright stars that could be seen between the clouds. "Or is it the Gufa Ashram, the one Sathya Sai Baba sent his people to?"

"Neither one. Lamayaru is on the tourist track, like much of Nepal these days. So many pilgrims were coming to Gufa that those monks moved from Nepal to Ladakh."

"Then where is Prema living now?" Abraham asked.

"A group of Buddhists offered us a large cave high above their monastery, and some have even joined us." Rumi pulled a bulky embroidered coat and a pair of heavy, lined boots out of his backpack. "Prema said you would need these. With those shoes, your feet would soon freeze or blister or both. Here, let's put the boots on."

Abraham was too tired and dizzy to resist as Rumi helped him into the coat and changed his footgear, carefully checking his toes and ankles for any abrasions. "When we're walking so far, and on such rough ground," Rumi said, "a single blister can give you a boot full of blood in a day. Let me know if you feel the slightest pain. I feel I've done this for you before, but you were much smaller then. Another lifetime, maybe." He laughed and patted Abraham on the shoulder, "Are you sure you're all right?"

"When I breathe, the air feels like broken glass," Abraham admitted, "and my head aches. Otherwise, I'll live."

Laying his palm on Abraham's forehead, Rumi frowned. "We'll stay at Lamayaru for a week. Longer if you need it."

"Then I'll be able to read the Notovitch manuscript? The one that tells about Jesus' stay at the monastery." Abraham was beginning to feel stronger, even though the air and wind slashed at his tongue when he opened his mouth. The top of the world was not a place for idle conversation. When mouths are open, heat escapes and the cold invades. Still, he had much to learn and was willing to risk gulping the icy air to hear more.

"You'll have to wait for that until we reach Hemis Gompa, twenty-five miles from here," said Rumi. "Hemis has manuscripts dating back to the ancient Indus civilizations more than five thousand years ago. Prema says they are hymns to Brahman, pure spirit, and teachings on how to become one with spirit. All the great religions began with these precepts, but over the years people have added this or that comforting local notion."

"Along with the concept of exclusive truth," Abraham added sadly, thinking of the three religions that over time had torn his country apart. "Yes, I want to see those manuscripts. Have you heard that similar documents were recently smuggled out of the Vatican's secret collection? About early Christian and Jewish beliefs in reincarnation."

"No, I haven't heard that. We get little news up here. But of course the Jews of biblical times believed in reincarnation, otherwise why would they have asked Jesus if the blind man was born blind because of his sins?

Obviously the poor fellow could not have sinned in the womb, so they must have been talking about past lives."

Rumi cupped his hands over his mouth and breathed the warmed air. "Try this," he said in a muffled voice. "It will be good for your lungs." From that point they were silent until inside the monastery walls.

⌘

Two weeks later, they left Lamayaru behind to begin the long climb toward Namila-La Pass. As the towering mountains pressed in on them, Abraham's breath was whistling in his throat, and it became harder to breathe. Struggling to keep up, he asked what he had been longing to ask since he arrived, "What is it like to live with Prema Sai?"

Rumi stopped for a moment and leaned close to Abraham, shouting to be heard over the wind. "No matter how high we climb," he said, "these mountains are always higher. It is like that with Prema. We meditate sometimes eighteen hours a day, then he insists that we eat with him, take a walk, anything to bring us back to our bodies. They are temples, he says, given to us by the Great Mother, our divine source." As the sun blazed through the thin, dry air, parching their cheeks, Rumi took off his coat.

Abraham looked toward the snowy, cloud-capped peaks, visible between the cliffs on either side of the path. With every step, he felt as though he was wearing lead boots and carrying a basket of broken rocks, like the peasant women they had passed along the way. "Is it true he is like a mother? One of the Vatican manuscripts says that in the Golden Age there were no weapons or wars, and the goddess energy ruled for a hundred thousand years in the name of love. Can Prema teach men how to love like that again?"

"That is why he came," Rumi said. "Prema is entirely mother, yet he says divinity is beyond our little ideas of man or woman. The best we can do is combine strength with kindness, as he does. Sometimes he sings old songs from the first sages who lived in these mountains, and we meditate on the times when women lived to give life and men lived to protect it. That was the origin of human love."

Abraham carefully pushed a tiny gray salamander out of the way with the point of his walking stick. "And what does Prema say about divine love?"

"He doesn't say anything about it. He simply *is* that love. You feel it naturally, the way a baby feels its way to its mother's milk. I can't tell you. It's something you'll find out for yourself." Rumi shifted his pack, which was attached to a large, flat package wrapped in plastic.

"What's that you're carrying?" Abraham pointed with his stick.

"Art materials. A folio."

"You do that sort of work in your cave?" Abraham glanced around at the pink granite shining against the fiercely blue sky, thinking that an artist could hardly ask for more.

"I will be starting soon," Rumi said. "You and I are to write and illustrate a book about these years in the cave. Someday people will want to know how it was."

Abraham shivered, remembering all the years he had spent studying holy scriptures written by others. Now Prema was asking him to write such a book. The high walls of the narrow pass seemed to close in on him, and his breath caught in his throat. He had a sudden urge to weep, fearing that he was not enough of a scholar, that there would not be enough time to learn. To write such a book, he would need to become utterly pure, however unlikely that seemed. "How long do you think we'll stay up there?"

"I don't know. Probably many years," Rumi replied. "Prema says that while we are being transformed, the world is also being transformed, invisibly remade, like old cells dying while new ones are being born. It's all part of the plan." As they came out of the pass, staggering in the strong winds that rolled down from the massive white slopes, Rumi pulled out his wool mask and put on his coat again.

"The sun sets early here." He gave Abraham the mask. "It'll

start to turn cold, so you'd better wear this."

They plodded on, slanting against the wind that groaned as it whipped across the crags cutting into their path. Far below, in the valley running east to west, Abraham could see patches of grass where snow had melted along the rushing gray river. A haze of green drifted around the still-bare branches of trees, anticipating spring.

"We have leaves for only a few months," Rumi said. "It's good you're coming in May. This is the best time." He stopped in front of a sparkling sheet of snow. "But dangerous because of the snow bridges. Here. Tie this rope around you."

Rumi tied the other end of the rope to his own waist, allowing about fifteen feet between them. "Now, we must go carefully. This time of year, the river underneath carves out such a big tunnel that the bridge can collapse. A fifty-foot drop onto jagged rock is not part of the plan."

Following Rumi's lead, Abraham lay on his stomach and half-wiggled, half-crawled across the snow bridge. Just as Rumi clambered up the rocky outcropping on the other side, Abraham heard an ominous creak. He remained still for a moment, then inched forward, his gloved hands turning wet and cold as they instinctively tried to grip the shifting snow. Again Abraham heard a creak, and this time he felt as though the bottom had dropped out from under the world. Just behind him, a part of the bridge had fallen, and he lay shaking, afraid to move.

"I'll brace myself against this rock," Rumi called. "Hang onto the rope with both hands and don't try to crawl anymore. I'll haul you in."

As Rumi pulled, the snow bridge collapsed entirely, leaving Abraham in free fall. Dangling fifty feet over the rushing river and its rocky shoreline, he clutched the rope with freezing fingers and tried not to look down. As Rumi slowly hauled him up, Abraham scraped his chest against the ledge, and his breath tore through his throat.

After dragging his companion to safety, Rumi untied the sodden rope. "It happens every May or June," he said, "We're the last ones across this year."

"Why not build a footbridge?" Abraham heard his chattering voice and realized he was shaking all over. "Surely you need to get out more than a few times a year?"

"Only to bring you." Rumi smiled. "The cave is our heaven. Who would want to leave? Here, take my gloves. You'll get frostbite now that the sun's going down."

Abraham wondered why Rumi's hands were not even red, though his gloves had been stuffed in his pocket, and how he could leave the front of his jacket open to the wind. Then he remembered stories of naked Tibetan monks, snow melting around them as they sat deep in meditation. His own body, used to the warmth of the Middle East, felt like it was shutting down, as the numbness moved up from his feet, threatening his heart. He hoped they would stop at the Hemis monastery, but his companion went on without slowing down.

"Only a little farther up to Prema's cave." Rumi pointed above them to an irregular black opening in the side of the mountain. "There's a rope to hang onto, and I'll be right behind you."

As Abraham dragged himself up the icy precipice, hand over hand, he heard the howl of a wolf echoing from the valley. The sound bounced back and forth against the sides of the mountains, ending in a roar that filled his ears and made his head spin. For a moment he didn't move. The full moon had already appeared in the eastern side of the sky, while the sun turned the west a pale lavender. Snow glistened on the distant mountains, and the wind carried the tinkling sound of ice falling on ice. His breath caught in his throat, and tears came to his eyes.

"Go on," Rumi said, with a gentle push. "What you see is nothing. He is waiting for you."

16

Spring had come to the Himalayas, and soon the snow bridges would no longer support travelers. For the last twenty years, Rumi had watched this cycle of the seasons, always surprised at how rapidly they passed. Lying on the pallet in his dark little room, he slept fitfully, finally drifting into a strange dream. As the air turned a brilliant blue, streaks of light flashed by like falling stars. A tall woman, whose limbs were long and shapely, floated gracefully toward him. Rumi shifted his body, then moaned when his elbow struck a sharp rock. "Your face has haunted me since I saw it at the monastery," he whispered. "Without you, how can I learn to love?"

As the woman's figure began to fade like a smudged drawing, she said, "You must ask Prema. If you suffer because of me, it is because our souls chose this path before we were born."

Rumi awoke with a start, sweat forming on his forehead. With trembling hands he lit a fire on the hearth. His breath was so short, he had to blow twice to put out the match. Since rocks had been piled six feet high to separate each man's space, he did not fear that his neighbors would be awakened. Instinctively reaching for his sketchbook, Rumi began to draw the woman's picture while it was fresh in his memory. As her small, triangular face emerged onto the paper, a slight shadow formed at the corners of her delicate mouth. Her hair was blowing as if in a fierce wind, like the one that howled outside.

Looking at the portrait, Rumi dimly recalled another picture he had painted long ago and hidden at the bottom of his portfolio. It was the same woman, Kori, his mother's friend. What power did this woman have to stir depths in him that only Prema had touched before? He held his head in his hands.

"I am not disturbing you?" Prema's voice was soft, and at first Rumi did not realize the curtain that hung between the rock walls had been pushed aside.

"Lord, come in," Rumi said, arranging the blankets in a neat pile for Prema to sit on.

In the years they had been in the cave, Prema had grown only a little. Though he seemed taller because of his graceful bearing, he was only five feet five. He now had a beard, which was kept short, and his wavy black hair reached his shoulders.

Prema sat on the blankets. "You are troubled," he said, looking sad himself. "Ask me what you need to ask. I would not have you grieving, *bangaroo.*"

"It is this woman in my dream." Rumi held up the drawing. "Many years ago, I saw her picture over her grave. Now, my heart is eaten up with longing for her. How can this be, Lord? I have given myself to you. A woman has no place in my life."

"Do not be so sure." Prema took Rumi's hand. "Perhaps it is my will that you should love a woman so much that you are better able to love God."

Rumi curled his fingers around Prema's. "Is there more than I have given you?" He shook his head. "I cannot believe it. You know you have all my love."

"There is more, dear one, more than you can imagine," Prema said. "This woman will teach you. Allow yourself to learn what you could not learn in previous lives. Without the grace of this vision, you could not bear what is to come." He let go of Rumi's hand and stood up. "Joy will result. Believe that."

Rumi laid his forehead against Prema's warm feet. "I believe, Lord. But help me never to love another more than I love you."

"All will be well with you," Prema whispered, touching Rumi's head in blessing. "Now, wake the others and gather in the pujah room. We must prepare to leave at once, while the ice bridges are still strong."

"We are going back to the world?" Rumi stood unsteadily, leaning one arm against the cave wall.

"It is time. The one who has brought evil to the world ever since the time of Ravana, since the Son of the Morning fell from heaven, comes again to earth. If he is not stopped, none will be able to breathe the air, and fire will parch the ground so that it cannot bear life."

Rumi closed his eyes for a moment, envisioning the earth as Prema had described it—seas boiling in their beds and human beings crowded together like ants, consumed in flames that swept across the planet.

"Come," Prema said, "We have little time. My heart burns with love for my children, and I do not want them to grieve a moment more than is necessary."

Rumi gathered up his sketchbook and pencil, intending to record this last meeting with as much fidelity as he had the others. He quickly turned the page, so he could no longer see the woman's beautiful face.

When Rumi had finished drawing, he went to the room next door. "Wake up, Eddie," he said, his voice ringing with joy. "It is time."

∞

Taking deep breaths of cool spring air, Radha watched the sun rising through the purple streak of sky above the hills surrounding Prasanthi Nilayam. After waiting twenty years, she had almost forgotten what she was waiting for. Her days were filled with volunteer work at the hospital and tending the vegetable garden behind the house Tewati had left to them. At the end of each day, she would walk with Murali and Philo to the great mandir Sai Baba had built toward the end of his life. Together they would pray and watch the sun set behind the hills, as schoolchildren chanted bhajans and bulbul birds wheeled and sang above the dome.

Though now in her sixties, Radha looked and felt barely middle-aged. Her dark golden hair had grayed at the temples, and her dimples were now deep creases with tiny tributary lines. She was still slim and energetic, able to pull clean sheets under hospital patients and help them onto gurneys. Every morning she did t'ai chi exercises on the patio in front of the house, imagining Eddie beside her.

On this morning, she went down the steps and turned to face the house. After a few warm-ups, she began slowly pushing her hands against the air, feeling her fingers tingle at the resistance. The rising sun was already bright enough to cast her shadow against the whitewashed wall, and she watched herself move, thinking that the shadow looked no different from the one she had cast as a young girl. What seemed most changeless, she smiled to herself, was least permanent.

As she swung her arm toward the house, Radha thought she saw another arm, longer than hers, shadowed on the wall. She moved again, and it moved with her. Then she stood still, arms dropped to her sides, her heart beating wildly. "Eddie?" she whispered, without turning her head.

"I'm here, Radha." His hands were on her shoulders, swinging her around.

She was almost afraid to look at him, afraid he would be old and broken, ready to die. But as they stood at arms' length, she saw that he looked no older than when he had left. His eyes were shining, and his finely lined skin seemed luminously gold, as if washed in sunshine.

"Don't be so surprised, my love," he said in a voice deeper than she remembered. "Prema has told us that people will live a hundred years longer than in the old days. Evidently, we are being given more time to learn who we really are."

"It seems like you just left," Radha said softly, as he held her close. "I've lived so much in the moment, that there doesn't seem to be past or future anymore."

"Still, a great deal must have happened," Eddie said, taking her hand and leading her into the house. "I want to hear it all, but first I will tell my news. Prema has come back into the world. He will meet us in Jerusalem at the end of the month."

"Jerusalem?" Radha held her throat, feeling the pounding of her heart. "Why not here?" She took him into her little room and closed the door.

"He has work to do there. If he does not go, there will be another war."

"We've heard." Radha smoothed a place for him next to her on the rolled-up sleeping mat that also served as a couch. "It seems like such a small thing to be fighting about. The Israelis have built a city on the Lebanese border, with apartment buildings to house Arab refugees from the camps. When they invited the Arabs to live there, most wanted to move, after years in those miserable tents where Nazim lived with them. But, since Nazim was their hero, the Arab leaders think nothing he did should be changed. Their honor won't allow the refugees to move unless the Israelis give back their original homes. Of course, that's impossible. Nobody can prove where their ancestors used to live."

Radha leaned against her husband's hard, thin shoulder, feeling the bones under his skin. In the years away, he must have eaten very little, she thought. She would feed him well to make up for it.

"If war does come," Eddie said, holding her hand, "Prema says the Arabs will hit Israel with enough toxins to kill every man, woman and child, and the Israelis will salt every Arab country with hydrogen bombs. Disease and radiation would spread around the world, until no one is left."

"What can Prema do?" Radha's eyes burned with tears. Mankind was already suffering so much, like a woman in labor, seeing no end to the pain. The earth was becoming a greenhouse, with soaring temperatures melting the polar ice caps. Some coastlines had receded by twenty-five miles, and many cities had drowned in the rising oceans. Miami, Boston, New York and Long Island no longer existed, their epidemic-ravaged populations having fled inland to higher ground.

Outside Brom Strassbourg's industrialized world, most of the barren lands he had emptied of wealth were now controlled by fundamentalists. The common people waited patiently for the coming of God to save them, reluctant to revolt, fearing the rage of merciless leaders who preferred power over peace.

"No one knows what Prema will do." Eddie said. "He has asked me to bring you and the others to Jerusalem, where he will do what he must to stop the destruction of the world."

"Strassbourg's men killed Devi and Shanti," Radha said, tears filling her eyes as if the loss were yesterday. "They killed Narayan, too. Because they wouldn't tell where Prema had gone."

"I know." Eddie closed his eyes, leaning his head back, as if looking into a great inner space. "Prema told us they were Bodhisattvas who were born for one purpose, to nourish and protect him. When they died, we had a celebration along the road, and Prema showed us in a vision what had happened. We saw a burst of light, like lightning, and their forms were gone."

"Murali saw the same thing. She's now a grown woman, you know. Though she's a great comfort to him, poor Philo is still grieving." Radha suddenly wanted to tell Eddie everything she had stored up, and the words tumbled out. "Murali is beautiful in the way my mother was. Tall and slender, with a face like an angel's. Not the gentle kind, but like the angel of Exodus, who passes over bloody doors with a sword. A Jewish sort of angel, not a Christian one."

"Not married yet?"

"She's too powerful for the men here. Also too tall." Radha smiled. "I think they're afraid of her, because she's so aloof and wary. Besides, I think she wants a life of prayer, not marriage. Like my mother, she's something of a nun."

"Not like my dear Radha," Eddie said, both arms around her, his brilliant eyes shining into hers. "Full of passion you are still. I will love you as long as I live."

Radha closed her eyes, her lips opening against his. There would be time to talk later. This moment was one she wanted to savor for as long as it lasted.

⌒ゝ⌒

Abraham stood amidst the bare ruins of Megiddo, the ancient Israeli city which Christians called Armageddon, the place of the Last Battle. He wished that Prema had not decided to meet Brom Strassbourg and his army of bodyguards on this barren, rocky site, where their small group would be completely vulnerable. Underneath them, like rodent burrows, were caves dug in the hillside by archeological workers looking for signs of ancient life. But the excavators had left early, and the windswept hilltop looked as it had for a thousand years, stark and dead, except for the Exhibit Building.

Abraham had once taken his family there to see a computer-graphic version of the Last Battle. One Christian tourist had burst into tears, lamenting the fate of unbelievers who would not stand with Christ in the war between good and evil. The woman's minister had patted her on the shoulder, telling her to remember that on this very spot, the Lord's kingdom would be restored. When Solly had looked up at his father, astonished at what he heard, Abraham whispered to him that God's kingdom had always been and would forever be. God certainly had no need to fight wars of retribution against humanity.

Buffeted by the cold wind, Abraham brushed back his hair with both hands. "Why here? What an awful place."

Prema stood quietly, hands at his sides. "The people must have their prophecies fulfilled." His large brown eyes reflected the light of the setting sun. "It matters to them. And you are here so you can record what happens."

It was a place Abraham knew well, for he had worked on this dig and many others when he was studying Hebrew history. Situated in the heartland of Israel, the ancient city of Megiddo had been fought over for thousands of years. He could almost hear the screams of the dying and smell the acrid odor of fire destroying the city once again. Yet the people had continued to build, layer upon layer, finding this hill a good place for farming and high enough to defend. As the climate changed, they finally gave up and left the desert to cover their homes with a fine dust that eventually compacted, creating a grazing area for goats and sheep. Now, it was not even that, for the stripped soil had turned to sand.

Abraham saw no armies, just their handful of monks and Brom Strassbourg leading his henchmen up the twisting stone steps. Brom's massive body, with its glittering, metallic clothes, reminded him of a machine, sleek as a torpedo heading for its target. As Brom's men approached the flat stretch at the top of the hill, Abraham smiled when he saw that they were armed, thinking how little their weapons mattered. During their trip from the Himalayas, he had seen Prema Sai render a hunter's torp useless as the man was about to kill a rare snow leopard.

In his white cotton robe with sleeves to the wrists, Prema looked almost childlike, except for his full mustache and black fringe of beard. He had a long nose and high cheekbones, narrowing toward the chin. It was a face people said was all eyes—wide, dark-lashed eyes that looked deeply into the soul. Abraham had once told Rumi that a man would weep at the thought of any darkness in him that might offend that pure gaze.

Even Brom Strassbourg stopped short, ten feet away, and stared down into the face of Prema Sai. Taking a step back, as if his path had suddenly been blocked by a mountain lion, Brom reached for the torp that hung from his silver-studded hip belt. He opened his mouth, but no sound came.

"Well, old friend, here we are together again," Prema said, smiling slightly. "Have you nothing to say to me?"

"I don't know you," Brom's voice was thick, as if he was unable to clear his throat.

"But I know you. The demon killed by the goddess Chamundi. The Roman soldiers who crucified Jesus. The beast who murdered my six million holy innocents only a century ago." Prema's eyes never left Brom's face. "You remember being none of these?"

"I am I. No one else." Brom shook his head, wincing as if in pain.

"Very good. 'I am I.' You do know more than you did in the old days. It is a beginning." Prema's voice was gentle, as if speaking to a child.

A tall, pale man with thinning gray hair stepped up beside Brom. "Can't we just shoot 'em and get it over with? Who needs all this talk?" Moving quickly, a woman in a long black caftan, wearing a gray scarf over her head, reached out to restrain him.

"Consuelo," Prema called to her. "You may come to me now, dear one. I release you from your task."

Although Jason tried to hold Consuelo back, she left the loose black garment hanging from her husband's hands and came running to Prema. She bowed low before him, her long, white dress clinging softly to her slender body as her dark braid fell across his feet.

"No tears, *bangaroo*." Prema raised Consuelo to look into her eyes. "We have never been apart. Do you know how I have wept with you in your sad times?"

"Get your hands off my wife, mister," Jason yelled. "Come on, Brom, when we gonna take them? That little guy in white is all mine."

Pulling out his torp, Brom stepped forward.

"Wait." Prema moved in front of Consuelo. "I am giving you another chance, old warrior. You can give up your madness and open your heart. I told you this when you fell from heaven, and I tell you again. Will you repent, or will it take another lifetime? I assure you that your next life will not be as easy as the one you are ending now. Will you drop your walls and let me come in?"

Brom choked and his words were hardly audible. "You have taken what is mine," he muttered. "I will not serve you." Suddenly his fingers stiffened involuntarily, as if he had suffered a stroke, and the torp slid from his hand. He stared for a few moments, first at the weapon, then at his hand, not understanding how the connection had been broken. Brom fell to his knees, his entire body rigid as he gasped for breath. His bronzed face had turned a mottled red.

Prema stepped up, his face level with Brom's. "It's not too late." Though soft, his clear voice carried on the wind. "How many times must I ask? Poor man, aren't you tired of the fight?" He sounded like a mother trying to coax a troublesome child into bed.

His tight mouth sagging open in a dark, empty O, Brom shook his head and fell face down in the dust.

Bending over Brom's body, Prema sadly stroked the wiry blond hair. His face did not look as if he had just won the Last Battle of the Kali Yuga. He slowly turned and began the long walk down the hill, saying nothing.

The little group of monks followed Prema and Consuelo down the winding steps of the hillside, stepping carefully over the sharp stones that were now in deep shadows. Jason and his soldiers remained motionless, their weapons still raised, perhaps waiting for their leader to rise again. But this leader, Abraham knew from the prophecies, would lie buried in the dust for a thousand years, along with the spirit that had animated him for all this long, unhappy age.

Ali, who was just behind his father when Brom Strassbourg fell, was amazed that no one had moved. Used to taking orders, these men were helpless once they were unplugged from their leader. It was the way he himself felt when he fell into sin and cried out to God to save him. But Jason no longer prayed to God. He had made Brom his god, and now Brom was dead. Ali had never seen his father so despondent.

During their return to Jerusalem in Brom's military copter, Ali wanted to comfort Jason with scripture, maybe lead his sinking soul back to God. He thought of quoting the Psalmist, who had been as dejected as Jason, crying from out of the depths. But then he thought better of it. Jason did not know his son was a Christian.

"That little guy in white," Jason muttered. "He's gonna ruin everybody's life like he's ruined mine. Grabbing other men's wives. I shoulda shot him myself."

"Why didn't you?" Ali really wanted to know. With so many men on that hilltop, why had none of them used their weapons? For him, it was

more than an idle question, since he had recently been given an official
mandate for the mission which had obsessed him since boyhood. In his
pocket was a letter from Waynel Masters, head of the Healies in America,
approving Ali's request to represent the organization at the coming world
meeting called by Prema Sai in Jerusalem. Ali had hinted that this meeting would provide the perfect opportunity for an assassination.
Although Waynel understood, he had written only that God's people
would praise whoever brought down "the Beast."

"Can't figure it." Jason pushed the visored military hat back on his
head. "I was just standing there, looking at Brom to be sure he was dead.
When I looked up, those monks were outta there, like they got beamed
up or something."

"That one in white is the Antichrist," Ali burst out, for once feeling
confident in his father's presence. "He can make people disappear or
even die, if he wants to. The Lord has given the world over to Satan for
a little while, to test his people before the Judgment." Ali's long, bony
face was flushed and his hands jerked awkwardly as if they were con-
ducting an orchestra of words.

Jason squinted at him, his mouth curving up tightly on one side.
"What's that stuff you're talking, boy? You keep watching those crackpot
preachers on the telecon and I'll whale you good, y' hear?" Jason still
called Ali "boy" though his son was a grown man.

"I only meant that the guy has some kind of magic that can make
people disappear, like you said." Ali felt his throat tighten and his eyes
started to water. For a moment he had felt close to his father, but now
Jason seemed to be on the other side of the moon.

"Aw, shoot. Now it's magic. You never did have much in the way of
sense, boy," Jason muttered, pulling out his chewing tobacco. He hadn't
been using much chaw, since Consuelo hated it. At least now he could
chew up a good spit whenever he wanted to. "Now it seems like you lost
what little sense you had."

Ali clung to the fraying thread of conversation, his longest with Jason since he could remember. "You'd like to see that guy dead, wouldn't you, Father?"

"You got that right." Jason spat some of his chaw into the plastic cup on his food tray.

Ali leaned over and peered into his father's face. "What would you think of the one who did it?"

"Did what?" Jason's teeth grimly pounded the chaw, while his lips hung slack. His mind was clearly drifting out to sea, probably in search of Consuelo.

"Killed that guy," Ali said, pulling desperately at his father's sleeve.

"Good," Jason jerked his arm away. "I'd think he was real good, anyone who could do that."

Knowing he had gotten from Jason all he was likely to get, Ali lapsed into thought. He was now satisfied that his mission had been blessed not only by his heavenly father but by his earthly one. Jason had taught him as a boy to use a torp and insisted he practice once a week. Now, he was as good a shot as anyone. Of course, aiming a torp was easy, since the weapon's computer did most of the work. Ali was proud that he could shoot a bird in flight taking scarcely a second to aim. Yet, in this struggle against the Antichrist, he would be a David going into battle with Goliath.

Prema Sai was a master magician, so it would be necessary to sneak up on him in the crowd that would gather the next day on the Temple Mount. Take him before he could work magic with those shining eyes, Ali decided, leaning his head back. As the rotocopter descended, Ali softly repeated King David's words from the Psalms, "The Lord punishes the wicked but loves good deeds. Those who do them will live in his presence." Imagining the pride Jason and the Healies would take in him when the execution was done, Ali was happier than he had ever been. His good deed would cause him to live in the presence of the Lord forever.

17

A fine spring rain was turning the trees of Jerusalem a faint, hazy green as the delegates assembled around the Temple Mount. Waiting in the great square between the Dome of the Rock and the smaller mosque, El Aqsa, where the women prayed, Murali covered her hair with a plastic hood. Beside her stood cousin Sol, in his traditional black coat and hat. He was barely her height, with a curly black beard and mild, thoughtful eyes.

When Murali had first met Abraham's son a few days before, he hardly looked at her and spoke rapidly, with quick gestures. Today, Sol talked very little, but glanced at her often, as if trying to figure out where he had seen her before. When their eyes met, he would flush and turn away. According to Aunt Radha, Orthodox Jewish men believed that looking at women causes evil thoughts. Since he hoped to become a rabbi, Sol was trying to keep his thoughts pure. Still, he couldn't help staring at her delicate, tanned face and slender body.

Murali paid polite attention to what Sol was saying but found her eyes straying over his shoulder to Rumi, who stood near a group of Arab sheikhs, their robes fluttering around them in the damp breeze. His tall body was relaxed, but she observed a taut energy, as if he were facing a dangerous, unfamiliar world. Rumi reminded her of Radha's husband, Eddie. With their firm, lean bodies and gleaming, watchful eyes, they looked like warriors amidst this crowd of soft, scholarly men.

She had met Rumi only yesterday, when Abraham introduced the handsome young Arab to his family at Havdalah, the Saturday night dinner that concludes Shabbat. Aunt Sarah had lit the traditional braided candle and lifted it so people could hold their fingers next to the flame and see the light through their nails, reminding them that they were both body and spirit. When Murali held up her hand, she found herself staring across the table through the pluming smoke into Rumi's dark eyes, entirely forgetting that she was spirit. The look he returned burned inside her, and she almost tangled her fingers in the six strands of flame. Now, standing beside Sol on the Temple Mount, Murali found herself hoping Rumi would turn toward her again as he had that night. When he suddenly did so, his flowing white caftan twisting around him, Murali had a hard time pulling her gaze away. Only when she saw Prema coming up the wide stone steps, could she put Rumi out of her mind.

All the religious leaders, who had assembled from around the world, turned toward Prema. Some had been invited personally. Others learned of the meeting from announcements passed by satellite and through the worldwide Internet. Delegates had been sent by all the major religions and from hundreds of splinter sects within each one. Murali noticed that the various delegates stayed carefully apart from their rivals. Little groups of men and women dressed in saffron or black garments, or even feathers, in the case of some African and Native American leaders, stood uneasily along the edge of the Temple Mount. Down below were massed crowds of eager bystanders, some waving palm branches, others singing chants. Many had their own telecams, not relying on the professional newsmen lining the walls of the Mount.

Instead of arriving by rotocopter, like most of the religious leaders, Prema had chosen to walk up the steps with the other pilgrims, jostled by the crowds trying to touch him through the protecting arms of his Tibetan monks. Once on top of the Mount, Prema took time to greet the representatives of each faith, his clear voice carrying above the continual roar of news copters flying overhead. At first, most of the delegates and spiritual leaders held themselves aloof, not sure what to do. If this man, Prema Sai Baba, was a fraud, they did not want to make fools of themselves.

They were waiting for him to perform a miracle, Murali guessed, before laying aside their wary skepticism. Since their followers were watching from around the world, a dignified image must be maintained. A few among the clergy, mostly women, fell weeping at Prema's feet and were pulled away by their more cautious colleagues. Some Christian leaders were looking up into the sky, for it was said that when Jesus returned he would come upon a cloud.

Abraham pointed out to Murali the stooped figure of his father-in-law, who stood with a handful of black-suited rabbis in the center of the Mount, as far away from both mosques as possible. "He is miserable, poor man," Abraham said. "After what happened at Megiddo, Sarah and Sol told him that they believe in Prema Sai."

Philo and Consuelo stood hand in hand, leaning together as if sharing secrets. Murali watched her father hold an umbrella over Consuelo's head, just as she remembered him doing for her mother. Murali had thought her aunt might be a little jealous, since over the years she and Philo had grown close, but Radha was smiling, her face peaceful. She didn't even reach out for Eddie's hand, as she always used to do.

It began to rain harder, and people were covering their heads with sheets of plastic. Murali felt the sweat trickling down her neck, mingling with the rain. What if nothing happened, she suddenly wondered, swallowing hard. What if these people were so filled with doubt and ego that Prema could work no miracles? After all, Jesus had not performed miracles among crowds of unbelievers. She watched the small figure in white passing casually among the assembled visitors, as if he were a host in his own home. He looked so vulnerable, almost childlike. What would these people do to him if he failed, if for some reason he decided the time was not right for miracles? They would mock him, maybe even attack him. Murali's eyes filled with tears and her hands clenched into fists.

When a short, fair-haired man rushed toward Prema from behind, Murali's legs melted beneath her, and Sol reached to hold her up. This man was going to kill Prema. She could sense it, like an event written in a book she had just read. Murali tried to cry out a warning, but her voice was choked and small, as if she were shouting in a dream. Eddie and Radha started to run across the court, but Prema waved them back. The blond man stood a few feet away, the sparkling head of his torp pointed at Prema's heart.

"You are the Beast," the young man cried, his thin voice dissolving in the cool, wet wind. "The Antichrist come to deceive even the elect. You must not live."

A telecaster pushed his lens between Murali and Sol, hissing at them to get out of his way. When Murali refused to move, he stomped on her foot.

Prema turned, offering his hand, palm up. "What is your name?" he asked gently, as if the torp was not there.

Shifting his weight from one foot to the other, the blond man hesitated, his voice uncertain. "My name is Ali. I've been sent by true believers all over the world to kill the Antichrist."

"Do you think," Prema said kindly, his eyes on Ali's, "that your Lord Jesus could not come again as a dark little man from a country where God is worshipped under a thousand names?"

"He would not." Ali kept his weapon trained on Prema's slender body. "He will be tall and white, and he will come on a cloud."

"Like this?" Prema made a sudden gesture toward the sky.

Ali looked up and shouted something Murali could not hear. She wondered what he saw but could see nothing herself, though she stared at the sky until her eyes hurt. Prema had once told her that because of the grace she had enjoyed growing up close to him, she would not see visions. And, except at the time of her mother's death, she had not.

Murali would not trade away her years with Prema for any lesser blessing, so she remained content to see nothing, now that others were seeing the Lord in his glory.

Eddie Szu was pointing at the sky, crying out that he saw Jesus. Sol's face was transfigured. "It is the Moshiach," he murmured. "The clouds fell apart and there he was."

The rain had stopped during the moment they all looked up, and Murali heard the rustle of plastic, as thousands of people dropped their head-coverings. Voices were softly singing, "Jesus, Jesus," while others chanted, "Moshiach."

His mouth hanging open in confusion, Ali dropped his weapon. "I saw Jesus. But his face was your face," he stammered.

"I know you did not expect it to happen in just this way," Prema gently touched Ali's cheek. "Come, dear one, love me as I have always loved you."

Ali fell trembling to his knees, his face turned up like a bedraggled flower looking for light. "I am a filthy sinner," he groaned. "I am garbage."

Prema pulled Ali to his feet as if he were a rag doll and embraced him. "You are my friend," he said. "As much a part of me as my heart. Think, Ali. Can anything I have created be evil?" Prema produced a handkerchief, apparently out of the air, since he had no pockets. After wiping Ali's face, he whispered something in his ear and walked on. The young man stood gaping after him, sniffling as he held the handkerchief to his face.

Prema walked over to the rabbis who stood apart, looking as uneasy as birds feeding on the ground. He greeted them in Hebrew, which Radha had taught him as a child. Murali had learned along with him, always wanting to be at his side, to do what he did. But the Hebrew he now spoke was much more fluent and complex than what they had learned, and she wondered if little Amar had simply been letting Radha play at being teacher because it made her happy.

Glancing at Abraham, Murali whispered, "How will he win them over, Cousin, since they believe God is pure spirit? There is no way Jews can believe that God would take human form and live among us."

"If Prema Sai can convince Rabbi Ordman," Abraham replied, tucking Sarah's arm under his, "he has the whole world in his hands."

Though gentle, Prema's voice could be heard all across the Temple Mount. "You have waited for so long, my dear friends, through incarnations and avatars, waiting until you were sure, so afraid have you been of offending Ha-Shem by worshipping anyone but him. Through all the ages you have laid down your lives for me in obedience to the laws I gave you. You have suffered for the whole world, just as I suffered when I came among you."

Rabbi Ordman was pale, his voice shaking, "Bring back the Temple," he cried. "Give us our Temple, and we will believe you are the Moshiach."

A chant rose from below, as many Jews in the crowd lifted their faces to the rain and cried in unison, "Give us our Temple."

The rabbi's lined face looked more sorrowful than when his daughter had decided to marry the son of a murderer. "How can you, from another world and tradition, know the task Ha-Shem gave us thousands of years ago?" he shouted over the chanting voices.

Prema approached the rabbi and leaned toward him, as if telling a secret, but everyone could hear. "You were asked to carry the truth of one spirit, one God through all the ages. This you have done."

"And at what cost?" Rabbi Ordman started rocking back and forth, as in prayer. "We are hated, persecuted. Our children have been murdered before our eyes because we will bow to only one God, our God, Ha-Shem, who could not become flesh."

The chant had died down, and the crowd strained to hear.

"Could not?" Prema reached out to Rabbi Ordman, then dropped his arms. "You think there is anything the omnipotent God could not do?"

"Not exactly," the Rabbi said, his voice low, "but surely he would not take on this human flesh that has so desecrated other flesh. Speak, tell us."

"I understand," Prema said, folding his hands behind his back, as if to keep them from touching these people with love, as he clearly longed to do. "But you must understand also. It is time to forgive those who have hurt you, to love them as you have loved God and free them from their guilt. They are your children. You have heard how the Buddha came out of the mother faith of Hinduism to share his universal truth? So it was with the Christ who came out of Judaism and made its truth simple, so the world could grasp it. As the child must revere the parent, the parent must be patient and loving with the child."

"And have you no word for us who have loved and obeyed Allah, the one God?" A sheikh in a billowing black and white robe stood in front of the other Muslim leaders. "Our faith is purer than any other. We demand that our men bow five times a day to Allah. Who else in the world is so devoted as we Muslims? So pure from the sins of immodesty and greed and drunkenness? Answer, if you are who you say you are."

Prema turned to face the golden dome that rose like an inverted cup over the Mount, spilling out blessings. He held up both hands, palms toward the immaculate blue and white tiled walls of the mosque. "You have always worshipped the pure spirit that underlies all that is, the spirit whom you call Allah. But only your Sufis have understood that on the human plane, infinite spirit manifests itself as love. Most of you have loved only the followers of Allah, even excluding many of them. Shiites fighting against Sunnis." He shook his head. "That must stop. Now I ask you to love all beings as your family. You will do this now, because I ask it." Prema raised his voice, but his face was kind and full of light.

A fiery-eyed Islamic leader from Mexical stepped forward. "We, like the Jews, do not believe that Allah, the formless God, would take on a human form. Even our great prophet, Mohammed, is not worshipped as God."

Prema came closer. "Yet Mohammed was and is a Divine Incarnation. The Koran came to the Prophet in the same way that the truths of the

Vedas and the Bible were revealed to mankind. Does the Koran not teach the same truths as I do? Mercy, truth, forgiveness and tolerance." As he spoke, Prema approached the Muslim leader and put his hands on the man's shoulders. "Do not fast from food and drink only, but also from anger, envy and violence. The inward fast is what you shall make, cleansing your spirit so that you will love others as you love Allah."

"These are just words," an imam shouted. "Show us proof." Other Muslims took up the cry. "The holy Mohammed is our prophet, and Nazim is our saint in this age. We need no other."

Murali wondered as she looked around if anyone would step forward and stand with Prema Sai. Dhattu and the young Dalai Lama stood to one side with the other Buddhists. They said nothing, but only smiled. One of the younger monks began to giggle, but was nudged into silence by an elder one.

As the Muslims jeered, Prema walked toward the empty center of the Mount, his head down. The rabbis had silently withdrawn toward the sacred Kotel, the last remaining wall of their ancient temple. Below, the crowd was restless, and some of the telecasters began to pack away their gear. They had deadlines to meet, and half a story was better than none. Her breath shallow and harsh, Murali stood close to Sol, afraid she was going to cry out loud like a child. Seeming to have forgotten the prohibitions against touching women, Sol put his arm tightly around her.

The crowd began to jeer. It wasn't fair, she thought. They all expected Prema to break his own natural laws just to satisfy their lust for miracles. Muslims, Christians and Jews raised clenched fists. "A miracle, a miracle," the people chanted, stamping their feet in rhythm with the words. Murali feared he would allow the crowd to kill him, as Jesus had let himself be killed.

Prema stood in the middle of the Mount, the dust rising around his sandaled feet as the wind blew it into tiny, swirling clouds. For a moment, he glanced at the Buddhist monks. Though he was smiling, his great, shining eyes looked sad. Murali held her breath as Prema raised his arms. She blinked at first, thinking that it was her tears making the air between the two mosques appear to shimmer. Or perhaps it was the bright sun coming from behind the clouds that was suddenly turning all Jerusalem into a golden haze. She remembered once before how Prema had transformed a heavy mass into mist. Her father had explained that matter is simply vibration, the energy of sound and light briefly confluent as a material thing. Now Murali watched, feeling her own body turn as weak as vapor.

Rabbi Ordman was slowly davening, his face wet with rain or tears, as he rocked back and forth in prayer. Feeling the intensifying energy, Murali wondered if perhaps everyone sensed, as she did, that Prema was a kind of divine transformer, changing energy into spiritual food. The holy communion he offered to the world was turning men into gods, whether they knew it or not.

When, at last, the crowd's roar died away, Prema's clear voice could be heard. "You will have the temple as it stood in the days of Solomon. But I must have your promise. Muslim, Christian, Jew, Buddhist and pagan. Everyone must promise. No more bloody sacrifices. You will no longer punish others for your guilt. You will stop hurting women and children. You will no longer bar women from praying with you, but honor them as holy guides, for they will teach you how to love. You will lay down your weapons, renounce your luxuries, feed the poor, and walk lightly upon the earth, returning to her all you take. You will treat each other as the gods you are and be one family, my people. Will you do this?" His eyes shining like stars, Prema reached out to them. "How often I have wanted to take you under my wings as a mother hen gathers her chicks, but you would not. You would not love me."

After a long silence, many in the crowd began whispering, "Yes, yes." Some people were uncertain, Murali thought, not sure if they could give up their castes, their slaves, their superiority, above all, their rightness. They knew that to such a being as Prema they must keep their promises. If they knew him as she did, Murali thought, breathing so fast she was dizzy, they would know he was all that was best in them, all that was loved and lovable. Then they would gladly do what he asked and be set free.

As Prema faced the sparkling, golden haze, his hands still held high, the earth shook underfoot, and Murali heard the sound of bells and thunder. Jerusalem's brilliant sun shone down upon them, and a rainbow arched overhead, spanning the entire Mount. Suddenly a luminous shape was shimmering above the sand. Taking solid form, it became a golden box that rested on two long poles. Angels knelt at each corner, the tips of their outstretched wings touching. "The Ark of the Covenant," Murali whispered aloud. The Ark that had carried the essence of God among the Israelites for a thousand years had returned to bless the world.

It seemed to have risen out of the earth, but the ground looked as solid as ever. Little clouds of dust were whipped into spirals by the wind and spread across the Mount, as a massive rectangular structure of cedar and gold coalesced around the Ark. At first Murali could see the sun shining through it, but within a few seconds, the sunshine became soft and diffused as if seen through tears. She wiped her eyes, aware that the tears were not only hers but everyone's.

"Come," Prema Sai addressed the silent confusion in the faces around him. "Do not be afraid. You are all priests. Today, like every day, is holy. You may all approach to touch the Ark and you will not die. I have spent many years preparing your bodies and souls for divinity."

He began walking toward the temple, then stopped to beckon the still-frightened crowd with the same smile Murali remembered from childhood. "Come, nothing will harm you. All of you are here because you have loved me in this and other lives. Where I am taking you is a safe place."

His feet crunching on the sand of the courtyard, Prema kept walking, not looking back to see if anyone followed. Murali began to run, knowing in her heart that she would be the first to walk in his footsteps, the way she had as a child. From the other side, Rumi came striding to meet her, the sleeves of his robe flying behind him like wings as he took her hand.

A crowd of children followed them up the stone steps, singing in high, thin voices that trembled like the strings of violins, *"Mi melach molachai hamlochim? Hakodosh Boruchu.* Who is the king of kings? The blessed Holy One."* Behind the children came all the others, their voices low and shy as they sang. But Murali hardly noticed them. Her eyes were on Prema Sai as he passed through the golden pillars and led them into the Holy of Holies.

EPILOGUE

The persons and events in this novel are a blend of truth and imagination, as are most things. Shirdi Sai Baba lived in a small town near Bombay, where he died in 1918. Sathya Sai Baba is alive today in Puttaparthi, India.

Except for Prema Sai Baba, other characters are fictional. The Golden Age, set in motion by Prema Sai in the novel, has been foretold by many cultures around the world. Such people as Murali, Rumi and Abraham will be part of it. But that is another story.

GLOSSARY

Adoni—*Lord, Sir (Hebrew, polite form of address)*

Al Fatah—*Arab political movement*

Amrit—*nectar*

Ashram—*a meeting place for religious instruction or exercises*

Avatar—*a divine incarnation, an appearance on earth of the Supreme Lord*

Bar mitzvah—*Jewish ceremony bringing thirteen-year-old boys into religious maturity*

Baruch atah adonai elohainu melech haolam—*Blessed are you, Lord, King of the Universe*

Bhagavad-Gita—*sacred Hindu text, considered the paramount scripture of the Vedic tradition*

Bhajans—*sacred songs of India*

Bismi-llahi al-rahman al-rehim—*in the name of Allah, the merciful, the compassionate*

Brahman—*impersonal all-pervasive aspect of the Supreme Lord*

Brahmin—*a Hindu born into the highest religious caste*

Bodhisattva—*one who chooses to incarnate in order to help humanity*

Challah—*a bread traditionally served on the Jewish Shabbat*

Chapati (plural Chapatis)—*a flat bread*

Cherimoya—*a fruit that resembles a combination of pineapple and banana, mainly grown in Mexico and southern California*

Dahl—*a lentil stew*

347

Darshan—*a viewing of a holy person*

Davening—*bowing during prayer by Orthodox Jews*

Desertification—*the gradual change of arable land into desert*

Dhoti—*Indian loincloth*

Diaspora—*the first-century dispersal of the Jews from the Holy Land (by the Romans)*

Dingo—*a jackal-like animal living in Australia and Tasmania*

Dybbuk—*a "bad" spirit that attaches itself to a living spirit*

Falafel—*a Middle Eastern chickpea paste*

Falafel roll—*Falafel in pita bread*

Gayatri mantra—*the most sacred hymn of the Hindu tradition*

Guru—*a highly evolved teacher, a spiritual master who speaks and acts in accordance with the Scriptures*

Halvah—*a Middle Eastern sweet*

Ha-Shem—*the name of God among Orthodox Jews*

Imam—*a Muslim religious leader*

Inshallah—*if God wills*

Jai—*Victory, the equivalent of Hallelujah*

Japamala—*Indian rosary, prayer beads*

Jihad—*holy war*

Kabbalah—*Jewish mystical book*

Kaddish—*Jewish prayer for the dead*

Kali Yuga—*latest cycle of human history, associated with iron, greed, immorality and degeneration of human civilization*

Karma—*Hindu and Buddhist belief that retribution or reward for actions will occur in this life or another to come*

Keffiyeh—*Arab headdress*

Koran—*Muslim scriptures*

Kotel—*Wailing wall*

Lassi—*yogurt drink*

Lehitra'ot—*until we meet again*

Mandir—*Indian temple*

Mantra—*a short (often two-syllable) holy phrase repeated in order to clear and focus the mind*

Maranatha—*Come Lord Jesus (in Greek)*

Mazel tov—*congratulations*

Matzoh—*Jewish yeastless bread, eaten at Passover*

Medhi Moud—*sacred Muslim book*

Menorah—*Jewish candelabra used in worship*

Mudra—*Oriental hand position with religious significance*

Meshugge—*Yiddish term meaning crazy person*

Mikvah—*Jewish ritual bath*

Minyan—*the required number of Jewish men for worship*

Moshiach—*Jewish term for Messiah*

Muezzin—*Islamic prayer leader who sings from a tower*

Nagarsankirtan—*singing bhajans at daybreak, while walking around the grounds of an Indian ashram*

Namasté—*I salute the divinity within you*

Parousia—*the Rapture, a Christian (Greek) term meaning the taking up of true Christians at the time of the Second Coming of Christ*

Paten—*flat brass or gold plate on which the communion bread lies*

Pesach—*Passover (Hebrew)*

Prana—*air or spiritual breath*

Pranayama—*breathing practices used by yogis*

Prema—*love of God that is free from any selfish motive*

Pujah—*personal prayer before devotional altar, place used for devotional practices*

Rishis—*Indian holy men*

Sadhus—*Indian spiritual seekers, often ascetics*

Sakina—*spirit in Arabic literature*

Samadhi—*spiritual ecstasy*

Sanskrit—*ancient, sacred language of India*

Shabbat—*weekly Jewish holy day, sundown on Friday to sundown on Saturday*

Shul—*Hebrew school*

Soma—*the food of the gods in Europe and in Eastern mythology*

Stetl—*Jewish farms in Poland*

Sufi—*Islamic mystic*

Sura—*any of the 114 chapters of the Koran*

Talmudic—*refers to the Talmud, the body of Jewish teaching passed on through oral, and eventually written tradition*

Tambura—*Indian stringed instrument*

Tefillin—*ritual objects worn by Jews on forehead and right arm*

Torah—*five books of Moses, also known as the Old Testament*

Tsizsit—*plural of tsizi, ritual fringes on the corners of an Orthodox Jew's vest-like garment*

Tulsi—*Indian plant with medicinal properties*

Tzaddiks—*Jewish holy men*

Vedas—*the entire body of sacred Hindu scriptures*

Vedic—*referring to Vedas*

Vibhuti—*sacred ash manifested by Sathya Sai Baba*

Yechiri—*beloved (Hebrew)*

Yenta—*Yiddish gossip*

Yeshivot—*plural of yeshiva, an Orthodox Jewish school*

HOFFMAN
FAMILY TREE

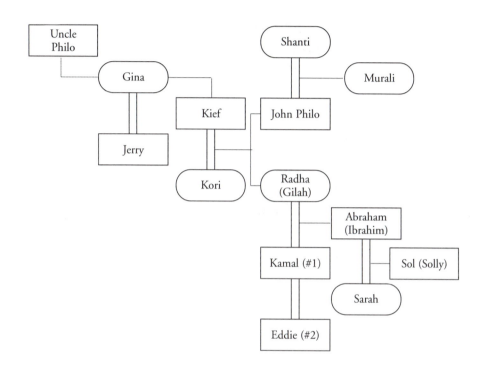

ANNIE & DAVID
FAMILY TREE

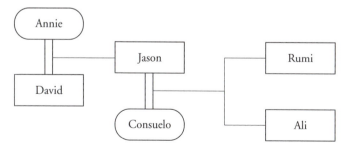

REINCARNATIONS

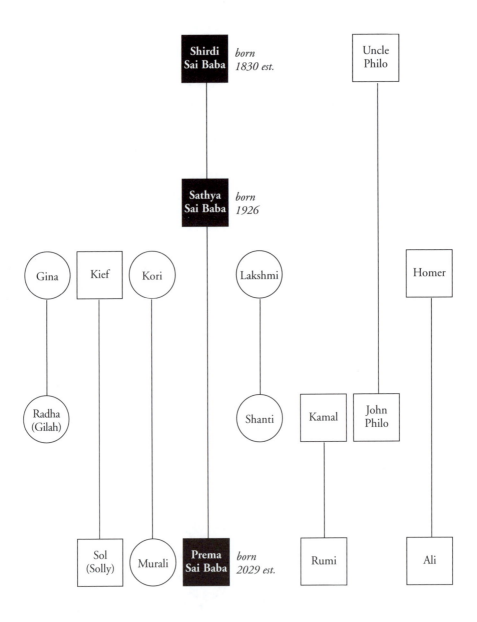

About the Author

Barbara Gardner holds a Ph.D. from Rutgers, and has taught literature and mythological studies at several universitites. She has authored a number of articles for academic journals and has written ten books, including two novels: *The Doomsday Scroll* and *Project Web*, both published by Dodd, Mead.

Ms. Gardner's love of international travel and her study of world religions are reflected in the broad scope of *The Sai Prophecy*. Her book, *In the Center: The Story of a Retreat*, was published by Ave Maria Press, Notre Dame University. Together with George Maloney, she coauthored *Loving the Christ in You*, Crossroad/Meyer-Stone Books.

When not writing, Barbara loves to take long walks in the forest or by the ocean. She plays the Celtic harp and enjoys creating ceramic sculptures, which have been exhibited in several professional shows.

Chicken Soup for the Couple's Soul

Whether single, married or separated, everyone wants to find and keep this elusive thing called "love." Bestselling author and foremost relationship expert Barbara De Angelis teams up as a co-author of *Chicken Soup for the Couple's Soul*, a collection of heartwarming stories about how real people discovered true love with the person of their dreams. A sweet spoonful of this enchanting Chicken Soup collection will warm the hearts of romantic readers everywhere.

Code #6463 Paperback • $12.95

New Chicken Soup for the Soul

Chicken Soup for the Golfer's Soul

This inspiring collection of stories from professionals, caddies and amateur golfers shares the memorable moments of the game—when, despite all odds, an impossible shot lands in the perfect position; when a simple game of golf becomes a lesson in life. Chapters include: sportsmanship, family, overcoming obstacles, perfecting the game and the nineteenth hole. This is a great read for any golfer, no matter what their handicap.

Code #6587 • $12.95

A 6th Bowl of Chicken Soup for the Soul

This latest batch of wisdom, love and inspiration will warm your hearts and nourish your souls, whether you're "tasting" *Chicken Soup* for the first time, or have dipped your "spoon" many times before.

In the tradition of all the books in the original *Chicken Soup* series, this volume focuses on love; parents and parenting; teaching and learning; death and dying; perspective; overcoming obstacles; and eclectic wisdom. Contributors to *A 6th Bowl of Chicken Soup for the Soul* include: Erma Bombeck, Edgar Guest, Jay Leno, Rachel Naomi Remen, Robert A. Schuller, Dr. James Dobson, Dolly Parton and Cathy Rigby.

Code #6625 • $12.95

HCI's Spring Spirituality Series

"Let go of all things and allow yourself to become true and clean. We now have the opportunity to change our attitude and perceptions. Time is calling us, the world is calling us and, if you listen, your own inner voice is calling you."

—Dadi Janki

In this inspiring collection, framed by the stunning color images of French artist Marie Binder, Dadi Janki will guide you on an awakening spiritual journey. Chapters on Humility and Empowerment, Living the Vision, God, The World, Meditation, The Art of Living and Angels, will provide you with the tools to remove mental and emotional obstacles to self-fulfillment. Dadi Janki shows how every one of us can find our spiritual identity and make a very practical contribution to a better life and a better world.

Code # 6722 Paperback • $10.95

HCI's Spring Spirituality Series

Qigong

You carry within yourself the ability to heal. Learn to tap into this innate gift and dance your own dance of life. You are sure to find this book fascinating, even life changing. A must-read for anyone intrigued by the mystique of ancient Eastern healing arts or seeking a daily practice that promotes and maintains full-body well-being.

Code #6749 Paperback • $12.95

The Tao of the Ride

A deft interpretation of the two worlds of motorcycling and Eastern spirituality, and the relationship between them. The motorcycle becomes the metaphor for freedom— whatever it is that returns us to our natural selves—to illustrate principles of Eastern spirituality, including such timeless Chinese philosophies and concepts as Tao and Qi, to name but a few. This handbook for the Ride of life will take you beyond motorcycles and into the mechanics of your own spirituality.

Code #6706 Paperback • $9.95

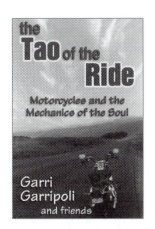

HCI's Spring Spirituality Series

Code #6781 • $7.95

The Man Who Couldn't See Himself

Whimsically illustrated, this is story of a man who has lost sight of who he is. Filled with loneliness he buys himself a dog, but before long, they are both lonely. Thus begins a sublime journey of a man to rediscover himself. In time and almost imperceptibly he realizes a shift in consciousness and becomes open to the mystery of love.

Ignite Your Intuition

Extraordinist Craig Karges is known to millions of television viewers for his remarkable demonstrations of extraordinary phenomena on *The Tonight Show with Jay Leno, Larry King Live*, and many other TV shows. In his new book, Karges reveals how to unlock the power within your own intuition—what he calls your natural psychic abilities. Be awakened to the possibility of realizing your own potential.
Code # 6765 • $10.95